# Lacrosse Fundamentals

## 4th Edition

Jim Hinkson

TRIUMPH
BOOKS

Library of Congress Cataloging-in-Publication Data

Hinkson, Jim.
  Lacrosse fundamentals / Jim Hinkson.
     p. cm.
  ISBN 978-1-60078-693-8 (pbk.)
  1.  Lacrosse.  I. Title.
  GV989.H563 2012
  796.34'7—dc23

                         2011052141

This book is available in quantity at special discounts for your group or
organization. For further information, contact:
  **Triumph Books LLC**
  542 South Dearborn Street
  Suite 750
  Chicago, Illinois 60605
  (312) 939–3330
  Fax (312) 663–3557
  www.triumphbooks.com

Printed in the U.S.A.
ISBN: 978-1-60078-693-8
Design by Patricia Frey
Photos courtesy of John Smith

*This book is dedicated to my wife, Cynndy, for her great support, and to my family whom I'm so proud of: Maggie and Jeff Webb, Kate Hinkson and Chris St. John, James Hinkson and Sarah Digby, and my two granddaughters, Sophie Webb and Elyse Webb*

# Contents

# Key to Diagrams

○ = player

● = ballcarrier

Ⓡ = right-shot player

Ⓛ = left-shot player

**G** = goalie

**C** = coach

Ⓧ = pylon

△ = net

——————▶ = path of player

- - - - - - ▶ = path of ball

∿∿∿▶ = path of ballcarrier

# Foreword

Lacrosse is more than a game among members of my family and among the families of the Longhouse on the Territory of the Onondaga Nation.

I remember the first time that my father and I played catch. I was about five years old when he asked me to come out with him. He handed me a lacrosse stick and a ball. He showed me how to throw the ball. We played catch. That day, although it was more than 55 years ago, is still in my mind as if it were yesterday. I received my first stick when I was about 10 years old. It was made of white ash and was the stick that I used until it broke during a game when I was 17 years old. I played league lacrosse until I was 41.

During these years I learned what the game really meant. I watched my father as he prepared to leave for games in arenas in Syracuse, Geneva, and Rochester, New York. He played professional box lacrosse during the '30s. He also played field lacrosse against colleges in our area. His team was good enough to try out for the 1932 Olympics in California. My grandfather played field lacrosse until he was 60 years old. My three sons have also played box and field lacrosse. Each has had a stick in his hands since he was two years old. One is presently playing for a college and one played pro box with the Buffalo Bandits. All three have played high-school lacrosse and all three play for the Iroquois Nationals, a team composed of members of the Haudenosaunee (Iroquois Confederacy). Someone from my family has been on the lacrosse field for the past 100 years.

As my boys grew up I taught them the same respect for the game that my father had taught me. The game was given to us by the Creator for his enjoyment. We believe that when there is a game being played here on earth there is a game being played in the land of the Creator at the same time. The game is for the spiritual and physical peace of mind of our people and gives us a chance to display our gifts for the Creator: the gifts of being able to run, catch, and throw; of being able to think and make split-second decisions; and most importantly, it gives us the opportunity to work together as a unit. Lacrosse is a very intrinsic component of our heritage and spiritual culture. When I play lacrosse it makes me feel like I am playing the game with all of my ancestors. It also makes me proud that it was our people who gave lacrosse to the world. For these reasons, lacrosse is more than just a game.

Dawnaytoh,
Chief Irving Powless
Onondaga Nation

# Preface

This book is an accumulation of my ideas from 34 years of playing, coaching, and instructing for the Ontario Lacrosse Association.

I was introduced to lacrosse in 1962 by Hall of Famer Jim Bishop, who knew only one way to play the game: Fast-Break. From these special roots I've grown and added my own ideas, as well as other coaches' ideas that I've borrowed, stolen, and imitated about how to play the game.

Lacrosse may be called by different names—box lacrosse, indoor lacrosse, inter-lacrosse, and field lacrosse—and it may be played in different environments with different rules. But the bottom line is that in all these different forms, a player still has to pass and catch, beat a defender, and shoot at a net, with only a lacrosse stick and a ball.

Lacrosse is a very simple game. Its object: to put the ball into the net. It is a game of tempo and rhythm, with two teams running up and down the floor; yet, like all sports, it is a game made up of fundamentals. It's through repetitive practice of these fundamental skills that teams are successful. There is an old saying: *It's not what you do, but how you do it*. In lacrosse this translates to: the type of system a team plays is not as important as how well a team executes the fundamental skills within that system.

The execution of these fundamentals is presented in this book: how to beat a defender one-on-one, how to throw a perfect pass to a teammate, how to catch a ball in traffic, how to score on a goalie, and many other skills.

I've tried to describe the fundamentals as clearly and simply as possible. I've tried to break the skills into a checklist of key points. Remember, these fundamentals are not just any fundamentals thrown together, but ones that complement the Fast-Break system. So, as you read, keep in mind that I'm giving you one proven method. Take from the book ideas that you can use and feel good about that reinforce what you are doing already.

I've also presented some basic strategies and tips on how players should think and act in certain situations. At the end of each chapter are drills presented in simple step-by-step progressions from the easiest to the most difficult. Practicing these drills will refine a player's skills.

By breaking the game into basic skills, the player, coach, and fan can analyze and thereby better understand and appreciate this great sport.

Finally, a special note to the parents: this book is written not only for the player, coach, and educator, but also for you. It's a tool for parents who want to work with their sons and daughters on their own time. Even if you can't handle a lacrosse stick, take this book and the ideas presented in it, grab a baseball glove, and practice passing and catching with your child. Having a stick yourself isn't essential. Understanding skills and techniques of the game is.

Jim Hinkson, 2011
Whitby, Ontario, Canada

# Introduction

Like most Canadian youngsters, I played lacrosse and hockey. The speed, the keen competition, the sheer exuberance of these sports allowed for the development of athleticism in a young boy. As I grew older, I began to recognize the tactics and strategies of these games; I became a student of sports. Later, as a teacher and coach, I tried to channel those spirits in my students, to impart to them the elementary rules, to instill in them the love of the game and respect for the opponent. Teaching fundamentals, increasing knowledge without destroying or limiting one's enthusiasm for a subject, is sometimes difficult for a teacher and a coach to accomplish.

In a sport like lacrosse there is a continuous movement, a flow that exhilarates the player and arouses the spectator. It is difficult to take that energy and slow it down to examine its creation. A step-by-step re-creation of the fundamentals is needed—like watching a film in slow motion to capture the subtleties of each player's abilities. We watch every move; we observe the hand-to-eye coordination so needed to succeed in this sport. Jim Hinkson has known the ebb and flow of such play and has put it into words, using instructional photographs and diagrams to complement them.

This book is designed to benefit everyone: the coach, the player, and the spectator. It puts in concrete terms the manner in which the sport works, purely and simply. It will make a player more aware, a coach more expert, a spectator more informed. *Lacrosse Fundamentals* will inform everyone who reads it; each individual can take it from there.

Knowing Jim Hinkson as a player, as a teacher, and as a coach, and knowing his dedication to the sport of lacrosse, I wholeheartedly recommend this book to you.

Mike Keenan
Former NHL coach of the New York Rangers,
Philadelphia Flyers, Chicago Blackhawks,
Vancouver Canucks, and St. Louis Blues

Chapter 1

# Terminology, the Stick, and Equipment

*(Thanks to Bill Fox, a referee in the OLA and NLL, for his input on rules, sticks, and equipment.)*

## I. Terminology

### Terminology of Playing Surface

*(See Diagram #1)*

**Center Face-Off Circle**—is a two-foot radius circle. *Note: In the NLL there is an eleven-foot radius.*

**Dot or "X"**—a two-inch dot found in the center of the two-foot Face-Off Circle.

**Parallel Lines**—two lines parallel to the sideboards touching the two-foot Face-Off Circle.

**Restraining Lines (also known as Defensive/Offensive Line)**—players not involved in the actual face-off must take a position outside the Restraining Lines, which are 22 feet apart. On the whistle to start play all players can pursue the loose ball. *Note: In the NLL there are also two Restraining Lines and a Center Line. The Restraining Line is 42'6" from the Center Line. This creates a smaller area for the Offensive/Defensive Zone for the players to play in.*

**Offensive Zone**—the area where the attacking team tries to score. This area is inside the Offensive Zone Line.

**Offensive Zone Line**—the line that stretches across the width of the arena from sideboard to sideboard to distinguish the Offensive Zone.

**Defensive Zone**—the area where the defensive team plays to stop the offensive team from scoring. This area is inside the Defensive Zone Line.

**Defensive Zone Line**—the line across the width of the arena from sideboard to sideboard to distinguish the defensive area.

**Neutral Zone**—the area between the Defensive Zone Line and the Attacking Zone Line.

**Imaginary Center Line**—an imaginary line down the middle of the floor, parallel to the sideboards, that makes the shooter aware of shooting around this area. This line also helps to break the offensive area into ball side and off-ball side.

**Imaginary Three Lanes**—imaginary lines that divide the floor into three lanes: the Middle Lane and the two Outside Lanes. The Middle Lane consists of two imaginary lines parallel to the sideboards and a little wider than the goal crease; the two Outside Lanes are measured from these two imaginary lines of the Middle Lane to the sideboards. These three lanes help to teach offensive positioning, Fast-Break positioning, and defensive positioning.

**Imaginary Semicircle Shooting Line**—an imaginary line that players should be aware of

**Diagram #1**

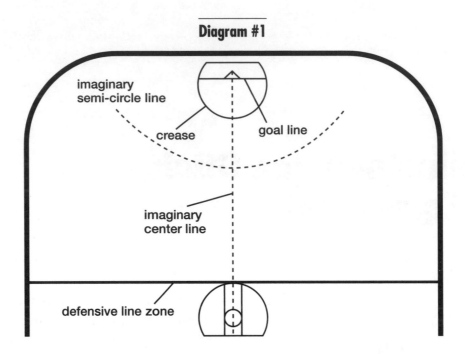

because around this 15-foot radius a ballcarrier should be a threat to score.

**Line Change Area**—a rectangular area made up of two lines (three feet wide) extending out from the boards and another line as long as the players' bench.

**Crease**—is a nine-foot radius from the center of the goal line in a semi-circle pattern. Offensive players cannot step on this crease line or they lose possession of the ball. The crease area is considered to be an imaginary vertical cylinder going up from this crease line on the floor. A player cannot put his stick inside this cylinder or the goal will be disallowed.

*Note: In the NLL the crease is a 9'3" radius and a player can score a goal with his stick over the imaginary crease plane.*

**Net or Goal**—made up of two metal goal posts four feet high and a metal cross bar four feet wide covered with a netting made of heavy mesh. *Note: In the NLL the goal size is 4'9" wide and four feet high.*

**Goal Line**—a line from goal post to goal post. If the ball goes past this line it is a goal.

## Terminology of Floor Areas *(See Diagram #2)*

- Corner area of floor (low) or creaseman's spot
- Mid-side area of floor, or wing area, or cornerman's spot
- Top-side area of floor or pointman's spot in the 3-2 offense

## Diagram #2: Terminology of Floor Area

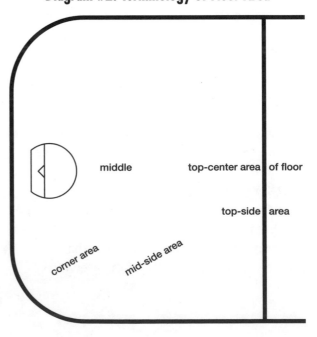

- Top-center area of floor or pointman's spot, or "X" spot in the "X" offense or 1-2-2
- Middle area of floor is in front of net, the Prime Scoring Area.
- Center area of floor is higher up from the middle area of the floor.

## Terminology of Offensive Players' Positions on the Floor

*(See Diagram #3)*

1. **Left Creaseman, Right Creaseman**—these are names of the offensive players who play in the so-called forward position, and are usually near the net at the front of the break or on offense at the beginning.
2. **Left Cornerman, Right Cornerman**—these are names of the offensive players who play behind the creasemen with about 15 feet of spacing and bring the ball up the floor most of the time. One of these players is usually the centerman on the team.
3. **Pointman**—this is the name of the offensive player who plays at the top-center or top-side of the offense. He can be either a left- or

right-hand shot and creates the strong side for that particular line or group by lining up behind one of the cornermen or playing in the "X" spot.

## Offensive Terminology

Go over the terminology so the players will understand what you are talking about when you say a certain word.

**Stick-side**—the side of the body where the stick is held over the shoulder

**Non-stick side**—the side of the body where the stick isn't

**Right-shot**—a player who holds his stick over his right shoulder and plays on the left-side of the floor

**Left-shot**—a player who holds his stick over his left shoulder and plays on the right side of the floor

**Bench-side shot**—player who receives the ball on his proper side of the floor and is also on the bench side of the floor

**Off-bench-side shot**—player who receives the ball on his proper side of the floor and is also on the off-bench side of the floor

### Diagram #3

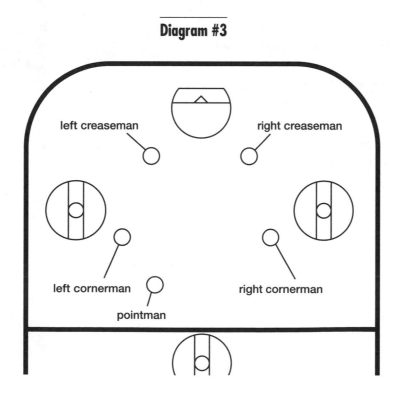

**Strong-side**—the side of the offense with three players of the same shot

**Weak-side**—the side of the offense with only two players of the same shot

**Ball side**—the side of the floor where the ball is

**Off-ball side**—the side of the floor opposite the ball side

**"Passing" or "Shooting" Pass**—best way to move the ball. The perfect pass is high and outside on the stick side.

**Getting in the "Clear" to receive a Pass**—popping back out to get open to receive a cross-floor pass or a down pass. The receiver now can pass to a cutter, execute a one-on-one, or set up a play.

**"Cut" or "Go"**—used usually as an element-of-surprise movement to get "open" for a scoring opportunity. A player runs in front of his check through the middle of the floor looking for a pass and shot on net.

**"Backdoor Cut"**—movement to get "open" for a scoring opportunity. A player runs behind his defender looking for a pass and shot on net. The defender is either overplaying or playing even with the cutter.

**Give-and-Go**—when the ballcarrier passes the ball to a teammate and then cuts to get "open" for the return pass and a possible shot on net.

**One-on-One Move or Penetration Move**—the ballcarrier tries to beat his defender to attack the net for a scoring opportunity.

**"Circling" movement**—on the off-ball or on-ball side, where three or two players cut for a pass by "circling," "cycling," or interchanging positions on their side of the floor.

**Picks**—when an offensive player goes to his teammate's area and sets, with his body and stick, interference on his teammate's defender, or at least gets in the way to set his teammate in the clear for a pass or shot on net.

**Screens**—when an offensive player goes to his teammate's area and with his stick and body and interferes or gets in the way with his own defender to stop him from switching so his teammate can use this screen to rub out his check to get in the open for a pass or shot on net.

## Manufacturers for Box Lacrosse

- Brine—manufactures sticks and equipment
- Warrior—manufactures sticks and equipment (subsidiary of New Balance)
- STX and Nike—manufactures sticks, equipment, Canadian mesh, and Nike shoes
- Gait and deBeer—manufactures sticks and equipment

**Photo 1:** Parts of the Stick

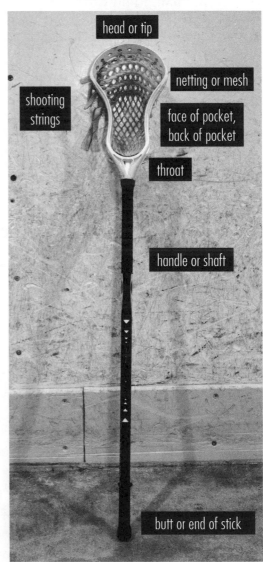

- Reebok—manufactures sticks, equipment, and shoes (supply the NLL with sticks)
- Harrow—manufactures handles, sticks, and equipment
- Marc Mesh—manufactures mesh only (supply NLL)
- Mohawk International Lacrosse (MIL)—manufactures sticks only
- Nami—manufactures goalie equipment only
- Boddam—manufactures goalie equipment only
- Cascade—manufactures field helmet only

## Canadian Lacrosse Association Rules About the Lacrosse Stick

1. The lacrosse stick head and handle shall be designed and manufactured of a framework of wood, plastic, or other materials. On this frame shall be woven a netting of soft leather, nylon, or other material. Replaceable handles of the lacrosse stick must be specifically designed and manufactured for the game of lacrosse. All designs and materials shall be approved by the CLA.
2. Referees shall not allow the use of any lacrosse stick that, in their opinion, is liable to cause injury due to its construction or repair.
3. For players above the 12-years-of-age level, the stick shall measure not more than 46", nor less than 40" in overall length.

**Notes:**

– *For players up to 12 years of age, i.e., Pee Wee level, and all lower divisions, the minimum length of the stick shall be 34" and the maximum length of a stick is 46".*
– *A few years back the minimum length of the stick was 42", but today the minimum length of the stick is 40", so minor/youth players can use one stick for both the box game and field game.*
– *In field lacrosse the minimum length is 40"–42" for attack players and the length of sticks for defensemen is between 52"–72".*

## II. The Stick

*(I would like to thank Mark Brown for his input about box lacrosse sticks and lacrosse equipment. He is the owner of Blades Custom Skate Care Inc., a sporting store in Whitby, Ontario, who has been in the hockey and lacrosse business for 30 years. I would also like to thank Andrew Faric of Lax Shack, in Pickering, Ontario, for his knowledgeable input.)*

"The stick is everything."

A player has to believe in his stick. If he doesn't have confidence in his stick, he won't have confidence in himself. A player wants to feel more of the ball and less of the stick so he wants a lightweight stick. And this is okay if he just plays offense, as in the NLL, but in minor/youth box lacrosse players must play both ways—offense and defense—so the stick has to be light and durable for checking. *Note: In field lacrosse each position requires a different style of stick.*

Many coaches do not take the time to talk about the stick, yet the stick is like a carpenter's tool: the better the tool, the easier it is to work with. So spend some time going over the finer points of the stick with the players and have the players' parents on the floor so they understand about the stick as you explain it to the players.

### I. The Plastic Part of the Stick—the Head

**Width of the Head**

The young lacrosse player should start with a wide face or open head so it is easier to catch the ball and scoop up loose balls. The youth players and parents look at the sticks with the narrow head and like them, but if they are not experienced or good at catching the ball, they shouldn't be going into a narrow "pinched head" stick until they are very proficient at passing and catching.

It is a player's preference at the older levels if he likes to use a narrow or wide mouth of the stick. Narrow is better for accuracy, but wide is better for scooping up loose balls. So there is a trade-off between narrow and wide and a player has to decide which one suits him best.

*Note: The CLA rule for the width of the stick is the stick cannot be more than 8" wide and cannot be narrower than 4½" in width. The measurement for width is to be inside the frame measurement. Nothing may be added to or attached to the outside of the stick.*

*Note: Minor/youth field lacrosse uses FIL rules (Federation of International Lacrosse), but in minor/youth box lacrosse pinching a stick has no effect.*

### Pinching the Head

Today the majority of the players do not pinch their heads anymore, although there are a small few that still pinch them, because now there are a very good variety of "pinched" heads from the factory, which are pinched properly and those are the ones that survive on the lacrosse market. Mark Brown has seen some "pinching" of the stick that kids have done on their own and they are pinched too narrow, pinched wrong, pinched off center, or they put a scoop on the end, which messes up the tip of the stick.

*Gavin Prout of Edmonton Rush of the NLL:* If you are going to pinch the head of the stick make sure you take [all of the] stringing and mesh out of the stick. Do not use the microwave because it will burn and ruin your stick. Use the oven at a lower temperature: 5–10 minutes at 350 degrees Fahrenheit. Then squeeze the head together and let it sit for a day. Then you can re-string it and you are ready to go. I still pinch my heads.

One problem with the new STX box stick is that most of the minor/youth kids are playing field and box and the stick is an illegal size for the field game as the "box stick" is smaller, shorter, and narrower. *Note: The field lacrosse head is narrow at the bottom for face-offs and ball* retention, and wide at the top for easier catching ability and obtaining loose balls.

All the heads below that are mentioned here can be used in both field and box lacrosse. But the better ones are strictly for the box lacrosse game. Here are some of the more common sticks in no particular order recommended by Andrew Faric at the Lax Shack:

**The Gait Torque Head**—This is one of the best sellers in the lacrosse stores as it is a stick that both youth players and experienced players can use.

**The Brine Clutch Head**—A stick for everybody at all levels of lacrosse. Brine makes one for field (wider head) and one for box (pinched into narrower head).

**STX Proton Power**—This is a light, stiff head that can be used for the youth player and experienced player.

**Warrior Evolution**—This stick's head is for everybody. Warrior also makes a stick for field and one for box (pinched) lacrosse. This is a stiffer plastic, which makes it good for playing defense and stops the ball from rolling around a lot.

**Warrior Razer**—This is also a stiff plastic head and is a good stick for youth players.

**MIL (Mohawk)**—This is a stick for new players to the game. It is only for the box game.

**Reebok 9K and 10K**—The Reebok is also a stiffer plastic with holes in the head to reduce wind resistance to give a player a faster shot.

**Notes:**
- *In the NLL the players use Reebok sticks and Reebok equipment because the league is sponsored by Reebok. The Reebok stick is used more in Canada by kids because players in the NLL use them.*
- *Andrew recommends for minor/youth players the Gait Icon Jr. and the Gait Bedlam.*
- *Here are some of the more common sticks which Mark Brown thinks are popular: the Brine "Edge," the Brine Junior Canadian (for kids), the STX "Ball Hog," the Mohawk International*

*Lacrosse (MIL) Mach One, Warrior, deBeer, and the Torque stick in the Reebok series.*

*– STX makes offset heads, including the K18, G22, and the X3 10, which is a 10-degree offset. But it is not as popular in the box game.*

## 2. Type of Mesh or Netting of the Head of the Stick

There are still a few lacrosse stick heads that come flat when you buy them, that is, there is no pocket and they're not game ready. When Mark Brown sells a stick he loosens the pocket to form some semblance of a pocket. More lacrosse stick manufacturers are starting to pre-pocket the sticks, that is, they're game ready for the kids because most kids end up making the pocket right at the throat, which is not where you want your pocket for box lacrosse.

At the Lax Shack, most of their heads come without the mesh, as a lot of players like to pick their own mesh and color. Andrew Faric then strings the mesh to the type of head the player picks out, making it almost game ready.

Some young players like the hard Marc mesh because of the color and flash; others like the soft, white mesh. It boils down to one's preference with the type of color and softness of the mesh. The junior and major players use a white mesh more because they feel the white mesh hides the white ball better. The experienced players also like Marc mesh because it keeps the pocket consistent and it actually feels like a soft mesh. Some players use a hair dryer on the Marc mesh to make it softer.

Mark Brown feels all beginners should start with the soft mesh, not the hard mesh. Some players use more of a medium-hard mesh. The hard mesh was made for the long defensive pole in field lacrosse. STX manufactures the Canadian mesh, which is a medium mesh and is best for the box game.

In box lacrosse there are still only a few guys using the traditional stringing pocket, i.e., leather runners and nylon cord. This traditional pocket is not very popular now since most players do not actually know how to make—and, more importantly, maintain—a traditional pocket. The mesh pocket is easier and requires less upkeep, thus it's the major choice.

*Gavin Prout of the Edmonton Rush of the NLL,* says, " I do not believe using the soft mesh is the case anymore in the NLL. The majority of the players use Marc mesh, or use the hard mesh just worked in very well."

*Note: This year players are using Marc Mesh in the NLL because the league is sponsored by Marc Mesh.*

## 3. The Shaft or Handle of the Stick

When picking out the shaft it is just a preference of which handle feels better over another handle. Players pick a stick because it just feels right. The more a player plays the game, the better idea he gets of all the makes of the sticks and through trial and error he will finally come up with the stick that feels most comfortable and he has the most success with. For the youth/minor lacrosse player, there is a junior stick that is a light-aluminum handle, making it easier for them to handle the ball and thereby having more success with it. Plus at the younger age they will not break it as there isn't a lot of hitting. As young players get older, around 11–13 years, they have to start to get into the adult handles, such as the titanium handle, as the junior-aluminum sticks are not strong enough for them and the stick will break or bend on a cross-check.

Mark Brown sometimes tells parents that their son is too big for the handle, but they like the light-handle stick and still buy it. He knows they are going to bend the handle in a game or practice and bring it back later, bent.

**Remember:** Lacrosse sticks are made "neutral," which means the middle of the tip of the head is lined up exactly in line with the handle. Unlike a hockey stick, where there are left-handed sticks and right-handed sticks.

### Types of Shafts or Handles

Certainly the weight of the stick is a factor when picking a stick. The lighter the stick the faster the motion of the stick head, which increases the speed of the shot. But in minor/youth box lacrosse, where players play both ways, offense and defense, a light stick-shaft might break when checking. A minor/youth player needs a stick-shaft that is light, but durable and strong.

There are three types of shafts: light weight, medium weight, and heavy weight. There is a fine line when youth players reach 11–13 years old and it comes to bending the shaft. Some smaller youths can still use a light stick and never bend it while the bigger youths need a heavier shaft so they can't bend it.

Here are some shafts that Andrew recommends:

- The **aluminum shaft** is the lightest shaft and most manufacturers make these. Young kids use this handle. It is an entry-level stick and comes with no warranty.
- The **platinum alloy** is a medium-weight shaft and is made by Warrior (the Warrior Kryptolyte) and STX (the STX Scandium).
- The **composite or graphite shaft** that is made of fiberglass is made by Reebok (K9 and 10K), Brine Swizzbeat, Gait NRG, Harrow, and Warrior Fatboy.
- The **titanium-alloy** shaft is the best on the market and most manufacturers make it. It is not only stronger and more durable for the older players, but quite light to handle and tough to bend.
- The Gait Orange Crusher is the thickest and strongest shaft there is. STX Scandium and Warrior Fat Boy also make a strong handle. If players bend their shaft in box lacrosse, the Lax Shack automatically gives them the Gait Orange Crusher.

The experienced player mixes up the plastic head and the shaft sometimes, but there are some good head and shaft combinations for box lacrosse, such as the Reebok 10K head and shaft, the Warrior Evolution head and Warrior Fat Boy shaft, the Brine Clutch head and Swizzbeat shaft, and the Gait Torque head and Gait NRG shaft.

### The Bend in the Shaft

Some players still like to bend the handle slightly to give deception to the goalie on their shot where the goalie thinks the ball is coming out normally on the release, but it comes out later because of the stick being farther back behind the shooter's body. Although some players still do this, it's tougher to do nowadays because a lot of companies are using composite shafts that won't bend.

The STX "SSH Katana" is a new performance shaft with a slight bend in the middle of the shaft. The Gait brothers used to bend their sticks when they played in the NLL; not in the middle, but just below the mid-point to get a better whip in their shot.

STX make the Crankshaft system handle which dips at the end of the handle at the insertion of the plastic head. There is a 10-degree bend at the end of the stick. This bend causes a later release of the ball and a better feel of the ball.

### Grip for the Shaft

Most players do not put any tape or the likes on the shaft as it makes it harder to slip the hands up and down the shaft in certain situations. Some manufacturers put a grip on the shaft for better handling and less slippage; some put ribs on the shaft for better grip. STX has the Vanadium grip, which makes it easier to handle the shaft.

### Knob at the Butt

Some players like to wrap tape around the butt of the stick to form a knob to give support for the bottom hand to prevent the hand slipping off the end of the handle; others wrap their bottom hand around the knob. It is all in one's preference on how the knob feels when he handles the stick.

*Note: The Western Lacrosse League (BCLA) has now disallowed any wood sticks in their league.*

## 4. The Length of the Stick

**Notes:**
– *The CLA rule for the length of the stick from the head to the end of the handle is for players above the 12-years-of-age level shall measure not more than 46", nor less than 40" in overall length.*
– *The reason the CLA changed the rule length from 42" to 40" was so that a player can use the same stick for both the box and field games and it appears that most kids do use the same stick for both.*
– *In the NLL players also use sticks between 40" to 46".*
– *For players up to 12 years of age (Pee Wee level) and all lower divisions, the minimum length of the stick shall be 34" and the maximum length of a stick is 46".*
– *As the players get older they seem to have two sticks: one for the outdoor game and one for the indoor game to maintain a pocket for box and to keep clean.*

**Length Affecting Shot**
The length of the shaft is another factor in determining the power of the shot. Minor/youth players are encouraged to play with a shorter stick as it will make it easier to catch, throw, and control the ball, but with a short shaft a player gets less wind-up and therefore less speed and power. With a longer shaft a player might get more power in his shot as the ball will travel more on the wind-up, but it might take too long to get the shot off, plus he will lose out on his ball-handling skills.

**Length Affecting Maneuverability**
If the stick is too short he will lose power on his shot yet be able to maneuver his stick better in traffic. If the stick is too long he will

have more power on his shot, but he will find it cumbersome to maneuver when in traffic and possibly get checked off the ball. Also if a coach sees a player "choking up" on his stick, bringing his top-hand up closer to the throat and his bottom hand up from the end of the stick, he is trying to compensate for the length by making it shorter to maneuver, which means the stick is too long. A player has got to use a stick that is comfortable for him and easy to handle.

The older players feel "the shorter the stick, the better they can control it" so the offensive players like to cut the handle near the 40" mark, but a short stick does not give a player as much power on the long shot. For the defensive player the length of the stick could range from 42"–46" to give that extra length for checking. The average length for an older player's stick is around 41"–43".

A minor/youth player has to experiment to find the proper length that feels right and that suits him best for ball-handling and shooting. Some minor/youth coaches cut their players' handles off at 36", no matter what their body size is. But if a young player is a big kid he could use a longer length from 39"–42". It all depends on what the player is capable of using.

## 5. The Depth of the Pocket

The criteria for depth of pocket:
a. If a player can see a space, about a width of a finger, between the top of the ball and the bottom of the plastic sidewall, the pocket is pretty deep, but this seems to be more common in the game today. Usually a player has to put in 3–4 shooting strings to make sure the ball has a smooth path to run out on the release.
b. If a player can see the whole ball between the top of the ball and the bottom of the plastic sidewall, the pocket is still considered normal for today's game. Usually a player has to put in 2–3 shooting strings to make sure the ball has a smooth

**Photo 2:** Depth of Shooting Pocket—ball depth plus finger

path to run out on the release. A lot of times the depth depends on the type of game a player plays—a fast passing game or a slow one-on-one game.

c.  If a player can see three-quarters of the ball below the bottom plastic sidewall, the pocket is considered shallow.

**Notes:**

– *In box lacrosse there is no restriction in regards to the depth of the pocket. But even though there is no pocket depth restriction in box lacrosse rules, the ball must dislodge normally and a pocket cannot be formed to withhold the ball.*

– *In NCAA field lacrosse the rule for pocket depth is a referee cannot see light between the top of the*

**Photo 3:** Depth of Shooting Pocket—ball depth

*ball and below the bottom plastic siding when viewing the ball on a horizontal position.*

– *Minor/youth field lacrosse in Canada uses FIL rules.*

– *Minor/youth players are encouraged to start with a shallow pocket, but this is harder to keep the ball in the pocket.*

How to determine the pocket depth: if a player wants to have a shallow pocket then he has the pocket just deep enough to see three-quarters of the ball below the bottom plastic sidewall. This pocket is not too deep and not too shallow. If a player can see the total ball underneath the bottom plastic sidewall, it is considered a fairly deep pocket. Definitely a ball-depth pocket allows a player to bring the stick-head back farther in an attempt to exert a greater force on the ball upon its release, but the ball might end up "hooking" on the release and take longer to get the shot off. With this deep pocket a player will need time and space to shoot, which goes against the trend of today's game of less wind-up for a quicker release on the shot.

The depth of the pocket could depend on the type of system a player plays in, the type of player he is, and the type of shooter he is.

Usually, for a player in a ball-control system or a player who likes to hang onto the ball more and go one-on-one more, the pocket is fairly deep, a ball depth plus a finger width below the bottom plastic sidewall, so that it's harder to "cough up" the ball.

A player in a running Fast-Break system usually likes to pass the ball more and cut for return passes, so the pocket is about as deep as a ball depth, the criteria is usually that one can just see daylight between the top of the ball under the bottom of the frame. This type of pocket gives players the ability to throw a quick release and get more velocity on their shot. Some players like to have very shallow pockets, but not as flat as a tennis racquet. Most overhand shooters have average three-quarter depth pockets; whereas the sidearm and underhand shooters like depths of a ball or more.

## 6. Where the "Shooting Pocket" Is Formed

Players should catch and throw from the same spot in the netting all the time. Usually the spot, called the "Shooting Pocket," is found at the edge of the last or bottom shooting string at the beginning of the slope (middle of the pocket) or near the tip of the stick (slightly forward from the middle of the pocket). It is best to form the shooting pocket just below the last or bottom shooting string so there is a nice, short, smooth path for the ball to run out of. With the ball resting against or below the last shooting string a player has a quicker release, more momentum in his shot, and higher ball trajectory on the release and thereby less chance of the ball hooking, i.e., having the ball hitting the original shooting string that came with the stick and consequently going low.

A shooter in today's game, more so than ever, wants the ball to come right in and go right out for a quicker shot. He wants the ball to come out nice and smooth on the release. If the shooting pocket is at the back of the netting near the throat of the stick or in the middle of the pocket the ball has too far to run and by the time it exits the pocket the head of the stick is in front of the shooter's body, resulting in a low pass or shot.

**Remember**: A player can correct a low pass or shot by having the release point farther behind the body.

Often in a game, players catch the ball by accident in the middle of the pocket or near the throat rather than at the tip of the stick. There are two ways to get the ball to the tip of the stick if they have time: they can cradle the ball to the tip, and/or drop the head of the stick back so the ball will just roll down to the tip.

The overhand player can pass and shoot the ball from close to the tip of the stick because of his shallow pocket, while the sidearm and underhand passers/shooters who have deeper pockets to keep the ball in the stick usually have their shooting pockets in the middle of the pocket. These types of players have to use three to four shooting strings to give a smooth path for the ball to come out of the pocket.

For most players the ball should sit in the dead center of the pocket (equal distance from the sidewalls) so the ball has a straight path to come out of the pocket. This again complements the straight-line theory in teaching overhand passing. Sidearm and underhand shooters like the ball to rest close to the plastic frame, for example, for a left-hand sidearm passer he likes the ball to rest closer to the right frame and vice versa. They feel this is a better position for the ball when passing, faking, and shooting.

To test the position of the pocket, hold the stick horizontally or level to the ground. While holding the stick level to the ground a player can check the depth and position of the pocket by seeing if the ball sits slightly below the last shooting string. He can test the smoothness of the pocket by pulling the stick toward himself to see if the ball rolls easily and effortlessly out of the pocket up into the air lightly.

*Gavin Prout of the Edmonton Rush of the NLL,* says, "Forming the pocket all depends on where you want your pocket, if you're more comfortable with it at the bottom or throat of the stick then that's fine."

## 7. How to Form the Pocket for a Plastic Stick?

To form a pocket in a plastic stick with a mesh pocket, the sidewall string must be loosened to allow the mesh to sag more in the area that you want to place the pocket. To form a larger pocket you need to take out the side strings and re-string the mesh on the sidewalls. Leaving a space of one to two rows will allow the pocket to be even deeper.

To stop the pocket from forming at the throat of the stick for box lacrosse, pull in the string that goes across the back of the pocket to make it tighter so it helps to form the pocket more in the middle of it. Some minor players even put in a string or lace across the throat from the plastic sidewall-to-sidewall, about one inch from the end, to stop the ball from settling or rolling into the throat.

*Note: STX sells what it calls "game-ready" sticks because the pocket is pre-formed for the player. Some sticks come with a flat mesh and the player has to form his own pocket. Mark Brown of Blades and Andrew at the Lax Shack form the pocket for the player.*

## 8. The Shooting Strings

### Why Put in Shooting Strings

A stick "hooks" when the exiting ball hits or catches on the permanent shooting string that came with the stick, on the edge of a newly placed shooting string added by the player that is too tight or too loose, or on the plastic mouth of the head of the stick changing the direction of the ball as it leaves the pocket and forcing it down. A major cause of "hooking" is that the pocket is just too deep and the ball catches a shooting string as it leaves the pocket, forcing it in a downward projection. To compensate for this "hook," players put in extra shooting strings to make a smooth path for the ball to run out of the pocket.

The important thing to remember is shooting strings should be put in a stick for a reason, i.e., to get rid of a "hook." But once the shooting strings are in place, the player should always be checking the roll of the ball over the shooting strings to make sure the path is smooth. If there is a ridge or gully created by the shooting strings, they should be adjusted by tightening or loosening them.

On the release of the ball some players want to feel the ball hit the top shooting string as it leaves the pocket, not the plastic; some like it to tick the tip of the plastic; and others don't want to feel anything but a smooth release.

### How to Put in Shooting Strings

The player uses a hockey lace for the shooting strings because of its thickness and strength. First fold the lace in half of two equal lengths. Secure the joined end to the side of the plastic sidewall by tying the laces together, then, starting with one lace above and one below

**Photo 4:** Weaving Shooting Strings (one lace above netting and another lace below netting)

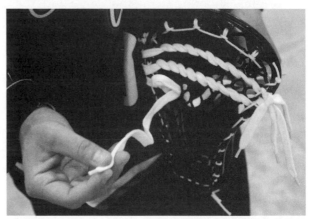

**Photo 5:** Weaving Shooting Strings (above lace went below and below lace went up to above and twisted around each other)

**Photo 6:** Weaving Shooting Strings (anchor laces to plastic frame)

the mesh, start to use a twisting pattern going through each hole of the mesh. Weave the laces in and out of the mesh and over each other all the way across the netting to the other side and end up tying the two laces again to the other plastic side. Attaching the laces to both sides of the frame gives the shooting strings stability to raise or lower the netting slightly.

### Number of Shooting Strings

Most players use basically two to three shooting strings, but players have to have a feeling of the stick to determine the number of exact shooting strings. Sidearm and underhand shooters sometimes use up to four shooting strings. Players try to use each shooting string to help another shooting string, so if a player puts in three shooting strings he wants them all touching or close to each other by skipping a row.

### Results of Putting in Shooting Strings

Putting in shooting strings allows the ball to exit the stick smoothly.

### The V-shooting Pocket

The V-shooting string is to help keep the ball in the center of the pocket, equal distance from sidewall to sidewall. To put in a V-shooting string a player starts to weave the laces in and out of the mesh from one side of the plastic side and works his way up to the center of the pocket about two holes from the last shooting string, then he comes back down to the other side of the stick, ending exactly across from where he started. Some minor/youth players use this new V-shooting pocket, which came from the field game, but most Juniors and Majors do not use it at all.

*Gavin Prout of the Edmonton Rush of the NLL* says this V-method is used so the "V" channels the ball up through the middle of the stick. It also compacts and squeezes the pocket for better ball control as there is not as much space for the ball to move around in the stick.

*Colin Doyle of the Toronto Rock of the NLL talks about his stick:* I use four shooting strings with Marc Mesh. I prefer nylon or skate laces as shooting strings. I like to catch the ball mid-to-high in the pocket so that I have a quicker release for passing and shooting. I also like to catch and throw the ball from the same spot as much as possible. My top hand does not move much whether I am passing or shooting. The criterion for my ball depth for my pocket is you cannot see the whole ball beneath the bottom plastic sidewall.

**Recall:** Great shooters like two to three shooting strings, a pocket at the tip of the stick, with the ball sitting in the pocket at a ball depth below the plastic bottom sidewall. Although most players have similar pockets to the explanation above, there is some flexibility as to depth and position of the pocket depending on how the release of the ball feels. *Note: Most factory-made sticks now come with two shooting strings, a V-string, and a soft mesh.*

## 9. Storage of the Stick

After a game or practice how does a player store his stick to maintain it? Where does he store it? Does he place a ball in it during storage? Does he stand it up? Does he lay it flat on the floor? Does he leave it in his parents' car? A minor/youth player should punch his pocket out lightly to maintain the pocket shape and face it standing up against a wall with the pocket away from the wall; this will make sure his stick is ready the next time he uses it.

It isn't used much in box lacrosse anymore, but if a minor/youth happens to be using a wooden stick with leather runners and cord netting he should not store it by hanging it. This can lead to deforming the shape of the head. A player should also untie the gut sidewall when not in use, this takes the stress off the sidewall and keeps it in better shape for play, so it's less apt to start to curl in. For long-term storage it's a good idea to place popsicle sticks in the gut to hold the shape.

## III. Putting on Equipment for the Lacrosse Player

The injury factor is still a concern in minor/youth lacrosse, but not as much as when the old wooden hickory stick was used to hit or cross-check. The key in minor/youth lacrosse in regards to equipment is to be well protected, while maintaining enough flexibility to handle the stick. If there is a question of too much protection versus taking it off to get more movement, go with the protection first.

With the older groups the philosophy with the arrival of the plastic stick and aluminum handles is to "dress down" in regards to equipment, because the plastic stick and aluminum handle does not hurt as much as the old wooden sticks. "Less is better" has become the motto. By not wearing as much padding the players have more flexibility and lightness, which gives the players better and quicker offensive moves and better control of their stick.

### 1. Gloves

When buying lacrosse gloves look first for a good fit; not too tight and not too loose. Most of the gloves fit fairly tight, which is okay, but STX makes a glove that is moderately loose. Then, look for good protection, especially around the thumb area and the back of the hand, which are the areas that get most of the hits. Players want

**Photo 7:** Lacrosse player wearing equipment (Front view)

**Photo 8:** Lacrosse player wearing equipment (Back view)

maximum mobility, flexibility, and protection. Finally, a player has to decide whether to buy the cheaper nylon or the more expensive leather for protection. Most gloves are now padded or have high density foam covering them.

For beginners, if the lacrosse player is not a hockey player, a parent should buy lacrosse gloves because they have a lot more flexibility, give better protection, and are lighter than hockey gloves. These give a player a lot more mobility to handle the stick properly. In Canada, parents are hesitant to buy lacrosse gloves because they already have hockey gloves, which they think will do the same thing: protect the hands. Also, the cost of lacrosse gloves is another deterrent to buying them, as they range from about $40–$65 in small sizes. A lot of parents want their sons to use their hockey gloves because they don't know if they are going to like the sport and don't want to invest everything in it. Of course, if a minor/youth player is not too sure he is going to like lacrosse he could stay with the hockey gloves until he has had a chance to say it is "my sport." But if he learns to like the game of lacrosse, then move on because you have a lot better stick control with lacrosse gloves.

Another reason lacrosse gloves are better than hockey gloves is players play in hot arenas and the mesh in the palm of lacrosse gloves helps the glove to breathe, which helps to keep the hands and glove dry. That means the gloves will last longer, and the soft dry mesh gives a player a better feel of the stick. Players do not cut the palms out any more as they used to do in the old days. Also, lacrosse gloves have much more movement and are lighter than hockey gloves. With the new type of lacrosse glove you buy them and wear them right away.

***Gavin Prout of the Edmonton Rush of the NLL***, says, "I disagree with the above statement. A hockey glove is way too restricting on the movements, especially with the thumbs.

I suggest parents buy equipment from Play-It-Again Sports [or a comparable resale sporting goods store] if they are worried about the price; besides they can always sell it back if the minor/youth player doesn't like the sport."

*Note: Andrew Faric feels some of the better gloves for box lacrosse are: the Brine King 3, the Warrior Mac Daddy, the STX K18, the Reebok 9K and 10K, and the Gait Recon.*

## 2. Lacrosse Shoulder Pads

Most of these are all the same, so again it is just a matter of preference on how the pads feel. Box lacrosse players are dressing down more in regards to equipment because of the use of the aluminum stick. Most shoulder pads are made for the field game. The lacrosse shoulder pads protect the chest, shoulders, and back area. Some shoulder pads come with a removable bicep pad or players can use a bicep-arm guard or bicep pad to protect the bicep.

If players play with their hockey shoulder pads, they usually tape on the plastic shin guard from their hockey pants on the upper arm of the shoulder pads where they receive most of their hits and cross-checks. But players should be aware that hockey shoulder pads are designed to keep the arms down, which is fine for hockey, but in the game of lacrosse the arms are held up in the air. The basic light-hockey shoulder pad can definitely be used for lacrosse, but the upper-end hockey shoulder pad is quite bulky, hard, and not nearly as good for lacrosse.

*Note: Andrew thinks some of the better shoulder-pads are: the Warrior Players Series (which is good for the box game as it has a thick bicep-pad), the Brine Esquire, the Reebok 10K, and the Gait Recon.*

## 3. Arm Guard (Slash Guard)

Arm guards are slightly longer and go all the way down the arm and below the elbow almost to the wrist area. The arm guard has a big plastic cap on the outside of the padding to protect the elbow and comes with a Spandex sleeve that a player can slide his arm through for better stability. Players use the field lacrosse arm guard (slash guards) because it gives protection that goes from the elbow area of the arm almost to the top of the glove. It is a good idea to add a padded arm guard with Velcro over the top of the slash guard to protect the bicep area. The field lacrosse slash guards are nice, but they seem to leave a lot of space above the glove where their arms can get hit.

Minor/youth players sometimes buy the shoulder pad and slash guard and put them together. Remember the shoulder pads are to hold the bicep guards on. This is a three-piece, curved-fiberglass pad that comes all connected to be flexible and to protect the forearm, the elbow, and the bicep area of the arm.

*Note: Andrew feels the better arm guards for box lacrosse are: the Gait Recon, the STX Assault, the Reebok 9K, the Brine King 3, Warrior Tank, the Warrior Flex, and the Brine Esquire.*

## 4. Elbow Guard (Slash Guard)

Elbow guards are similar to the arm guards, but have shorter protection up and down the arm. The elbow plastic cap comes with padding.

## 5. Bicep Pad

This pad helps to protect the bicep area. It comes with a fiberglass cover that forms to the bicep and is kept in place by a Velcro strap. Some players put tape over the strap for reinforcement as it stops the pad from moving around.

*Note: Andrew from the Lax Shack feels the bicep pad is crucial. Some players only wear one, depending on which side of the body they take a cross-check or hit to when they drive to the net. Andrew likes STX Bicep Pad, the Warrior Bicep Pad and the gait Bicep Pad.*

## 6. Wrist Pad

This is a padded wrist guard to cover the gap area between the glove and slash guard.

*Jim Veltman, formerly of the Toronto Rock of the NLL:* I wear as much light yet comfortable equipment as I can. I protect the areas where I tend to bruise a lot, especially on my forearms.

## 7. Kidney/Rib Pads

Mark Brown feels the single most important thing a minor/youth player wears is the kidney pad. This is the area where players get hit a lot, besides the arms and back. This jacket-like pad must fit properly for good protection; in fact, it can fit him a little big because it wraps around the entire back and side-hip area, and is adjustable. It's a hard plastic covered with nylon wrap. It is important that a player should wear a kidney pad in lacrosse just like he wears a jock in hockey. All the manufacturers make the kidney pad.

*Note: Andrew thinks the better rib pads for box lacrosse are the Brine Esquire, the Gait Intrepid, the Warrior Fatboy, and the Reebok 9K.*

## 8. The Jock

Mark Brown recommends the "jock" for protection of the groin area. It is made by Bike, and it's made for running like a baseball-type jock. There is a cup to protect the player in the groin area and Mark Brown finds most parents want their son to wear a cup. Most minor/youth associations make it mandatory to wear a cup. Mark feels if you forget your cup you can still play lacrosse, if you forget your kidney pads you can't play. Mark also feels that hockey jocks are not made for running and can chafe, irritate, and rub the skin.

*Note: Andrew likes the Warrior Players Club Nutt Hutt. They are a compression short-style jock with great flexibility and are comfortable for running.*

## 9. Helmet/Face Masks

It is important that the helmet fits properly and does not move or flop around. Most lacrosse players wear a cage to protect the face, not a full-face plastic hockey visor as the visor becomes too hot for summer wear. Players in lacrosse, when they breathe inside a hot arena with a visor, it will fog up, whereas on the ice a player gets the cool air to stop the visor from fogging up.

More minor/youth lacrosse kids are wearing the Calcoat/Maxsite lacrosse mask. It is like an old hockey goalie mask with wider spaces for better vision and stronger bars. This brand is the only one for minor lacrosse. Adult players can wear cages that are similar.

Hockey helmets and field lacrosse helmets can be used by an out-player in minor/youth box lacrosse, but must meet the standards and be approved by CSA (Canadian Standards Association) for ice hockey or by NOCSAE (National Organizing Committee for Safety in Athletic Equipment) for lacrosse.

Mark thinks the best helmet is the Bauer 7500 hockey helmet with the Nami lacrosse face mask attached to it. This wire-lacrosse face mask has bigger eye holes than the regular hockey-wire face masks and is curved around and under the chin. He also feels the Bauer helmet, the STX helmet, and the Gait helmet are all pretty good.

*Note: Andrew thinks the best face masks for minor/youth players are the Gait face mask and the Nami lacrosse mask. For the Junior-aged players and older, he likes the OTNY 20/20 face mask kit, and for helmets he likes Cascade CPX, Cascade Pro 7, and the Warrior Trojan.*

## 10. Mouthpiece

Mouthguards are mandatory in minor/youth lacrosse. Player can use a dentist-made or heat-and-mold mouthguard. It seems the "Shock Doctor" is rated higher than a dentist mouthguard for protection. The difference is the dental mouthguard is molded to your teeth and stays on your teeth a little nicer, has less gagging, is easier to talk with and easier to breathe than self-molded ones. Self-

molded cost between $4 (Fox 40) to $80 (Under Armour), while the dentist is about $200. The mouthguard is not only to protect the teeth from getting chipped and broken, but to help stop concussions by stopping the upper and lower jaw from jamming together which could cause a shockwave which could cause a concussion.

## 11. Knee Pads

A few players wear knee pads, which are made of a sponge material over the knee to protect the knees from bruises and scrapes. Andrew Faric of the Lax Shack feels that a good volleyball knee pad is the best due to its flexibility and comfort.

## 12. Running Shoes

Mark Brown suggests that players wear the three-quarter or high-cut basketball/running shoe, which gives better ankle support than the low-cut basketball shoe, because of all the cutting and running in lacrosse. Another suggestion Mark gives to players is to keep the shoes as strictly their lacrosse shoes and not to wear them as an everyday shoe. Wearing them every day will break down the sole of the shoe and get them dirty, giving a player less traction, which will cause him to slip and slide in a game.

The final suggestion from Mark is to make sure the shoe is a good fit because if it is too big a player could get blisters. In fact, some players wear two pairs of thick socks for absorption of sweat, prevention of blisters, and protection of their feet.

**Remember:** A player should make sure his socks are smooth when putting them on because any wrinkle could cause blisters.

*Notes:*
*– Brine and Warrior (New Balance) make shoes for the lacrosse game—Warrior for the field game and Brine for the box game. STX (Nike) and Reebok make shoes in general for box lacrosse.*

– *In 1968, Converse made the first leather running shoe for the Detroit Olympics of the NLA. It was a red-and-white high-top version of the Chuck Taylor Converse All-Star.*

## 13. Dressing for the Game

The order of putting on one's equipment for a game in lacrosse is very straightforward and simple. The player should put his cup, shorts, T-shirt, socks, and shoes on first. Then he inserts his kidney pads. Make sure the kidney pads' straps will stay in place and stay on by tying or taping them together. Then pull on the three-piece shoulder pads and slash guards. Some players like the straps of their kidney pads to go on the outside of the shoulder pads. It's a comfort and preference thing. Next, a player puts on his sweater. He wants the sweater to be big enough to go over his equipment, but not so big that it gets in the way of his ability to handle his stick and not so small that he plays stiff. Finally, he puts the helmet on, and then his gloves.

# Chapter 2

# Cradling the Ball

A player can go after loose balls, shoot the ball, pass the ball, and be able to go one-on-one, but he better be able to protect the ball from an opponent to be successful as a lacrosse player. Cradling is the art of keeping the ball in the stick without looking at it. So if a player can cradle the ball in his stick he will know where the ball is without looking, which is extremely important so that he can look at the net, see his teammates cutting, and concentrate on beating his defender without worrying about whether he has the ball in his pocket.

## I. What is Cradling?

Cradling is a side-to-side, up-and-down, or back-and-forth rocking motion of the stick, which:

- Keeps the ball in a player's stick and gives him the ability to run and get checked with the ball and still hang on to it.
- Tells a player by "feel" or by "weight" that the ball is in his stick.
- Tells a player where the ball is in his pocket without having to look at it.

## II. When to Cradle

A player cradles basically whenever he has the ball. In particular:

- When taking a check
- When running down the floor with the ball
- When protecting the stick after obtaining a loose ball
- When getting the ball to the tip of the stick for a shot or a pass
- When checking to see if the ball is still in his stick
- When unsure where the ball is in his pocket

## III. Position of Stick When Cradling

**There are four positions of holding the stick for cradling:**

1. Player can hold the stick high with both hands at a 45-degree angle to the floor when running down the floor just before passing or shooting. (See Chapter 4, Passing, and Chapter 8, Shooting)

2. Player can hold the stick high and horizontally to the floor with both hands in a cocked position when standing stationary or moving slightly, just before passing or shooting. (See Chapter 4, Passing, and Chapter 8, Shooting)

3. Player can hold the stick at waist level and horizontally in front of the body with both hands while running up the floor or just before he goes one-on-one. Most players have a natural tendency to run with the ball, carrying it at waist level, but it is more

practical to run with the ball while holding the stick up in a passing position.

4. Players can hold the stick vertically or at a slight 45-degree angle beside the body while taking a check.

## IV. Three Types of Cradles

Players practice three basic styles of cradling with two hands, depending on the game situation:

### 1. The Small Cradle

This small side-to-side or up-and-down rocking motion of the stick is used when a player standing stationary holds the stick horizontally, looking to pass or shoot while still knowing where the ball is in his stick, or when moving the ball to the tip of his stick in a horizontally cocked position for a shot or pass.

**Photo 9:** The Small Cradle—player is stationary, ready to pass or shoot using wrists

This continuous swinging action is mainly accomplished by the top-hand wrist and usually when the stick is held in the "cocked" position (i.e. horizontal to the floor). The top-hand wrist rotates lightly side-to-side causing the stick to rock side-to-side or the top-hand wrist rotates up-and-down causing the stick to swing up-and-down. This swinging motion helps a player to "feel" the weight of the ball in the pocket and to move it to the tip of the stick. The hand placements are the same for passing and shooting. The butt of one's stick just turns slightly in the bottom-hand grip.

### 2. The Medium Cradle

This is more of an up-and-down motion of the stick, and is a little more forceful than the small cradle, and is executed: 1) when just running the ball up the floor with the stick held in a horizontal position in front of the body with two hands holding the stick, not really looking to pass or shoot, 2) just prior to going one-on-one, 3) when running down the floor with the ball, holding the stick in a three-quarter horizontal position with two hands close together over the stick-shoulder, looking to pass or shoot.

**Photo 10:** The Medium Cradle (just before going one-on-one)

**Photo 11:** The Medium Cradle (running up the floor at 45-degree angle, looking to pass)

**Photo 12:** The Large Cradle (when ballcarrier is being cross-checked, stick is held vertically)

Players use the medium cradle when in heavy traffic, to let the player know by feel that he has the ball, plus this swinging motion creates a centrifugal force to help keep the ball in the stick.

This up-and-down medium cradle motion is created by the top-hand wrist and the forearm moving simultaneously upward and downward. The hand placements are wider than the passing and shooting position, with the top hand holding the shaft near the throat of the stick and the bottom hand gripping the butt. The stick turns slightly in the bottom-hand grip.

**Variation:** Another way players create this up-and-down cradle action is by just using the top-hand wrist fingers only. The players straighten the fingers and let the stick roll downward to the finger tips, then curl the fingers and the wrist upward, bringing the stick up also.

## 3. The Large Cradle

This back-and-forth rocking action of the stick is mainly used when taking a hit or being

checked while carrying the ball. The stick is held vertically to the floor while the body protects it.

This continuous back-and-forth swinging motion of the stick is created by the wrist flexing inward and outward. When the wrist flexes inward the forearm and the upper arm of the top hand also move forward; and when the wrist flexes outward the forearm and the upper arm of the top hand also move backward. It is important that the top hand grips the stick at or close to the throat. This motion of the wrist and forearm, as noted above, creates a centrifugal force, keeping the ball in the stick. The bottom-hand grip at the butt end of the stick is loose, allowing the stick to rotate within it. On contact from the cross-check, make sure the top-hand wrist is rotating forward. This will put the "face" of the pocket facing toward the direction of the impact, with the result of the netting of the pocket blocking the ball from falling out.

**Points to Stress When Taking a Check** (*See Chapter 6, Inside Slide Move*)
Player turns his body sideways, as a shield to protect the stick, and takes the impact of the

cross-check on the upper arm padding rather than on the back. He watches the checker over his shoulder rather than watching the ball in the stick. Make sure he chokes up on his stick, holding it at or near the throat, to cradle better. When a player executes the Large Cradle he should hold the stick vertically. On taking the hit he should lean into his checker and relax rather than tightening. Finally he should take a wide stance to keep good balance and stability on the hit. *Note: If a player merely holds the ball in the pocket when taking a check, the ball will simply be jarred out from the sudden impact of the cross-check.*

**One-on-One Cradling Drills (See Chapter 6, Individual Offensive Drills)**

# Chapter 3

# **Catching**

Stick-handling or ball-handling is the ability to catch and throw the ball accurately without a conscious effort and without looking at the ball when it is in the stick. Catching is part of ball-handling which is based on the feel or weight of the ball in the stick.

For beginners, catching gives them more problems than passing and it seems to be a much harder skill to master. Many times beginners will have the ball fall right into their stick and they will still drop it because they have not learned the proper way to catch. Beginners have a tendency to tighten up on their grip, which is opposite to what they have to do—relax and "give" with the stick.

Catching the ball may seem like a simple enough skill that a player should catch the ball every time, but this is definitely not true. Parents can help their child develop catching skills quicker by practicing with them in the backyard or at the local park. Parents, if not adept at lacrosse, can use a baseball glove.

## I. The Grip

- The position of the bottom hand, which gives the stick stability and holds it vertically, is placed at the butt of the stick, holding the stick lightly so it can rotate in the hand. The top hand is placed slightly below the mid-point of the shaft, about 8" from the bottom hand, and is for power and guiding the stick. This grip is important as a player doesn't have to change it to pass, catch, fake, or go one-on-one.

- Players wrap their fingers around the shaft with a loose grip when catching; by keeping the wrist and fingers of both hands relaxed, the wrists can rotate and turn freely. Grabbing the stick tightly restricts stick movement. If a player tightens up with his hands and arms, he will be stiff and rigid in his passing and catching, and will be "fighting" the ball when trying to move his stick quickly to get it in front of the ball. Remember to hold the stick with the fingers, snugly, but loosely, and not to grab the stick tightly.

- Some players like to place both their thumbs along the shaft to have more control and flexibility of the stick, others just like to wrap the thumbs right around the shaft. Again this is whatever feels comfortable and is an individual preference.

- A good player should not have to move his top hand up the shaft to catch and then move it down to pass. But a beginning player, who is having problems catching, can slide the top hand up the shaft to the throat to catch, like a baseball glove, then slide his top hand back down to pass.

*Note: When shooting, players typically slide their top-arm hand down, closer to the bottom hand, approximately 4" apart, so that they can get more of a whip (power) in their shot. (See Chapter 8, Shooting.)*

## II. Receiving Positioning of Body and Stick

### Body

• If the receiver has the opportunity, he should always face his passer with his body to receive the pass. As a player becomes more adept at catching the ball he can catch the ball with his body turned sideways, over his stick shoulder and in front of his body. Basically an experienced player should be able to catch the ball thrown anywhere around his body.

### Stick

• Always give a good target to the passer. In other words, always keep the stick up for a target. Line up the "face" of the pocket to the passer for him to aim at.

• Hold the stick out in front of the body, about one foot, and in front of the stick shoulder. By holding the stick out in front of the body, as opposed to holding it to the side of the body, a player can both catch the ball and still see the play in front of him developing and have the stick in a position to drop back over his shoulder on the catch.

• It is important to catch the ball with the stick in the same grip-position as a player would throw from. It is also important to catch the ball in the same spot in the pocket that he throws from. Both of these techniques allow for a quick release and do not waste time, such as "cocking" to shoot or "cradling" the stick before the pass.

**Photo 13:** Receiving position of stick—Stress the grip (hands), receiving positioning of stick (stick out in on front), and body for the catch (facing passer)

• Line up the "face" of the pocket in front of the ball and let the ball come to the pocket.

• It is very important to be physically and mentally prepared to pass the ball before catching it. Hold the stick in a "passing position," so as soon as the receiver catches the ball he is in a position to pass it immediately.

## III. The "Give"—Contact of the Ball with the Netting

• Before contact with the ball, keep the stick out in front of the body and wait for the ball to come to the stick. As the ball approaches the pocket, drop the stick gradually back as it absorbs the ball into the pocket. Reaching for the ball with his stick forces the player to cradle the stick by automatically bringing the stick around in front of his body so the ball will not fall out of the pocket. This movement wastes time, especially if he is executing a quick Give-and-Go play, because the player has to take his stick back to get it in a cocked position.

- On the actual contact of the ball with the netting, the stick should be beside the head.
- Similar to catching a baseball in a glove, the receiver must "give" with his stick on impact of the ball to cushion it, i.e., slow the ball down gradually. He gives by relaxing his grip or by dropping his top-hand arm backward and his top-hand wrist backward. This motion lets his stick head drop backward as the mesh makes contact with the ball and helps to cushion the impact of the ball in the pocket so that it will not bounce out. Players should think of catching the ball as if they were catching an egg.

Beginning players have a tendency to make certain common errors:
- They tighten up or "fight the ball" when catching. When they tighten up their stick, it becomes like a tennis racquet with the ball bouncing off of it.
- They try to catch the ball in front of their body by trying to stop the ball immediately, with the result that the ball bounces out of their pocket.
- They "twirl" their stick inward to help maintain the ball in the pocket.

## IV. Eye on the Ball

- Concentrate on keeping an eye on the ball as it approaches. Players often drop passes because of lack of concentration.
- Look the ball all the way into the pocket, but once in the stick, watch the play. As players get better at catching, they don't have to watch the ball all the way as it becomes instinctive. Remember, a player catches the ball with his eyes and feet first and finally with his stick.

## V. The Catch

By the time a player actually catches the ball, the stick is now in a horizontal position or slightly higher, and behind his body and over his stick shoulder. Now he is in a position to pass the ball back to his teammate or shoot the ball.

*Note: Players that drop passes regularly are not always suffering from poor technique. Sometimes they're simply thinking of shooting or passing before they actually catch the ball. As players become more experienced they can anticipate what they are going to do before they catch the ball, once catching is a natural thing and they do it without thinking.*

# Chapter 4

# Passing

The most important skill in lacrosse is passing, because it is the fastest way of moving the ball. Passing is the chief weapon for attacking any defense, so players have to take pride in their passing, both as an individual and as a team. The offense wants to pass to move the defense, so every pass must count. With constant body and ball movement it becomes harder to guard someone, and therefore, harder to stop the offense from scoring. They move the ball with the idea of getting the ball into their better shooters hands so that they can do something with it right away. The quality of a team's passing determines the quality of its shots.

It seems great passers have a great passing instinct which a coach cannot teach. They have the ability to see everything: players who are wide open, make accurate passes, hit the open man where he can do something with the ball, know where the opposition weaknesses are, know where the drives are, and know where everybody is on the floor.

## I. Stance or Ready Position

- The receiver, when catching the ball, was facing the passer. Once the ball is caught, the receiver turns his body sideways to his partner to pass back to him.

- Before passing, a player should take a baseball batter's stance with the front shoulder facing his target and standing sideways with his front foot forward. This is usually the stance taken in a game situation as the ballcarrier is usually being checked or slashed at and he must protect his stick with his body from the defender by turning it sideways.

    *Note: Although the player takes a batter's stance to pass, he does not hold his stick the way a baseball player would hold a bat. A beginning player has a tendency to use the same motion as swinging a bat in baseball when throwing in lacrosse, thereby throwing the ball sidearm rather than overhand.*

## II. Grip of Stick

- Remember for catching, the bottom hand is placed at the butt of the stick, holding the stick lightly so it can rotate in the hand. The top hand is placed slightly below the mid-point of the shaft, about 8" from the bottom hand. This is usually the balance point of a stick. This is the same hand position for passing.
- Another way to determine the placement of the top hand is to grab the stick roughly in the middle of the shaft, extend the top hand

only, making sure the butt of the stick is touching the elbow. Wherever the top hand ends up with the elbow touching the butt is a good placement. The hands do not move and as has been stated are almost in the same position as catching.

- Hold the stick loosely with the fingers to get "fingertip" control. A player wants this loose grip to get a good feel of the stick. A player certainly shouldn't grab the lacrosse stick like he would a hockey stick or an axe. Also, holding the stick with the fingers helps to keep the wrists flexible to rotate the stick when cradling and faking. Some players like to place their thumbs up along the shaft to get a better feel of the stick and to give the wrists more flexibility.

- The closeness of the hands—8" apart— makes it easier to control the stick for faking, passing, and shooting. If a player grabs his stick too high on the shaft the passing becomes stiff and jerky and he cannot completely fully extend his stick for a good follow-through.  If a player's top hand is too close to his bottom hand, he will not have good control of the head of his stick and it will be wobbly.

## III. Cradling and Cocked Position of Stick

### Cradling Position of Stick Prior to Pass

- The player holds his stick vertically at a slight 45-degree angle over his stick shoulder while doing a small cradle with the ball. (See Chapter 2, Small Cradle.)
- The top hand is beside his head while holding the shaft in the mid-point area and the bottom hand is below the top hand while holding the butt of the stick, putting the stick in a slight 45-degree vertical position.
- A player keeps the stick close to, but not touching, his body, with the arms slightly

flexed to protect it and to help move it more quickly from this position.

### Cocked Position of Stick

- A player cocks his stick when he is getting ready to throw a pass. As a player cocks his wrists backward, his top-hand arm moves his stick straight back with the butt of his stick almost pointing at his target. This horizontal position of the stick, plus the body weight on the back foot, puts the player in a good passing position. Some players like to hold their stick at a 45-degree angle to the floor rather than horizontally, but this depends on what is comfortable for each individual player.

**Photo 14:** Overhand stationary passing technique—throwing position before the release—stance or ready position (stand sideways), grip of stick, cradling position of stick prior to pass, cocked position

**Photo 15:** Overhand stationary throwing motion—picture of middle of the overhand throw

## IV. Throwing Motion

- Always start the throw off the back foot, then take a short 6" step with the front foot to help transfer weight from the back foot to the front foot. This movement is called "stepping into the pass" and helps a player get more power into his pass. A player should be certain he steps with the opposite foot to his stick-side. Some players like to stay stationary (no step) when transferring the weight on the pass.
- At the same time as he steps, his stick is brought straight forward by his top-hand arm and both cocked wrists are snapped forward on the release. The player does not want to bring his stick across his body with the butt of the stick ending up in the stomach area as this becomes a sidearm pass.
- A good ball handler will keep both hands stationary, and about 8" apart when passing

and catching. Some players like to slide the top hand down the shaft during the actual passing motion.
- It's important to find the point at which to release the ball from the pocket to get the perfect level on the pass. One of the main passing rules is "to release the ball soon, not late, from the stick." Releasing the ball "soon" means releasing the ball from the stick while it is still behind the head, which makes the ball come out high rather than low. The ball leaving the stick from the tip of the pocket also helps to produce this high-level trajectory.

   *Note: The top-hand creates most of the power on the pass or shot as it brings the stick forward. The bottom hand acts as a guide and is more for accuracy of the stick. The problem with beginner players is they try to push the ball out of the stick by extending both their arms.*

## V. Follow-Through of Stick

It's important on the follow-through that:
- The top-hand arm ends up fully extended while the bottom hand arm remains flexed. Be aware that a beginner will try to push the ball out of the stick by extending both his arms fully, rather than using just the top arm.

**Photo 16:** Overhand stationary passing—follow-through of stick, stick ends up parallel to floor, wide stance, tip of stick pointing at target (straight-line theory)

- The butt-end of the stick touches the elbow of the top hand. The elbow is only a reference point for a player to make sure that he has thrown a perfect overhand pass. In reality, the butt of the stick does not usually end up touching the elbow. It misses it by a few inches to the inside.
- The tip of the stick ends up pointing at the target, following the path of the ball.
- The follow-through of the stick is straight ahead, not across the body. Coach encourages players to "freeze" on the follow-through to exaggerate this action. "Freeze" means to hold the stick pointed at the target for a split second to get more accuracy in the pass.
- The upper body is turned from a sideways position to ending up facing his target (i.e., shoulders ending up square to the target).
- The body weight ends up on the front foot after the release of the ball.
- In putting all the parts together, stress throwing a continuous, smooth, overhand motion. The stick traces out the path of the top half of a Ferris wheel from the beginning of the pass to the end of the pass. The stick starts in a horizontal position to the floor, and during the throwing phase it follows a straight line forward, ending up again in a horizontal position to the floor. This "straight-line" theory makes the overhand pass the simplest and most accurate pass there is.
- Besides using the motion of the top half of a Ferris wheel in teaching passing in lacrosse, also use the analogies of the "swinging action of an axe" or the "throwing motion in baseball." *Note: When faking a pass turn both wrists inward quickly to keep the ball in the pocket while making it look like you are really throwing a real pass.*

## VI. Correcting the "Hook"
*(See Chapter 1, Shooting Strings)*

Every player, whether experienced or beginner, sometime in his lacrosse career "hooks" the ball in his stick (i.e., the ball comes out of the stick at a low trajectory). The hook may be caused by: sloppy netting, the way the player throws the ball, the ball hitting the permanent shooting string that comes with the stick, where the player has formed his shooting pocket, or his pocket is just too deep.

A player can correct this problem by forcing the ball to be released higher. He does this by doing one or all of the following:

- Smoothing out his pocket, especially making sure his runners or mesh and shooting strings are smooth and tight and not bulky.
- A player can pull in his side runners (i.e., the cords that are parallel to the sides of the stick) to make his pocket shallower.
- Putting in extra shooting strings to help the ball roll out of the mesh smoothly while not hitting the permanent shooting string.
- Making sure the shooting pocket is close to the tip of the stick rather than in the middle or at the back of the pocket near the throat of the stick.
- Releasing the ball from his stick when it is still behind his body rather than when the ball is beside or in front of his body.

## VII. Tips for Passing

- Teach only the overhand pass versus the sidearm or underhand pass, because it is the most accurate of all passes and it carries into the overhand shot nicely. It seems more players are passing with a three-quarter motion of the stick.
- Before passing, the passer must make sure the receiver is looking and is ready for the pass. Eye contact is a good way to signal for a pass. The passer is also "the eyes of the receiver," watching out for any defender

who might be looking to crunch the receiver, called a "suicide pass."

- Stress a "shooting pass" or a "passing pass." This is a pass in which a player has only to catch and shoot in one continuous motion. He does not have to move his stick from a catching position to another position for throwing or shooting.

    *Note: In today's game, besides the overhand pass and the three-quarter pass, players are now throwing a lot of sidearm passes, flip passes, and shovel passes.*

- Stress passing with a snap of the wrist. You want players to be wrist passers rather than pushers.

- Stress throwing hard, crisp passes, but not too hard. Passes are meant to be caught. Players must realize it takes two players to make a pass—a passer and a receiver. Most of the responsibility of a completed pass rests with how accurate and hard the passer should throw the ball. If a receiver drops the ball, the passer says, "It's my fault." The hardness depends on whether his receiver is a good or poor receiver; and how far away his receiver is. Throwing to an experienced player, a passer should throw a hard pass knowing he could catch it with no problem. Throwing to a beginner, a passer should take a little bit of the intensity off the pass so it would be easier for him to catch it. Great passers have a "softness" to their passes that makes them catchable.

- Stress throwing passes that are parallel to the floor or level passes. Coaches don't like semi-lob or "rainbow" passes thrown in a game, especially on cross-floor passes. Rainbow passes are high-arcing passes that take forever to reach their target. Usually by the time the receiver catches the ball he is being checked by a defender with no time to make a good play.

    But a "rainbow" pass is okay when throwing to a player who has a breakaway, or throwing to a player up the sideboards ahead of the passer on his own side of the floor. At one time coaches emphasize not throwing bounce passes since they come off the floor or carpet with back spin and sometimes spin out of the receiver's stick. But in today's game the bounce pass has become quite common.

- Stress throwing only short passes in the breakout and in the offense. The short pass is more accurate and travels faster and therefore there are fewer chances for interceptions. Throwing the long pass has a lower percentage of being caught.

- Stress quick passes and quick releases, but not to hurry the pass. Players have to learn to pass quickly, but not to sacrifice accuracy. By hurrying, a player might pass too quickly, pass out of control, pass off-balance, or make wrong decisions, any of which could cause bad passes.

- Stress accuracy over speed or power. Players should take pride in hitting the receiver's stick without him moving it. Once players become accurate then the next progression is in creating the power or throwing harder.

- Stress learning to use one's peripheral vision when passing. Avoid telegraphing passes (i.e., looking directly where the passer wants to pass) and be deceptive by faking a pass one way and passing the other way. When being pressured by a defensive player a passer should often fake before he passes. Many times the defender will react to the fake pass and the passer will now be able to make an unforced pass. This move will get a passer out of trouble.

- Concentrate on throwing to the "head" of the receiver's stick. Stress "a high outside pass on the receiver's stick-side."

- Players should know what a perfect pass is: "a pass into a receiver's stick without him having to move it eight out of 10 times."

- If a player makes a mistake on the height of a pass, the rule is "pass too high rather than too low." This rule is used because most players make the mistake of passing low too often. Therefore, this rule forces players to concentrate on throwing a high pass.

- The timing on throwing to a teammate on the run up the floor and who is across the floor from the passer is very important. Remember: the receiver's stick should be held over his inside shoulder as he runs down the floor. That is, the stick is held behind the runner not in front of him. By aiming slightly in front of the receiver's stick (to a spot), the ball should arrive behind him when it makes contact with his stick.

- When running down the floor with a teammate on the opposite side of the floor, another rule is: "If a passer makes a mistake, throw the ball too far in front of the receiver rather than behind him." The reason for this rule is that the receiver still may have a chance to catch the ball if he keeps on running and if the ball is out in front of him.

- A similar rule is employed when passing to a teammate on a breakaway. "Over pass rather than under pass," i.e., throw a semi-lob, soft pass in front of the receiver.

  **Remember:** When catching a breakaway pass, catch the ball over the inside shoulder by placing the stick with the "face" of the pocket parallel to the floor and in front of his body and let the ball come to the pocket to avoid breaking stride.

- A rule after catching a bad pass is "pause for poise." This means, before a player makes the next pass, he should get everything together (balance, composure). By hurrying the return pass, a player often creates the chain reaction of yet another bad pass.

- To make good game decisions, players must concentrate all the time, must keep their heads in the game all the time. Players do not want to catch the ball then think of what they have to do. Players have to be thinking on what they are going to do before they catch the ball.

- A very simple rule for passing is: "after you pass, move."

- If passing to a teammate who is partially denied or cutting out to the boards to receive a pass with a defender right behind him, just pass away from the defender and pass to the receiver's stick on his outside.

## VIII. Teaching Passing and Catching

To be successful, a team must be solid in fundamentals, especially in passing and catching. Coaches must be aware when doing drills that they have to fight boredom, lack of concentration by the players, and the fact that most players think they know how to pass and catch when they practice these fundamentals. So, it is important that the drills are fun, organized, competitive, short, varied, progressive, and game-like.

- Assume that all players know nothing in passing and catching, and teach everything from the ground up.
- Teach by having the players do the skill rather than having the coaches do too much talking.
- Believe that high repetition helps to builds confidence.
- Have the drills favor success rather than failure at the beginning.
- Concentrate on form first, accuracy second, and speed and power third.
- Follow this drill progression:
  1. Start the drills with both players stationary, then have one of the players running, then have both players running.
  2. Start with no pressure in the drill, then slowly create pressure by adding players for competition, adding time limits (race against the clock), or setting goals on the number of passes successfully completed.
- Make the losers of a competitive drill do token punishment.
- Have the passers call out the receiver's first name. Hopefully, this will help the players get into the habit of communicating on the floor.

- Have a criterion for the perfect pass: expect a player to hit a receiver's stick (without his moving it) eight out of 10 times at a distance three-quarters the width of the arena floor.
- State the key points before the drill starts.
- Stress "passing passes," which are quick, hard, and level.
- Run "team passing drills" to make the "star" players give up the ball unconsciously to anybody on the floor.

## IX. Passing and Catching Drills

### First Progression: Talk About the Stick's Pocket

Coach should go around the players and look at their sticks, checking their pocket depth and if their pocket is formed at the tip of the stick. (See Chapter 1, The Stick.)

### Second Progression: Teach How to Hold a Stick

(See section on Stationary Passing Technique.)

### Third Progression: Teach Catching With Partners

#### 1. Partner Throws Lacrosse Ball with His Hand

Teaching the proper way to catch first saves a lot of wasted time of players running around picking up balls off the floor from missed passes. So, first get the passers to throw the ball with their hand to the receiver's stick. This is a much more efficient way to teach catching as most beginning players can throw the ball more accurately with their hand than with the lacrosse stick and thus the ball will end up near their partner's stick where they can practice the skill of catching. Two things to stress to the thrower is to throw the ball overhand, not underhand, and try to get him to throw a level pass, not a rainbow pass.

#### 2. Partner Throws Tennis Ball with His Hand

In this progression now get the passers to throw tennis balls with their hands, as tennis balls are harder to catch because of the weight difference than a regular lacrosse ball. Tennis balls create "soft hands" because players must "give" more with their sticks to help maintain the tennis ball in their sticks or the tennis ball will bounce out. The players learn to catch with the proper technique first by "giving" without "cheating," i.e., using the additional information of the weight of the lacrosse ball to tell them if they have caught it.

#### 3. Partner Again Throws Lacrosse Ball with His Hand

Next, the passers throw lacrosse balls with their hands again and the receiver thinks when the ball makes contact with the pocket "to pretend the ball is an egg" and not to break it, just to exaggerate the "cushioning" of the ball in the stick.

### Fourth Progression: Teach the Breakdown of Passing Technique

#### 1. Form Passing

Players do "form" passing where they pretend to pass an imaginary ball and the coach corrects their technique. This allows the players to get the "feel" and total picture of passing.

#### 2. Isolate Passing Motion

Have partners pass while breaking down the fundamentals of passing. In this drill try to isolate the different mechanics of passing:

- **Throw with Top Hand Only**
  First pass and catch the ball with only the top arm. This is a swinging motion of the stick—straight back, straight forward. The analogies coaches like to use are "to make a motion like you're casting a fishing rod," or to make a motion like a Ferris wheel, or to make a motion like "you're throwing a dart" to get the proper form of the top hand.

- **Throw with Wrists Only**
  Next, get the players to throw the ball with only wrist movement to stress the "snap" in the pass. Cock the wrists back and snap them forward. Cocking the wrists is a great power source.

  Try this: hold both wrists as if you're going to box. Now cock your wrists backward and then forward doing this cocking motion quickly will give the snapping motion desired.

- **Throw with Arms Only**
  Next, get the players to throw the ball with just the arms, stressing the extension of the top-hand arm and keeping the bottom-hand arm flexed. The top-hand arm creates the power by taking the stick straight back and bringing it straight forward.

- **Stress Transfer of Weight**
  The legs create power by moving the body weight from the back foot to the forward foot.

- **Stress Follow-Through of Stick**
  The follow-through of the stick after the release of the ball is another power source. Make sure the tip of the stick ends up pointing at the target.

- **Throwing Motion Like a Ferris Wheel**
  Finally, go back to the total picture of passing by stressing to the players: to make a motion like a Ferris wheel, to snap the wrists, to fully extend the top-hand arm, to follow through with the "head" of the stick, and to step forward with the foot opposite to the stick.

  For beginners, get them to exaggerate the follow-through by having them touch the floor with the head of the stick.

### 3. Throw Darts

In their spare time, get the players to improve their passing technique and "touch" by actually throwing darts with their weak hand (i.e., top-hand arm).

### 4. Passing Against a Wall

Players concentrate on just the swinging motion of the stick rather than the target. Players start to develop the proper "feeling" of passing.

Passing against a wall is the oldest drill in any shooting or throwing sport, but this simple drill makes great players and great shooters. Throwing a ball against the wall for a couple of hours takes self-discipline, a burning desire to be great, and a great love of the game.

Players should be using two types of targets. One target could be a circle to represent the height of the stick of a receiver. This should be as high as he would want to throw a ball to a receiver's stick. The other target should be the shape of a lacrosse net, where he can pick the top corners and bottom corners.

## Fifth Progression: Teach Passing with Partners

To do these drills have the players line up opposite their partner down both sides of the floor. The players should be as far away from each other as they would be in a game on offense. With this formation the coach can keep everybody busy and still walk around giving feedback (positive or corrective) to individual players on what they are doing right or wrong.

### 1. Two-on-Zero Stationary Passing with One Ball Drill

*Partners Do Normal Stationary Passing*

- Two players just pass the ball back and forth from a normal offensive passing distance and concentrate on their form, technique, and accuracy. Start the drill with the players facing each other, versus standing the proper way of passing by standing sideways, until they get the proper overhand technique. Stress to players not to come across their bodies on the follow-through with their sticks, but to follow through straight ahead with the top-hand arm extended.

*First Variation of Different Passes in the Two-on-Zero Drill*

- Once the players throw with a perfect overhand technique, then, have them turn their bodies sideways to the receivers. This is the more natural stance taken in a game when they have the ball because the chances of them being checked or harassed by a defender are great; therefore, they must be in a position to protect their stick and still pass.
- A player "fakes" the overhand pass to his partner by starting the forward motion of his stick as if he is really going to pass, then he "checks" or stops his pass by rotating in, clockwise, strongly with his top-hand wrist and rotating in lightly, counter-clockwise, with his bottom-hand wrist. This turning inward motion of the wrists turns the stick clockwise, keeping the ball in the netting.
- Player "cocks" or winds up to fake a shot, then passes to his partner.
- Partners can move in toward each other and start passing a few feet from each other (short distance) still throwing hard, level passes.
- Then partners can move back close to the sideboards and throw passes across the floor.
- Finally, players go and stand near the end-boards and throw semi-lob passes the distance of almost the length of the arena or three-quarters the length.

*Second Variation by Putting Different Pressure in the Two-on-Zero Drill*

Coach puts pressure on the players in the drill by:

- Keeping track of how many catches the partners can make without dropping the ball.
- Keeping track of the number of catches in 30 seconds. Partners do "hot potato" passing, which is passing the ball back-and-forth, in which the ball goes in-and-out of the stick all in one motion.

- Acknowledging the pair that catches 20 passes first. Start the drill with all the balls on one side of the floor and as the players catch the ball they both call out the number of catches made. At the beginning of the drill, the partners can compete against themselves by improving against their last count, then, as the team gets better, the partners can compete against each other.

*Third Variation is Having Partners Throw Bad Passes in the Two-on-Zero Drill*

- The third variation of this drill is to get the passers to throw all the passes to their partner's off-stick side. Coach wants the players to learn to bring their stick across their body to catch bad passes and in return become comfortable catching the ball on the wrong side of their body.

*Fourth Variation is Having Partners Throw Tennis Balls in the Two-on-Zero Drill*

- The last variation to this stationary passing drill is to use tennis balls to pass back-and-forth to help the players work on the proper mechanics of passing and catching and to create "soft" hands.

## 2. Two-on-Zero Stationary Passing with Two Balls

In this drill both players must throw overhand passes concentrating on catching one ball while making a good pass with the other. The coach should make this a game to see which partners can keep the balls going the longest without dropping them.

**Variation:** One partner throws an overhand pass while the other partner throws a bounce pass, when the coach yells "change" the partners switch to the other type of pass.

## 3. Two-on-One Stationary Passing with Defensive Pressure—"Monkey in the Middle"

The partners stand about 15 feet apart. The defender standing in the middle of the partners attacks the ballcarrier trying to force a bad pass while attempting to get his stick in the way of the pass. The defender cannot cross-check, but he can interfere with the passer's stick in any way. If the defender touches the ball or forces a bad pass, he switches position with the passer on whom he forced the bad pass or the receiver who could have caught the ball, but dropped it. Passes cannot be lobbed over the defender's head, but must be a level pass or a bounce pass. The passer must pass around the defender's stick while staying in a small area. The fake pass really helps to relieve pressure in this drill. After the ballcarrier passes the ball to his partner the defender must follow the pass to try to force a bad pass by the partner. The defender keeps going back and forth until he forces a bad pass.

**Variation:** The coach gives the passer more room to move around while being harassed by a defender. In an actual game beginning players try to make passes while being checked, with the result that the ball is turned over. Giving the ballcarrier more room to move teaches a player not to panic when being harassed by defenders, but to relax and get in the clear with quickness, deception, and intelligence. One way to get away from pressure is to fake a step in one direction and step in the other direction to make their pass; another way to release pressure is to attack the defender and pushing off with his shoulder and arm, or back off from the pressure and throw around his defender's stick. Stress to the passer not to take a hit or be interfered with when making a pass.

### 4. Two-on-Zero Partners Passing on the Run Full-Floor

Make a line of right-shots and a line of left-shots at one end of the floor about three-quarters the width of the floor. Partners (a left- and a right-shot) will run to the other end of the floor passing the ball back-and-forth and wait at that end. As soon as the first set of

partners leave, the next pair goes and so on. This is strictly a passing drill and therefore no shots are taken. So that there are lots of passes on the way down the floor, state the rule: "a player cannot take more than two steps with the ball before he must pass it." Do the same thing coming back down the floor to the other end. Also stress calling out the receiver's name and keeping the stick up for a good target.

**Variation:** Make the width between partners narrow or wide as they run down the floor. A narrow width would be as wide as the crease around the net; a wide distance would be almost to the sideboards.

### Sixth Progression: Teach Passing in Team Drills

**1. Knock-Out Drill** *(See Diagram #4)*
In this drill, there are six players and two balls. Three players line up opposite the other three facing each other. Players pass the ball back and forth either diagonally or cross-floor as quickly as they can. If the receiver drops a good pass, or if the passer throws a bad pass that the receiver can't catch, they get a demerit point. The only rule is: "a player can't throw to another player who has a ball in his stick." When a player gets five demerit points, he drops out of the drill. The drill ends up with two players and two balls. Eventually one player with the lowest number of demerit points becomes the winner. Losers will run one sprint the length of the floor.

**2. Pepper Drill** *(See Diagram #5)*
Set up this drill with one player facing four others who are in a straight line. Using two balls, the group passes the balls back-and-forth to the individual passer. The objective of the drill is to make the lone passer work as hard as possible on his ball-handling skills. Stress accuracy, speed, and quick releases. Time the drill for 30 seconds and then rotate another player in as the lone passer.

## Diagram #4: Knock-Out Drill

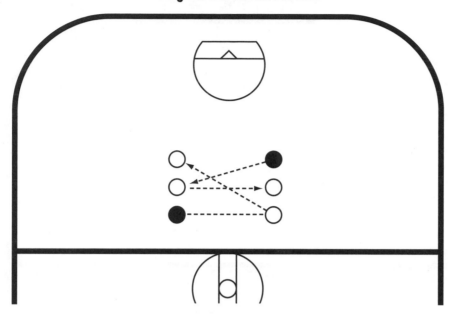

## Diagram #5: Pepper Drill

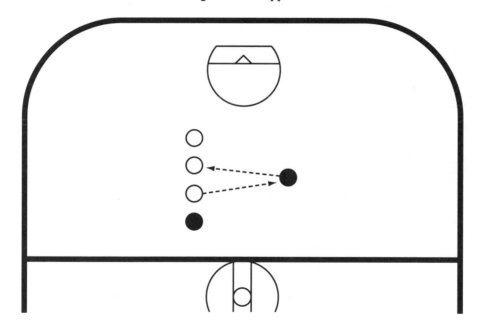

**3. Zig-Zag Stationary Passing Drill** *(See Diagram #6)*
Form two lines facing each other all the way down both sides of the floor, putting a full bucket of balls at one end of the line and an empty bucket at the other end of the line. The

drill can be run with the whole team or with groups of six.

- **Teaching Drill:**
  Players pass the balls down the lines in a zig-zag fashion (i.e., they pass the ball diagonally across the floor). The players

### Diagram #6: Zig-Zag Drill

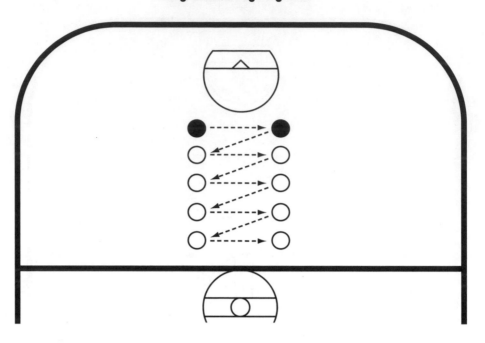

have no pressure on them giving them time to work on their passing technique and accuracy. This high repetition drill gives the coaches lots of time to walk around and give feedback to all the players while still keeping everybody busy.

- **Pressure Drills:**
  The next six variations of the zig-zag drill will help to put pressure on the players to make them concentrate more.

  a. **Pressure Through Punishment**
     A player sends all the balls down the line from the full bucket. Players who drop a good pass or throw a bad one must do five push-ups for every dropped ball. Players stay in the drill and do their push-ups after all the balls have been sent down the line.

  b. **Pressure Through Statistics or an Objective**
     Here, coach gives an objective, such as the following: out of the 20 balls thrown down the line, at least 14 must end up in the bucket at the other end. Do not stop the drill until the objective is met,

so be sure it is realistic and obtainable. Coach can give a reward for obtaining the objective or a punishment for not obtaining the objective.

  c. **Pressure Through Number of Times the Players Can Pass the Ball Down-and-Back the Line**
     Players count the number of times they can pass one ball down and back without dropping it. After they have done it once, they now have a standard that they will try to beat the next time. So, if they went down and back two times, they now want to go down and back three times. Another variation is that the players can set a pre-determined objective of the number of times they can do it.

  d. **Pressure Through the Time it Takes to Pass the Ball Down-And-Back the Line**
     This is a speed drill where the coach uses a stopwatch to time how long it takes a ball to go down and back the line without being dropped. The team is always trying to beat its best time.

e. **Pressure Through Competition (Group Against Group)**

Keeping the same type of formation put the players in groups of six. The lines compete against each other to see who can keep the ball going the longest without dropping it, or who can pass the ball the quickest down-and-back three times.

f. **Pressure Through Passing, Then Running to Replace the Receiver**

Put six to eight players in a zig-zag formation with the rest of the team with a ball at one end of the formation. The first ballcarrier passes the ball to the first player and follows his pass to the first player's position, the first player then passes to the teammate opposite him and also follows his pass to the second player's position. The players continue this follow-your-pass-and-replace-the-receiver procedure all the way down the line. The player at the end of the zig-zag line runs back to the end of the straight line with the ball. The drill is over when everybody returns to their original spots. Time the drill to see if the team can beat their previous best time.

4. **Shuttle Passing Drill** (*See Diagram #7*)

Form two lines: one group of three players lined up behind each other facing another group of three players lined up behind each other. Using one ball, the ballcarrier will pass the ball to the first player in the opposite line and run to the back of that line. This procedure continues until the end of the drill, which is either a pre-established number of passes caught in 30 seconds, or a contest by the lines to see who can keep the ball in the air the longest without dropping it. Players can pass and catch standing still or pass and catch while on the run. Players can work on short passes in close to each other; or long passes across the width of the floor to the sideboards; or normal passing distance in the offense, about three-quarters the width of the floor; or breakaway passes using the full length of the floor. Stress that players concentrate on the target (the stick head), give horizontal passes or "passing passes," keep their stick up for a target, and keep the ball in the air.

**Variations:**

• Run the Shuttle Passing Drill the length of the floor. The player who receives the pass

---

**Diagram #7: Shuttle Drill**

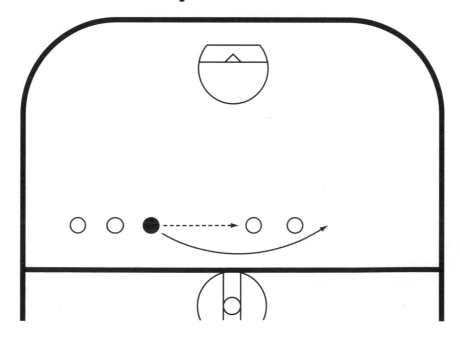

runs to center and beats his defender, who has just passed to him, coming from the other line. Then after he goes around the defender he passes to the next player in the opposite line and waits for the ballcarrier to go around him and then runs to the back of the opposite line.

- Shuttle Cutting Drill. This is the same formation as the Shuttle Drill, but everybody has a ball, except for the first cutter. The cutter runs hard toward the passer as if he is cutting for a pass into the middle of the floor for a shot. Passer throws an accurate, hard pass. After catching the ball, the player V-cuts back to his own line or continues across the floor to the back of the other line. At first no shot, then later players on catch can shoot.

### 5. Three-on-Two Pressure Passing—"Monkey in the Middle"

Three stationary players pass the ball around quickly in the offensive half-floor area, trying to score. The two defenders and the goalie do anything to stop them from scoring. The best opportunity to score is after one or two quick passes. Drill can last to a set number of goals, or how many goals in 30 seconds. Can also run a four-on-three drill.

**Variation**: The offense is allowed to back off from taking a hit to make a pass.

### 6.  Five-on-Five Half-Floor Keep Away

Start with three teams of five players: a resting line, an offensive line, and a defensive line. Play five-on-five with the two groups to see how many passes the group can make. The group that makes the most passes caught is the winner. The two losers run a sprint. The coaches count the number of passes made or caught. If the defensive team forces a bad pass or forces the ball to hit the floor, the offensive team that dropped the ball loses possession and goes to the rest station. Now the defensive team goes on offense and the resting team goes on defense.

**Variation:** This drill can also be run as a four-on-four Keep Away.

### 7.  Five-on-Five Half-Floor Borden Ball

Play five-on-five with the teams trying to score. The game has three rules: a player must pass the ball in three seconds, a player can only take three steps with the ball before he must pass it, and a team cannot drop the ball. Any violation of the three rules and the team loses possession of the ball. Teams can play for a certain length of time or until one team scores a certain number of goals. Stress that players must work to get open for the pass. They must move and not stand still, and the ballcarrier must see the whole floor. Coach runs this drill especially if his team didn't move the ball or the players didn't move in a game.

**Variation:** Coach can also run this drill full-floor, which is perhaps a bit more realistic to an actual game.

### 8. Four-on-Zero Four-Corner Fast-Break Passing Drill *(See Diagram #8)*

Four players stand in the two creaseman's positions and the two cornerman's positions and tic-tac-toe the ball around as quickly and accurately as possible. Stress to the players not to make the same pass twice in a row.

**Variation:** The ballcarrier pretends that he is being pressured by a rushing defender and backs off so he does not take a hit while passing. The new ballcarrier now backs off and passes to another receiver, etc.

### 9. Four-on-Zero Four-Corner Offense Passing Drills

These drills are to get the players into the habit of passing and cutting, or at least moving without the ball.

### I. V-Cut Drill *(See Diagram #9)*

#### A. Cornerman Receiving Cross-Floor Pass

This drill teaches the concept of getting

in the clear. Players in the cornerman's position must do a "down-and-back" V-cut before receiving a cross-floor pass from the ballcarrier in the other cornerman's position. This move stops the defender from intercepting the dangerous cross-floor pass and breaking down the floor. The receiver must fake a cut through the middle by looking at the ballcarrier as if he is going to receive a pass. Then he must stop suddenly, push off with his outside foot, and return to where he came from to receive the pass. The receiver must make sure his stick is extended fully outward to give the passer a good target

**Diagram #8: Four-Corner Fast-Break Passing Drill**

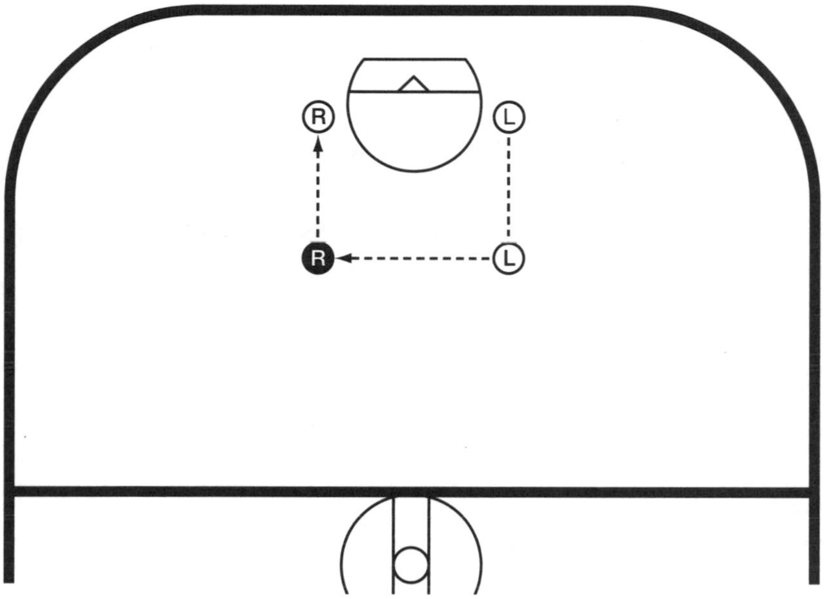

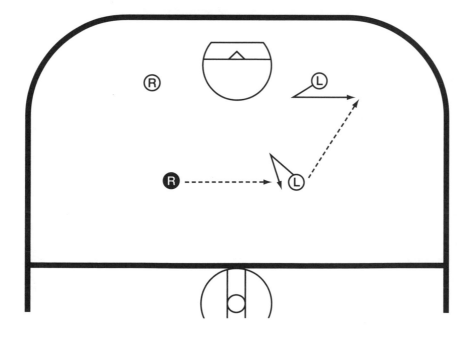

**Diagram #9: Four-Corner Offense Passing—V-Cut Drill**

and give him that extra edge so that the pass is not intercepted.

### B. Cornerman Receiving an Up-Pass From the Corner Area

Players in the cornerman's position must also do a "down-and-back" V-cut before receiving a pass from the ballcarrier in the creaseman's position. The player still fakes a cut to the net and looks at the ballcarrier, but stops on his inside foot and pushes off, backpedaling to the spot he left, giving his stick target inside his body which is the most natural position.

### C. Creaseman Receiving a Down-Pass From the Cornerman

Players in the creaseman's position must do an "in-and-out" V-cut before receiving a pass into the corner area of the floor from the ballcarrier in the cornerman's position on his side of the floor. It's best to receive the pass as close to the net as possible. To accomplish this he must fake a cut to the net to draw the defender, then stop suddenly on his outside foot, and break out to a scoring position or farther out

to the sideboards. Extend the stick to give a good target and to give the receiver an edge to prevent an interception. The four players make these moves over and over again with no shots as they swing the ball from one side of the floor to the other.

*Note: In today's game players play wider out toward the sideboards and higher up on the offense where the defense will allow these passes rather than deny these passes as they are not an immediate threat to score. These passes are more just to get the offense moving than looking to receive a pass that will give a receiver an immediate shot. The offense, after moving the ball, then starts to go into their attack mode.*

### II. Interchange or Exchange Drill on Off-Ball-Side Drill *(See Diagram #10)*

This drill helps players move on offense and gives them another option of throwing the cross-floor pass without the worry of an interception. Here the off-ball players just exchange positions from the cornerman's position to the creaseman's position (and vice

**Diagram #10: Four-Corner Offense Passing—Interchange Drill**

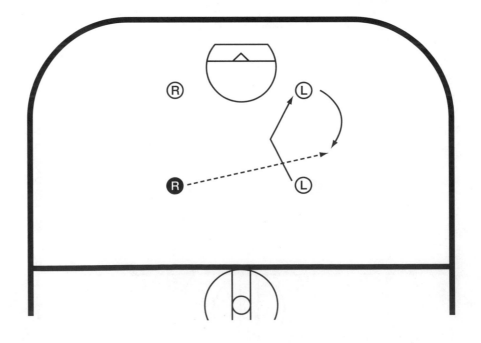

versa) while the ballcarrier throws a cross-floor pass from the cornerman's position. Once the ballcarrier throws the cross-floor pass, he then runs down to interchange with his teammate who should be in the clear for the next cross-floor pass. Timing is important as the ballcarrier must let the off-ball side develop. The players just keep running the drill over and over again. There is no shot in this drill. The player leaving the crease position cuts on the outside of his teammate while the player coming down on the interchange cuts on the inside of his teammate. The reason for this particular movement is that the player coming down may run into his teammate's opponent, thereby putting his teammate in the clear, or just by exchanging the players could cause confusion between the two defenders. Do they switch or stay with their checks?

### III. Down-Pick Drill on Off-Ball Side Drill

*(See Diagram #11)*

This drill is similar to the one above. It is a continuous movement drill with no shot. The picker runs an L-pattern cut, he cuts inside of the floor and then goes down and sets an imaginary down pick on the off-ball side on an imaginary defender. The creaseman comes off the pick looking for the cross-floor pass. Then, this creaseman now looks for the opposite creaseman coming off the off-ball down pick. The players just keep setting down picks and throwing cross-floor passes.

### IV. Down-Pick Drill on Ball-Side Drill

Again this drill is similar to the one above. The ballcarrier passes down to the crease on his side of the floor and sets a down pick on him. When the creaseman comes off the down pick with the ball he makes a cross-floor pass to the opposite cornerman who does the same thing, he passes down to the crease and sets a pick for him. The players just keep setting down picks on the ball side and throwing cross-floor passes.

**Diagram #11: Four-Corner Offense Passing—Down Pick Drill**

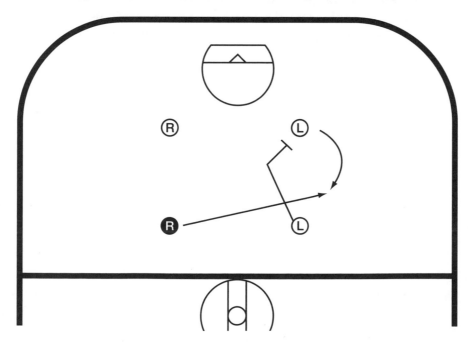

**Diagram #12: Four-Corner Offense Passing—Cut and Replace Drill**

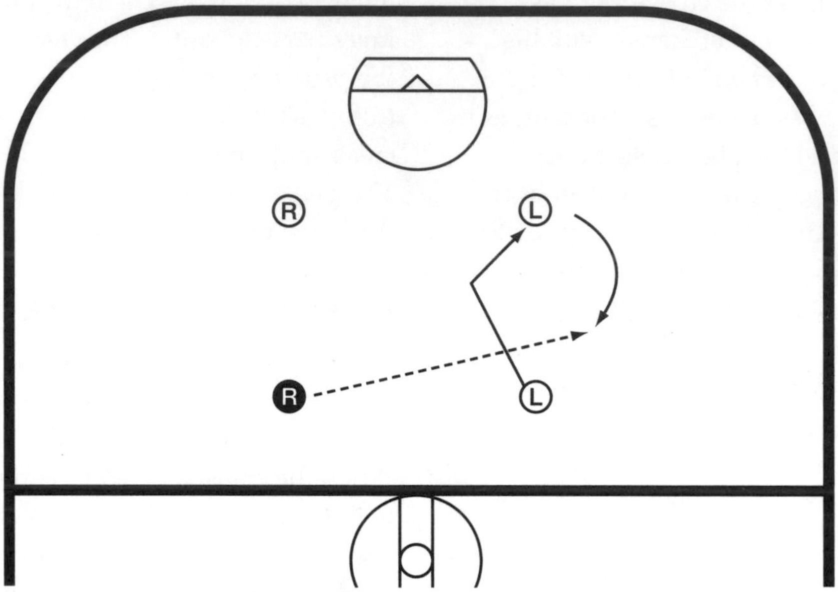

## V. Cut and Replace on Off-Ball-Side Drill

*(See Diagram #12)*

This is a good drill to get the players into the habit of passing and cutting. It is a continuous-movement drill with no shot. The ballcarrier in the cornerman's position throws a cross-floor pass, then cuts into the middle looking for a return pass (Give-and-Go). Once he gets to the imaginary center line in the middle of the floor, he cuts back to his own side of the floor and replaces the creaseman who has just replaced the cornerman's position. Just as the creaseman replaces the cornerman's position, he should be receiving the next cross-floor pass. The players just keep cutting and replacing each other on the off-ball side and throwing cross-floor passes.

## VI. "Circling" on Off-Ball-Side Drill

The ballcarrier in the cornerman's position throws a cross-floor pass, then cuts into the middle looking for a return pass, and then veers over to the crease area, followed by a second cutter coming from the crease area. So

the two players on the off-ball side just keep "circling" and cutting looking to get open. Players can run through the "circling" motion two times, then receive a cross-floor pass, and then the other side does the same thing.

## VII. "Circling" on Ball-Side Drill

The ballcarrier in the cornerman's position passes to the creaseman on his side of the floor. Cornerman then cuts into the middle, looking for a return pass, and then veers over to the crease area. The ball-carrying creaseman comes up and around looking to pass to the cutter or going one-on-one. The two players run the circle two times then pass the ball across to the other side of the floor, who in turn run the same thing.

## VIII. Four-on-Zero Corner Stationary Passing Drill

Players just stand and pass the ball around the square. This is an easy drill to improve ball-handling. Coach can use two to three balls eventually.

## IX. Four-on-Zero Four-Corners "Follow-Your-Pass" Drill

The players form a box formation about the distance they would have in a game with the players lined up evenly at each corner. They pass one ball in one direction, and follow their pass, going to the back of the line they passed to. As their proficiency improves, add another ball to the drill. Now, two balls are being passed in the same direction, so the second player in each line has to stay alert for a pass. Then, progress to three balls and possibly four. In this drill the players must concentrate on: communication (passers call out the receiver's name), precision passing and catching, and knowing whether they are passing in a clockwise or counter-clockwise direction because when the coach calls "change" the players change their passing direction.

## X. Four-on-Four Pressure Passing Drill

Same as above (Drill IX) except defense plays token defense. This is a passing drill but with defensive pressure. The players run the drill continuously moving and passing.

This drill teaches a team how to move the ball. A lot of times a team can't move the ball because all the offensive players are tight to their checks. The tendency for offensive players is to gravitate to their defenders. Now, the ballcarrier has to run around with the ball because nobody is open and therefore he has nobody to throw the ball to because everybody is tight to their check. This drill reinforces to the players to stay wide and spread so they can move the ball.

## XI. Single-Line Full-Floor Drill

*(See Diagram #13)*

Use six stationary passers: three on each side of the floor, spaced out along the sideboards. One passer is about a third of the way from the near end-boards, the next passer is at the center floor area near the sideboards, and the third passer is about two-thirds of the way down the floor near the sideboards. The

**Diagram #13: Single-Line Drill**

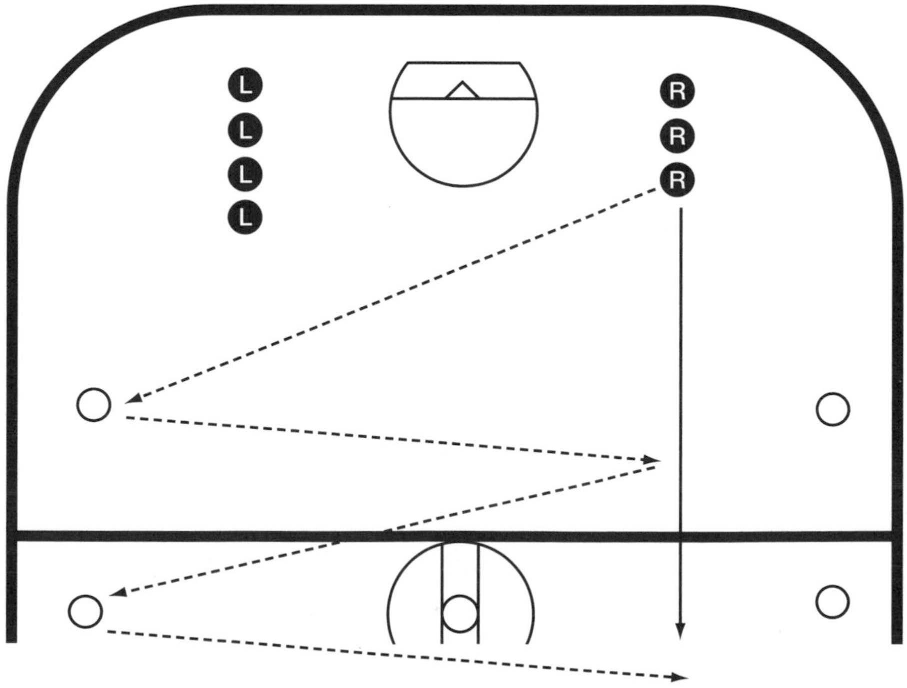

players with balls line up on their proper side. All the left-shots with a ball line up on one side of the floor (right side) and all the right-shots with a ball line up on the other side (left side). The first left-handed player passes to the opposite stationary passer and sprints down his side of the floor looking for a return pass. He then passes to the next stationary passer and looks for a return pass, and does the same thing to the third passer. In the beginning this is a no-shot drill. When the runner has caught the ball from the last passer, he runs behind the net, lining up to come back the other way. Once the left-handed player

leaves, the first right-handed player executes the same procedure. The lines can alternate with a left-shot going then a right-shot going until everybody has practiced the Give-and-Go technique down the floor. Then the players come back the other way doing the same thing.

**Variation:** The players can take a shot at both ends of the floor. Make a game of left-shots versus right-shots. The winning team is the first team that scores the most number of goals down and back in a certain time limit, or the first team to score a set number of goals.

# Chapter 5

# Loose-Ball Strategies

Usually, the team that controls the loose balls wins the game. Fighting for loose balls is one of the hardest things to do in any game because this involves effort, physical contact, composure, and technique.

## I. Techniques

### Trap-and-Scoop Pick-Up Technique

The "Trap-and-Scoop" is the most basic pick-up and should be taught to beginners and young players first. Coach gets the players to trap the moving or stationary ball with the "back" of the pocket, then pull the pocket backward over the ball, then scoop it or shovel it up with the mouth of the pocket. This should be done all in one motion. But for beginners it may take awhile for them to get the execution down. Even for experienced players there are times in a game where the "Trap-and-Scoop" comes in handy.

**Photo 17:** Trap-and-Scoop—Trap the ball first

**Photo 18:** Trap-and-Scoop—Scoop pick-up technique

### Indian Pick-Up Technique

The Indian Pick-Up is executed with one hand, held at the end of the shaft by the player's dominant hand, by turning the stick upside down and over top of the ball where the "face" of the pocket is facing downward. Then, with his natural hand he hits or bangs the ball off the inside edge of the plastic sidewall frame, while at the same time flicking or turning the wrist upward to turn the stick upward. If the player is left-handed he usually holds the stick with his right hand to execute this move. He hits the ball with the inside of the inside frame. This pick-up does give a player a slight advantage as he has the full length of his arm and the stick to quickly get on top of a loose ball and out with ball possession. If there is a lot of traffic around the loose ball, the player would have problems picking it up as his opponents would just slash his exposed stick.

*Notes:*
- *The outside frame is the side of the frame that is on the outside of the player's body.*
- *Finding out the dominant hand? Just let the kids pick up a stick and they will naturally hold it over whichever shoulder feels comfortable. If he holds it over his left shoulder, he is a left-handed player and vice versa.*

**Photo 19:** Indian Pick-up—Bang ball off inside of inside frame, stick upside down

**Photo 20:** Indian Pick-up—Flick wrist upward

## Scoop Pick-Up Technique

As players get more skilled with loose balls teach only the "Scoop" pick-up method. The "Scoop" is used when picking up a rolling loose ball, a stationary loose ball, or a bouncing loose ball. Here are some ideas to stress when teaching the "Scoop" pick-up:

### 1. Keep His Eyes on the Ball

The player should keep his eye on the ball at all times during the game, but especially when the ball goes loose.

### 2. Stance for Picking Up a Loose Ball

Bend the knees to get low, stay low, and take a wide stance. With a player's weight closer to the floor he now has a lower center of gravity, which helps him to maintain better balance. A wider stance gives him a more stable base so he can't be pushed around from the side or from behind. These two techniques will help him scoop the stationary, bouncing, or rolling ball up more easily. Also make sure the foot opposite the stick side is planted close to the ball for better balance and to protect the ball from the opponent's stick also trying to scoop the loose ball up.

### 3. Grip of Stick

Grab the stick at its throat with the top hand. This forces the player to bend over more to get closer to the floor and helps him to focus on the loose ball. Keep the bottom hand low to the floor so the stick is almost parallel to the floor. The player can then scoop the stationary ball or rolling ball into his stick using a "shoveling" motion. Stress to scoop "through" the loose ball into a cradling motion on possession of the ball and to always keep two hands on the stick when fighting for a loose ball. This is for control of the ball once in the stick and to muscle the stick away from opponents who will be trying to dislodge the ball from the pocket.

### 4. Approaching a Loose Ball

Try to approach a loose ball on the stick side of the body, especially if there is defensive pressure, as it is quicker to scoop the loose ball up on the run with the stick on that side of the body.

### 5. Protecting the Ball with the Body

When fighting for a loose ball against an opponent, whether it is lying on the floor, rolling, or bouncing, try to get the body between

**Photo 21:** Scoop Pick-Up Technique—scoop pick-up on the run, butt of stick

**Photo 22:** Protecting the ball with the body while picking up the ball against defensive pressure

the opponent and the ball. In this situation a player will be picking up the loose ball in front of his body, as he is shielding the ball with his body rather than trying to pick up the ball from the side of his body in which case his stick will be exposed to his opponent. So, he has to hold his stick on his natural side and in front of his body when scooping up the loose ball as he uses his body to protect his stick. Once he scoops up the ball bring it up to his chest area especially in traffic to protect the ball with his body.

### 6. The "Scoop" Pick-Up

On the pick-up, "shovel" through the loose ball with two hands on the stick, not a one-hand pick-up, then cradle immediately. Once a player gets the ball in his stick he protects his stick by keeping it close to his body.

## II. Loose-Ball Tips

- It seems when two players go after a loose ball one player will always get it and the other will never end up with it. They both may know how to pick it up, but only one gets it every time. It appears that desire is more important than technique when going after loose balls. Some coaches feel it takes 75 percent desire and 25 percent ability/ technique to be a great loose-ball player. So to be a great loose-ball player a player has to have a mentally tough attitude where he is not afraid of being hit. He has to be very persistent and have a determined attitude of "never giving up," thinking every loose ball is his. And he has to be aggressive and attack every loose ball like it belongs to him. Loose-ball players are true warriors.
- It is important to stress to players that they should never stand still and wait for a loose ball to come to them. They have to attack all loose balls.
- When going after a loose ball, a player has to believe he is going to be in a battle along the boards for possession of the loose ball. It

will be an all-out war! So, attack it with two hands on the stick, tuck it in, and protect it with the body.
- Because of the importance of loose balls, it is a good idea to send two players after every loose ball.
- A player has to fight for or contest every loose ball. He can never stand back and let an opponent just pick up a loose ball even if he is ahead of him. The most important aspect in going after a loose ball is "assuming that if the opponent is in first, he is going to miss it, fumble it, or mishandle it." So, pressure him, be aggressive, and never give up.
- Similarly, if the opposition gets possession of the loose ball, a defensive player has to continue to pressure the ballcarrier as a delay tactic so he cannot pass the ball down the floor to his teammates or even to stick-check him to steal the ball.

### Going into the Boards with an Opponent

#### 1. If a Player Goes into Boards Beside an Opponent

If an opponent is beside a player on going after a loose ball, he has to try and step in front of him to get his body between the ball and his opponent and then maintain the "ball-you-man" position by moving around to keep his opponent on his back. If he can't get in front of him, he has to bump his opponent out of the way or lean into him to equalize pressure so he can pick it up.

#### 2. If a Player Goes into the Boards First

If a player is in front of his opponent and he is right on his back when going after the loose ball, slow down so not to take a slash on the stick, but to take it on the body. By this maneuver the opponent will end up swinging his stick around the player's body and not slashing his stick.

So besides teaching a player to use his body to protect the loose ball before he actually tries

**Photo 23:** If in first, lean back into check to absorb hit

to pick it up; teach him to use his body to be ready for a check from behind by his opponent. He should lean back into his check with all his body weight to brace himself for the hit.

On possession of the ball, cradle and protect the stick with his body immediately. Stress keeping the stick in close to the body, in a vertical position, and keeping the body between the stick and the opponent.

*Note: Never stand up when pursuing a loose ball with an opponent in the same area. Bend the knees, get low, and brace oneself for physical contact.*

**3. If the Opponent Goes into the Boards First**
If the opponent is in front of the player and in first when going after a loose ball, the player must go after the loose ball by being "two-handed tough." He must give his opponent a hard two-handed slash on his stick to stop him from picking it up. Teach the player to play his opponent's stick to stop him from picking up the loose ball and to never stand back and let an opponent just pick up the loose ball. A player has to have discipline in not cross-checking from behind, since this type of move reveals selfishness, laziness, and stupidity on behalf of the player. On any hit from behind, the opponent will be awarded possession of the ball, or the hitter will be awarded a two-

minute penalty or a five-minute major penalty depending on the severity of the hit. A player wants his opponent to earn and pay the price of getting a loose ball.

- When a player gains possession of the ball and knows he is going to get hit along the boards, he should keep moving, absorb the check by leaning into it, and make sure he instigates the hit.
- Once a player has control of the ball, he has three options:
  a. He can look to pass the ball up the floor quickly to take advantage of any lapse by the opposition defense. The closest teammate can make himself available for a pass and calls out "here's your help" to let the ballcarrier know where he is.
  b. After picking up a loose ball, he can tuck it in and look to run the ball up the floor.
  c. He has the option of picking up the loose ball or not picking it up and knocking it back to his goaltender. Sometimes it is a good idea to just knock the loose ball back to his goalie rather than trying to pick it up.
- One of the team objectives or statistics for loose balls is to gain possession of at least 50 percent or more of them.

## Loose-Ball Thoughts

- Every great play starts with a loose ball. "For every loose ball there is a chance to score."
- To stress the importance of every loose ball in a game state that the difference of a loose ball is two goals: a possible goal for us and a possible goal for the opposition. A team must have the attitude of "we are going to dominate the face-off and loose balls." That's why a team should send two to three players after every loose ball.
- A team must control loose balls to control the tempo of the game. Slow-down or ball-control teams are always strong in obtaining loose balls.

- The game is very physical for loose balls. Players must attack every loose ball with intensity, toughness, hungriness, and with abandonment. Players cannot be afraid of getting hit when going after a loose ball. The best way to go after a loose ball is to go after it knowing one is going to be hit or slashed. Most teams slash the man first, then, play the ball. Toughness is taking a hit, not giving a hit. The question is who goes into the corner or boards first?

- One of the toughest things for a player to do in game is go after a loose ball knowing he is going to get hit. And the toughest battles are for loose balls along the boards and from face-offs. A player must fight for every loose ball because if he "wins the one-on-one battles (loose balls), he will win the war (game)."

- In the defensive zone if a player can get the loose ball cleanly, then he goes and gets it. But he must remember if he makes a mistake in going after a loose ball he might get "burned" by his opponent getting the loose ball, going by him, and scoring. By going after a loose ball in the defensive end and knowing he won't or might not get it, a player could end up chasing the ballcarrier. So a player doesn't go after a loose ball when he knows he can't get it. If a player questions whether he can get the loose ball, he stays back and protects his net rather than take a chance, where he might not end up with the loose ball and the opposition ends up scoring. A player should always err on the side of defense.

- When fighting for a loose ball a player should know how many seconds are left on the 30-second clock, if there is a shot-clock in the league. If there are only a few seconds left, he can let the opponent pick it up.

- If a player is a defender, on any loose ball or rebound off a shot, he should cross-check or "box-out" his offensive check to stop him from going after the rebound or loose ball in front of or around the net. The good teams beat their opponents on offensive loose balls in their own defensive end so "box out."

- Rather than fighting for a loose ball some players just cross-check their opponent from behind, which is lazy, selfish, and stupid. This is bad because nothing positive comes from doing this.

## Jim Veltman's Six Keys for Winning Loose Balls

*Jim Veltman, formerly of the Toronto Rock, was one of the top loose-ball players in the National Lacrosse League.* Here are his thoughts on loose balls.

1. Anticipate where the ball will end up before it becomes loose.
2. Get to the loose ball first going at full speed.
3. Know where your outlets are before scooping the loose ball up whether it be an outlet pass to a teammate or breaking away with the ball in your own stick.
4. If you get to the ball first, spread your legs to shield the ball from your opponent.
5. If you get there behind your opponent, hit his stick up just before he attempts to pick up the ball and hope the ball passes by him, giving you a chance to pick the ball up.
6. On anticipating a loose ball on the face-off, be mentally alert to the point where your timing is a hair-second ahead of the whistle; stay on the balls of your feet; keep your knees bent; and attack anything on the floor. It is a good idea not to play on the non-stick side of your opponent, play on his stick side to stop him from picking up a loose ball.

## III. Loose-Ball Drills

These are "attitude drills" to instill aggressiveness, persistence, and determination. These drills are done regularly, but more so if the team was not aggressive and hungry for loose balls in their last game. Work a lot of loose balls drills so players are able to pick up a ball in "traffic."

In all loose-ball drills stress to the players a never-say-die attitude, to attack all loose balls (obtaining loose balls takes courage and heart), and keep two hands on the stick on every pick-up.

**Drill Progression in Regards to Number of Players:**

Start with one-on-zero, then one-on-one, then two-on-two, then three-on-three.

**Drill Progression in Regards to Speed of Loose Ball:**

1. Start with a stationary ball and let the players run "through" the ball.
2. Players work on picking up a slow rolling ball going away from them.
3. Players work on picking up a rolling ball toward them either thrown by a coach or coming off the boards.
4. Increase the speed of the loose ball so that it is moving quickly away from the player, then coming toward him.
5. Eventually work on picking up a loose ball in "traffic," with lots of players around fighting for possession.

**Loose-Ball Drill Progression in Regards to Defensive Pressure:**

1. Start drill with no defensive pressure until the players are able to pick up the ball properly.
2. Add token defensive pressure to the drills. For example, start the defender behind the offensive player to give the offensive player an advantage.

3. Run a "live" drill, where there will be defensive pressure.

### 1. One-on-Zero Practicing Picking Up Loose Balls on His Own

A player shoots the ball off an outside wall and lets it roll back toward him along the grass. When the ball hits the grass it will do crazy bounces and hops. The player has to attack and react to the ball. It is harder to retrieve a ball coming off a rough surface such as grass and gravel than off a smooth cement floor or artificial turf. This drill will help a player react quickly to a loose ball in a game.

### 2. One-on-Zero Stationary Pick-Up Drill

Players line up in a single line of six players. In front of the line is one coach with a bucket of balls. He places a ball on the floor and the first player runs all-out and picks up the stationary loose ball. Another coach will give feedback on the player's "Scoop" technique. Players have got to learn to use speed to get in and out.

### 3. One-on-Zero Partners "Attack" Drill

Each partner faces the other partner standing near their sideboards. One partner rolls the ball across the floor toward his partner who runs all-out toward it, attacks it, and scoops it up. The ballcarrier then runs back to his original spot and rolls it toward the other partner who is now running forward the ball to scoop up.

### 4. One-on-Zero Partners "Chase" Drill

Partners stand side-by-side near the sideboards. One partner rolls the ball away from his partner who chases the rolling ball and scoops it up on the run. Then the partners change roles.

### 5. Loose-Ball Zig-Zag Drill

Use the same formation as the Passing Zig-Zag Drill. Stationary player with a bucket of balls will start at one end of the formation and will roll or bounce the ball down the line in a zig-zag pattern. Since the players are stationary, they are just working on their scooping up technique.

## 6. Five-on-Zero Loose-Ball Shuttle Drill

Use the same formation as the Passing Shuttle Drill. The first ballcarrier in the line rolls the ball toward the first player in the other line and follows the rolling ball, running to the back of that line. The loose ball player attacks the ball aggressively and now rolls it toward the opposite player. Coach makes sure the players pick up the loose ball on the run.

**Variation:** Players can pick up the ball and place it down in middle of floor. Or players can shuttle the length of the floor.

## 7. Loose-Ball Single-Line Drill

Use the same setup as in the Passing Single-Line Drill with six stationary passers, three on each side of the floor. Left-shots and right-shots line up on their proper side of the floor at one end with everybody having a ball. The first leftie passes the ball to the first stationary passer opposite him, who in turn rolls the ball in front of the runner who picks up the loose ball and then passes to the next player.

## 8. Five-on-Zero Rebounds Off the Boards Drill

Five players form a single line facing the sideboards about 15 feet away, around the center of the floor. The first player with a ball will approach the sideboards and bang it off the boards. Then the next player in line attacks the ball, but only after it hits the boards and not before. After a player bangs the ball off the boards, he goes back to the end of the line. The coach can control the type of bounce he wants coming off the boards by telling the players to bang the ball off the boards low-and-hard so it will roll along the floor or to bang the ball off the boards high-and-hard so there is a higher bounce. Coach should stress to players

that they should charge the ball with all-out intensity.

**Variation:** One player, near the side-boards, rolls or shoots all the balls off the sideboards, one at a time, players at center attack the ball, then put them back beside him.

## 9. One-on-Zero Partners Rebound Off the Boards Drill

One player faces the boards from about six feet out. The other player stands behind his partner throws the ball off the boards and his partner reacts to the rebound, picks it up, and passes it back to his partner.

**Variation:** Partners face each other and the rebounder does not turn to retrieve the ball until it hits the boards.

## 10. Two Lines on Opposite Sides and Opposite Corners Loose-Ball Drill

Form two lines on opposite sides of the floor and at opposite ends of the floor. The first player passes to coach in middle of floor who then rolls ball for player to pick it up and score on the run. Other line on opposite side of floor does same thing with a second coach in the middle of the floor. After a player scores or takes a shot they go to the back of the other line.

## 11. One-on-One Teaching Progression for Picking-Up Loose Balls Along the Boards

**a. One-on-One Protecting the Ball Drill**
Both players have no sticks. Players learn to protect the ball with their bodies. The offensive player (or the player in first) wards off or "boxes out" his defensive opponent (or player in second) with his body while shielding the ball along the sideboards.

**b. One-on-One Warding-Off Drill**
The defensive player has a stick while the offensive player has no stick. The defensive player starts immediately behind the offensive player. On the whistle the offensive player

moves around to ward off the defensive player who is trying to pick up the ball. The offensive player should keep his eye on the ball, stay low, and maintain a wide stance. Time the offensive player to see how long he can stop the defensive player from picking up the ball.

### c. One-on-One Defender Pushes with His Hands Drill

The offensive player has a stick while the defensive player has no stick. The defensive player makes it tough for the offensive player to pick up the ball. The defender tries to push the offensive player with his hands into the boards. The offensive player has to be low, anticipate getting hit, and lean back into the defender.

### d. Defender Leans on Offensive Player Drill

Both players have sticks. The defender can only lean on the offensive player's body with his stick. The offensive player leans slightly into the defender with his back or sideways with his arm as he tries to pick up the ball.

### e. One-on-One Defender Stick-Checks-Only Drill

Both players have sticks. The defender is restricted only to stick-checking the offensive player. Defender can't pick the ball up while the offensive player tries to pick the ball up. Defender starts behind offensive player, coach rolls the ball.

### f. One-on-One Defender Cross-Checks-Only Drill

Both players have sticks. The defender can only push and cross-check the offensive player to prevent him from picking up the ball. The offensive player starts a few feet ahead of the defensive player.

### g. One-on-One Live

Both players have sticks. The defender is a half-step behind the offensive player to prevent him from picking up the ball. On the whistle the drill is "live."

## 12. One-on-One "Courage Along the Sideboards" Game

This is an attitude drill usually done after a poor performance on loose balls from the last game. Coach picks two teams by pairing players by weight and quickness. Coach squats between the two teams lined up beside each other at center and facing the sideboards. First two players on each team face the sideboards with sticks ready to battle for the loose ball along the boards. The coach will roll the ball to the sideboards and the players will attack the ball on the whistle, on the release of the ball, or when the ball hits the boards. The player who gets the ball tries to score and the other player tries to stop him. The ballcarrier gets one point for possession and another point if he scores. The first team to ten points is the winning team. The losing team does ten push-ups or runs four sprints.

## 13. One-on-One "Courage in the Corner" Drills

### a. One-on-One Token Defense in the Corner Drill

Coach forms two lines—offensive line and defensive line—beside each other and has the first two players in the lines fight for the ball in the corner. The coach rolls the ball into the corner or places the ball in the corner. On the whistle, both players attack the loose ball. The coach can set this drill up by: starting the defender one step behind the offensive player and not allowing him to pick up the ball, by restricting the defensive player to play only "token" defense so that the offense can work on protecting the ball with his body while picking up the ball; and then have the players go "live."

Stress to the players that once they have possession they should pull the stick in close to the body and cradle it and to anticipate a hit when picking up a loose ball. So, do not expose the front of his body to the action or stand straight up, but keep his body turned sideways and lean into the defender in case of a possible cross-check by the defender.

### b. One-on-One "Courage in the Corner" Game (See Diagram #14)

This is another attitude drill done after a poor performance on loose balls from the last game. Coach picks two teams by pairing players by weight and quickness. Coach squats between the two teams lined up beside each other in the wing area. First two players on each team face the corner with sticks ready to battle for the loose ball in the corner area of the floor. The coach will roll the ball into the corner and the players will attack the ball on the whistle, on the release of the ball, or when the ball hits the boards. A player gets one point for possession. The first team to ten points is the winning team. The losing team does ten push-ups or runs sprints.

**Variations:**

- The player who gets the ball tries to score and the other player tries to stop him. The ballcarrier gets one point for possession and another point if he scores.
- The player who gets possession in the corner passes out to a passer, then, breaks by cutting in front of the defender for a return pass or by cutting "backdoor" (behind the defender) for a return pass. On possession he tries to score. A player gets a point for possession, a point for receiving a return pass, and a point for a score.
- Coach designates one line offensive and the other line defensive. If the offensive player gets the ball, he tries to score, if the defensive player gets it, he tries to score at the other end of the arena.
- This drill is similar to the other two games. The coach squats between the two teams and rolls the ball into the open floor. The first two players battle for the loose ball, then go one-on-one.

### Diagram #14: "Courage in the Corner" Game

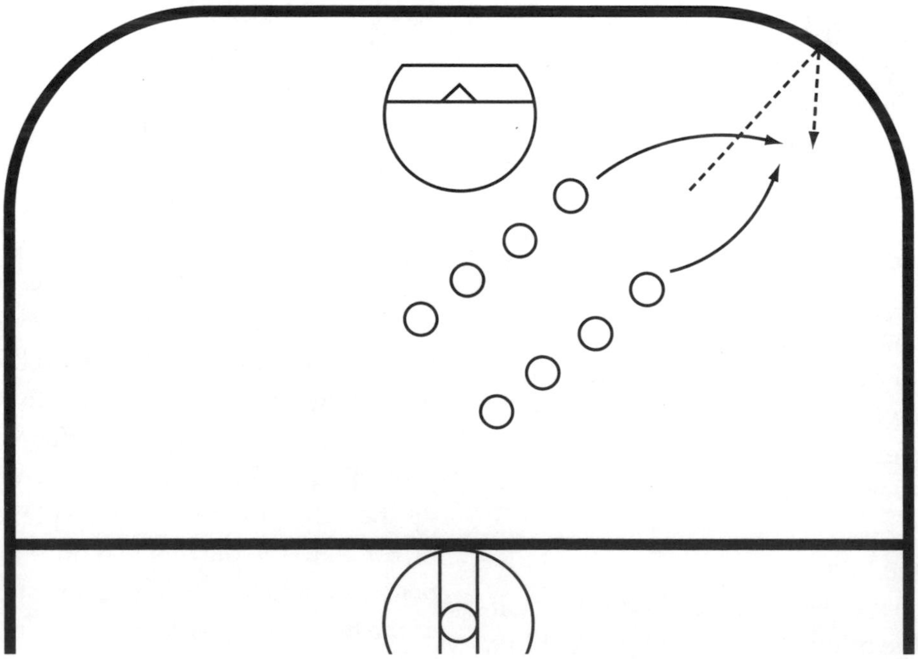

## 14. Two-on-Two "Courage in the Corner" Game

This drill is the same as "Courage in the Corner." Two teams lined up beside each other. First two players in each line (four total) battle for the loose ball in the corner. Coach stands beside the end-boards and drops the ball or he can stand back between the four players and roll the ball toward the boards. Teams get a point for possession. Play to eight points. Losers run.

**Variation:** The group of players who get possession try to score on the goalie at the one end. Other team plays defense.

## 15. Three-on-Zero "War" Drill

This is known as a tough, aggressive drill, almost like a "free-for-all" drill. Put the players in groups of four. One player throws the ball into the corner and the three other players fight for the loose ball in the corner. The first player who gets two loose balls is out of the drill while the thrower comes into the drill.

**Variation:** In this drill, once a player gets the loose ball he goes to score. Man who gets the loose ball becomes offense, other two players become defenders. The defense can almost do anything to stop the offense. This drill teaches the ballcarrier how to relax on contact.

Winner is the first player to score.

## 16. One-on-One "Animal" Drill

Put players in groups of three all over the floor. One player throws ball off the sideboards or end-boards. The other two players fight for the loose ball. Winner has to get three possessions, loser does 10 pushups. Winner becomes the loose-ball thrower, the loser goes again.

## 17. Three-on-Three Loose-Ball Drill

Have three players lined up to go after the loose ball and three defenders to stop loose-ball players from picking it up. The three defensive players have no sticks and stand in the corner area of the floor, along the boards, or in the middle of the floor. Later the defensive players can use their sticks, but inverted so they can't pick up the ball.

## 18. Three-on-Three "Cut Throat"

There are two teams of three players. Coach throws the ball off the end-board. Winner is the team that gets three possessions. Losers sprint the length of the floor.

## 19. "Get It" Drill

Put four balls on the floor while five players have to get them. The loser runs.

## 20. One-on-Three Loose-Ball Multiple Drill

Coach from the top of the offense area rolls the ball into the corner and the loose-ball player goes after it. A defender, with no stick, in the corner area, tries to interfere and stop him from picking it up. Once he gets possession he passes to the coach who then rolls it along the sideboards. Same thing happens again with defensive player trying to delay him from picking up the ball. On the second possession, he passes to the coach again, who then rolls ball into the middle of the floor. Again he goes after it, but is restrained from picking it up by a third defensive player. Once he gets it he goes to score. Work both ends of the floor. Rotate players in and out from different positions.

## 21. Five-on-Five Scrimmage

A team can practice loose-ball drills as much as it wants, but the most realistic drill is the actual scrimmage game in practice. So getting loose balls during a scrimmage involves effort, physical contact, composure, and technique.

# Chapter 6

# Individual Offense and Drills

## I. Offensive Terminology

**Strong-Side**—the side of the floor with three players of the same shot.

**Weak-Side**—the side of the floor with only two players of the same shot.

**Ball Side**—the side of the floor where the ball is.

**Off-Ball Side**—the side of the floor opposite the ball.

**"Passing" or "Shooting" Pass**—the best way to move the ball. The perfect pass is high and outside on the stick side.

**Getting in the "Clear"**—popping back out to get open to receive a cross-floor pass or a down pass. The receiver now can pass to a cutter, execute a one-on-one, or set up a play.

**"Cut" or "Go"**—used usually as an element of surprise movement to get open for a scoring opportunity. A non-ballcarrier runs or cuts in front of or behind his check through the middle of the floor looking for a pass and shot on net.

**Give-and-Go**—when the ballcarrier passes the ball to a teammate and then cuts to get open for the return pass and a possible shot on net.

**"Backdoor Cut"**—movement to get open for a scoring opportunity. A player runs behind his defender looking for a pass and shot on net. The defender is either overplaying or playing even with the cutter.

**One-on-One Move or Penetration Move**—the ballcarrier tries to beat his defender to attack the net for a scoring opportunity.

**"Circling" Movement**—on the off-ball or on-ball side where three or two players cut for a pass, and circle—or "cycle"—rotating their positions on their side of the floor.

**Playing on the Proper Side of the Floor**—means a right-handed shot plays on the left side of the floor and a left-handed shot plays on the right side of the floor. A player plays on his proper side of the floor because his stick is facing the middle of the floor, and therefore the ballcarrier is in a better position to score. Plus, in this position he can protect his stick with his body from his defender and still see the whole floor.

## II. General Offensive Moves

There are basically two ways for a ballcarrier to beat his defender and get a shot off at the net—going inside (middle) or going outside (sideboards). As you will see, a good offensive player has to have both these moves to be successful.

### Primary Offensive Move

This move is used when an offensive player goes one-on-one and cuts into the middle of the floor. The primary move does not occur as frequently in today's modern game because defenses now form the "Wall," which is taking a defensive position facing the sideboards to prevent the offensive player from cutting across the top. This move is the most natural move as the stick is held facing into the middle of the floor giving the player the best scoring opportunity.

### Secondary Offensive Move

This move is now as common as the primary move in today's modern game because it is a great countermove to defenses playing the "Wall" or overplaying the ballcarrier from going into the middle. This move is no longer considered a secondary move, but a countermove or even a primary move. By cutting to the outside and beating their check underneath it is hard for the defense to come across from the off-ball side to help defensively. By beating their check by cutting outside to the sideboards, the ballcarrier must eventually come back inside to get a good scoring position.

## III. Summary of One-on-One Offensive Techniques

### Outside Cuts

1. "Undercut" Move
2. Fake shot to an "Undercut"
3. Faking a shot while side stepping ("Drag") down the side into an Outside Spin-Around Move
4. Outside Spin-Around Move
5. Inside Body Fake Move
6. Outside Pivot Move

### Inside Cuts

1. Fake Shot to an Inside Slide Move
2. Faking a shot while side stepping ("Drag") down the side, into an Inside Slide Move
3. Inside Slide Move or Bull Move
4. Inside Spin-Around Move
5. Outside Body Fake Move
6. Inside Pivot Move

## IV. 12 Offensive Moves for a Ballcarrier Beating a Defender

These techniques are listed in priority, but a player may be more successful with one than another. So all a player does is experiment to see what works best for his size, quickness, and shooting technique.

### I. "Undercut" Move (Cut Outside)

This move is executed while on the move down the side of the floor. The ballcarrier turns his body slightly while facing the end-boards to take the cross-check on his stick-side shoulder. He leans on the defender and swings his stick outside with the outside hand in a vertical

**Photo 24:** Undercut Move—leaning on check to beat a defender outside, being checked on stick-side shoulder, stick held outside of body with two hands, facing end-boards

**Photo 25:** Undercut Move—get elbow and body inside defender to get underneath or weasel underneath, get low

position to protect it with the body, or he keeps it level to the floor with both hands protecting it with the body.

The battle is to get the body in front of or underneath the defender. A ballcarrier does this by using his free inside arm, elbow, and forearm to ward off, to push his defender behind him, or to "hook" the defender and then "weasel" his way underneath him. Some players just bend down and use their back to push their way around the defender.

He should be ready for an over-the-head check, a wrap-around check, or a defender just waiting for the ballcarrier to bring his stick back and stick-check him as he cuts back inside. So if the ballcarrier beats his defender he should keep his stick in front of his body to protect it.

If the offensive player runs out of territory or the defender stops him from cutting underneath, he just spins back around and cuts across the top as a counter-move. The offensive player can keep trying to beat his check by moving up and down the side trying to set him up so he can cut outside with an Undercut Move or back inside with an Inside Slide Move.

The Undercut Move is sometimes executed off an "Up Pick" when the back defender is

sleeping on the switch and the ballcarrier turns the corner outside and cuts below the defender. But if the back defender plays it right and switches hard on the ballcarrier, stopping him from turning the corner on the Undercut, then the ballcarrier has to stop and turn back around and cut across the top, either by himself or by a teammate setting a second pick—the "Cross" or "Down" pick. Some players, when cutting down the side off an "Up Pick," like to keep their stick down and low looking to throw an underhand pass to the picker rolling to the net.

From deep in the corner area, some players like to fake a one-on-one cut across the top, then swing the stick back inside and cut inside and underneath the defender.

*Note: Before talking about the "fake shot," here are a few general principles to follow when faking a shot:*

- A ballcarrier uses the fake shot to make his defender think he is going to shoot which might "freeze" or tighten up his defender, giving the ballcarrier a split-second advantage to go around him. It is a "fake" if the fake makes the defender think he is going to really shoot, while in fact he is going to do something else. Great players do a lot of faking, so do not look at their stick to check.
- The fake shot is used best when the defender tries to get his stick in the way of the ballcarrier's stick to interfere with his shot, or when a defender is rushing him.
- The fake shot is accomplished as the ballcarrier goes to shoot his overhand shot. He turns his top-hand wrist inward to "check" or stop his shot. Some players like to turn the stick outward with their bottom-hand wrist on the fake (See Chapter 8, Shooting). The important thing is the fake must look like the real thing, so the ballcarrier must pretend to actually shoot the ball, and then, at the last second, "check" his shot. It is important to "sell the fake" to the opponent to get a reaction by making it

look real, i.e., look at the net, and fake hard and quick.

• From the fake shot a player can execute two main moves: an Undercut or an Inside Slide Move.

• The other type of fake shot is a similar move to a "Face Dodge" in field lacrosse where the player pretends to shoot by bringing the stick completely across his body with his top-hand arm while turning his wrists inward, then the player cuts to the outside. The difference here is the offensive player that uses only his wrists has two options cutting across in front of the net or cutting to the outside.

• Another fake move is the fake Underhand shot. Because the stick is upside down this fake is accomplished by turning the top-hand wrist, which is now the lower of the two hands, upward to "check" the shot.

## 2. Fake Shot to an Undercut (Cut Outside)

This move is carried out when a ballcarrier fakes a long shot or pretends to wind-up for a shot and then pulls or swings his stick across his body and cuts to the outside and works his way back inside by going underneath his defender for a close-in shot. The great players keep it simple by facing the net and just faking a long shot, then pulling the stick outside, cutting outside to the sideboards and back in for a close-in shot.

*Notes:*
– *Some players like to just run down the side, fake the shot, cut outside, and shoot a long-shot to the far top corner without cutting underneath.*
– *Defenders have to be aware of players that look to fake their shot and Undercut all the time. If they play their stick to check them, they will get beat.*

**Photo 26:** Fake shot to an Undercut—fake shot and pull stick across body (wrists and arms)

**Photo 27:** Cut outside

**Photo 28:** Fake shot to an Undercut—lean with inside or stick-side shoulder to beat a defender outside and underneath, stick held by two hands

## 3. Inside Slide Move or "Bull Move" (Cut Inside Across Top of Floor)

This is one of the simplest, but also the most effective, of all the one-on-one moves.

### Protect the Stick

Just before going one-on-one the ballcarrier holds the stick low and horizontally in front of his body. As he gets to the defender in this move his first priority is to protect his stick before trying to shoot or score. He does this by turning his body sideways to take the slash, poke, push, or cross-check on the upper arm of his non-stick shoulder, thereby using his body as a shield for his stick so he can watch the checker, the floor, the play, and the net over his shoulder rather than watching the ball in the stick. The great players are always facing the play even with their back turned to take a check, while looking for off-ball plays with their stick in a shooting or passing position.

**Photo 29:** Inside Slide Move—turn body sideways to take a hit on non-stick shoulder, lean into defender as ballcarrier cuts inside across top of floor

### Stick Position When Being Checked

Before the check, a ballcarrier could choke up on his stick, i.e., moving his top-hand up the shaft close to the throat of the stick. He now brings up his stick vertically while executing the Large Cradle. This position gives the ballcarrier better protection of the stick and better control of the ball when taking heavy hitting. But with this wide grip a player has to keep it until the exact moment he is going to shoot or pass at which time he will slide his top-hand back down to the middle of the shaft.

A more common position for the ballcarrier in today's game is holding his stick horizontally over his shoulder with his hands closer together in a position to shoot, pass or go one-on-one, called the "triple-threat" position, while being slashed or cross-checked. Be aware that by holding the stick horizontally makes it easier to be stick-checked, and there is also a higher probability of the ball falling out on the jar of the hit.

*Notes:*
- *Do not pass when being cross-checked unless one is an experienced player.*
- *When the ball is in the stick, never keep it stationary, always keep it cradling.*

### Contact When Taking a Hit or a Cross-Check

On contact, a ballcarrier should have a solid wide base, i.e., feet spread wider than shoulder-width apart to maintain balance, dip his inside shoulder, get low, lean into his check with his body weight, and relax his body, "like a sack of potatoes," on the impact of the cross-check instead of tightening up and possibly coughing up the ball on a jarring hit.

*Note: If the ballcarrier is stronger and bigger than the defender, he makes contact by driving through the defender's stick to overpower him and knock him off balance, or pushes him back to create a gap. On receiving a cross-check, some of the bigger*

*ballcarriers like to initiate the contact with their upper arm and body weight to see if the defender is good enough to stop him.*

### Point of Contact When Sliding

On executing the Inside Slide Move the ballcarrier's objective is to try to make contact at the "head" area of the defender's stick or off-center of the defender's stick so he can slide off his check by leaning into his check's stick to equalize pressure with his relaxed body weight, called "dead weight," and eventually sliding or muscling his way past the defender and getting a step in front of his check for a shot on net.

*Notes:*

— *By the ballcarrier hitting the stick at an angle, rather than dead on or a direct hit, it is easier to slide past the defender when his force is on the side of the stick.*

— *Do not resist a cross-check, relax on the hit, resisting a hit is counter-productive.*

— *Great players keep it simple by just cutting straight across the top, leaning into their defender while taking a hit, and shooting.*

### Tuck Stick In

If the ballcarrier beats his defender down the middle, he should remember to tuck the stick in front of his body and keep it in this vertical position to protect it until he shoots. Some defenders play what is called the "Matador Defense," where they let the ballcarrier go by, then stick-check him from behind.

### Variations of the Inside Slide Move by Great Shooters

- Great shooters like to shoot around their defenders and use them as screens when there is a long gap (two steps) between themselves and their defenders.

- Great shooters like to lean into their check to equalize pressure then step back or push off, creating a gap for a screen shot around their defender.

- Great shooters like to cut across the top, stop, fake to go back outside, and then come back around for a shot or a screen shot.

- Great shooters like to just shoot long even when leaning into the defender.

  As the shooter leans into the cross-check, he tries to pick up his defender's rhythm. Then as the defender commits to cross-check, he steps away from the opponent so that the latter ends up reaching for air or becomes off balance with the result of the shooter stepping around him.

  The ballcarrier puts his back into the defender then rolls back and forth or from side to side trying to get the defender to commit to cutting him off in the direction he is rolling. Once the defender commits, the ballcarrier rolls back the other way going to the net. In this rolling motion, use the upper body, lean with the body weight, keep the feet moving, and use deception to beat the defender.

- Another option of rolling back and forth is that when the ballcarrier is cutting across the top he fakes a half-roll by leaning with his back into the defender and fake rolling to the outside. When the defender commits by trying to stop the ballcarrier from beating him to the outside, he then rolls back across the top for a shot or Slide Move to the net.

## 4. Fake Shot to an Inside Slide Move (Cut Inside Across Top of Floor)

The fake shot in this move is a little bit different than the fake to an Undercut. The ballcarrier fakes a shot using only his wrists with his stick parallel to the floor over his shoulder to "freeze" the defender. When the defender tightens up, the ballcarrier just cuts across the top for a long shot. A good time to fake a shot is when the defender appears he is going to try to stick-check you. Remember to make the fake look real. The great players are always looking to fake a shot and cut straight across the top for a shot.

## 5. Faking a Shot While Side Stepping ("Drag") Down the Side into an Inside Slide Move (Cut Inside Across Top of Floor)

In this move the ballcarrier turns his body sideways to take the hit on his non-stick side while looking at the net. He keeps the stick parallel to the floor over his shoulder with the ball behind him and hands close together, in a "cocked" position or a "triple-threat" position: looking at the net to go one-on-one, looking to pass, or looking to shoot. He then side steps down while faking to shoot all the time, but what he really is looking for is to

**Photo 30:** Fake shot (wrists only)

**Photo 32:** Faking a shot while side stepping ("drag") down the side—turn body sideways, taking hit on non-stick shoulder, triple-threat, look to cut into Slide Move

**Photo 31:** To an Inside Slide Move to beat a defender, then a cut inside across top of floor

**Photo 33:** Then cut using Inside Slide Move to beat a defender cutting inside across top of floor

cut across the top for a shot, using a Slide Move.

**Variation:** From this position he can also side step down the side of the floor faking an outside Spin-Around move into an outside Undercut Move then, stops and spins back in and cuts across the top for a shot.

### 6. Faking a Shot While Side Stepping ("Drag") Down the Side into an Outside Spin-Around Move (Cut Outside)

Ballcarrier again turns his body sideways to take a hit on his non-stick-side shoulder while keeping his stick parallel to the floor over his shoulder, in a "triple-threat" position: looking at the net to go one-on-one (Inside Slide Move), looking to pass, or looking to shoot. As he takes a hit on his inside non-stick shoulder, while side stepping down, faking to shoot all the time, but really looking to Spin Around, making a 180-degree turn into an Undercut Move, i.e., cutting underneath or below his defender and back inside for a close-in shot.

**Photo 34:** Faking a shot while side stepping ("drag") down the side, taking a hit on his non-stick shoulder—player facing net, stick in triple-threat, make it look like he wants to cut across the top, then spins back

**Photo 36:** Continue Outside Spin

**Photo 35:** Start of Outside Spin to come back

**Photo 37:** Outside Spin-Around Move to beat a defender—cut outside into an Undercut

## 7. Inside Spin-Around Move (Cut Inside Across Top of Floor)

While moving down the side of the floor, facing the corner, the ballcarrier takes a hit on his inside or stick-side shoulder, or on his back, maybe looking to try an Undercut Move. If the defender commits to the Undercut, he then stops and makes an Inside Spin-Around Move, 180-degree turn with his back on his defender's body, back into middle of the floor to an Inside Slide Move for a shot.

## 8. Outside Spin-Around Move (Cut Outside)

While moving down the side of the floor, the ballcarrier will turn his body sideways to take a hit on his non-stick-side shoulder or on his back, then stops and makes an Inside Slide Move to cut across the top. If the defender reacts and overplays him from cutting across the top, the ballcarrier stops and does an Outside Spin-Around Move, 180-degree turn, with his back on his defender's body—or an Undercut Move—for an immediate shot on net. Here the defender has either stopped him

**Photo 38:** Moving down side of floor takes a hit on inside or stick-side shoulder, looking to Undercut (player usually facing corner), then starts an Inside Spin-Around Move

**Photo 40:** Continues Spin

**Photo 39:** Continues Spin-Around

**Photo 41:** Beat defender by cutting across top of floor using Inside Slide

from cutting across the top or the ballcarrier is setting him up to make this Outside Spin-Around Move.

*Note: Before talking about the "body fake," here are a few general principles to follow when faking with the body:*

### The Actual Body Fake

The body fake is a move of lateral quickness with little or no contact while facing the defender on the run. The ballcarrier initiates an action to get a reaction from the defender. The fake move is to make the defender move in one direction while the ballcarrier goes in the other. It is important to make the fake look convincing. All the ballcarrier needs to do is to get his opponent leaning in one direction and therefore off-balanced or committing himself totally to the fake by reacting to the move. Then the ballcarrier takes a quick step in the other direction. Although this is a change of direction move, the ballcarrier runs straight at the defender and beats him in a confined area while maintaining this path of a straight line rather than running wide and possibly giving the defender time and space to recover.

### Moving the Defender for a Body Fake

The fake is to get the defender slightly off-balance by making him take a step in the fake direction. The success in beating a man is "moving the defender." If both players are standing still and the offensive man makes a move the defender might still be able to react quickly enough to stay with him. But if the ballcarrier is walking or jogging, the defender will be moving backward or moving alongside him. Then, when the offensive player suddenly fakes and cuts sharply (changes direction), the defender has to fight the lag of his physical reaction time to stay with him. Also, the defender having to overcome his momentum from one direction to another might unbalance

him while the ballcarrier will be balanced and under control. This will give the ballcarrier the half-step he needs to beat him.

### Footwork for the Body Fake

Stress that a ballcarrier beats his man with his feet rather than faking or bobbing with his head or moving his upper body around. To set the defensive man up, the ballcarrier works on the jab step. He plants his foot as if going in a certain direction—to look believable, the fake step has to be convincing. Then, pushing off the faking foot, he takes an explosive step with his other foot in the opposite direction (V-cut).

So, when a ballcarrier wants to go one way, he will take a fake step before he goes there or he will take the defender down the floor two or three steps in the opposite direction he wants to go and then make his move. Again, the important thing is to move the defender so he will be vulnerable to fakes and quick changes of direction.

### Execute the Body Fake Quickly

The ballcarrier must make his move quickly. He can set up a defender by appearing to relax a bit so that the defender will also relax. Then, a quick fake step, followed by a quick "first" step. Remember to stay low. Making the first step explosive and longer than normal will give the ballcarrier a half-step on the defender, permitting the ballcarrier to drive to the net. If possible, the ballcarrier wants to make this quick move before contact, so he can try to keep time and space between himself and his defender before starting his move.

To make matters worse for the defender, the ballcarrier chooses the moment to make his move, thereby providing an element of surprise. The defender's reaction must make up for a mental reaction-time lag—besides the physical reaction-time lag—because of the suddenness of the move.

## 9. Outside Body Fake Move (Cut Inside Across Top of Floor)

### Get the Defender Moving Backward

The Outside Fake is the most common fake, and the most logical choice, as the ballcarrier ends up in a good scoring position quickly in the middle of the floor. The ballcarrier, on entering the Offensive Zone, tries to get his opponent moving backward, before giving him the Outside Fake Move, i.e., stepping outside and then cutting back in. He fakes as close to his check as possible, without being slashed or cross-checked, so that his defender has less chance of recovery. This is a move of quickness while on the move, therefore, there is very little contact. The key though is to get the defensive man moving sideways or moving backward since he can't go in two directions at the same time, i.e., backward and laterally.

### Protect the Stick with the Body

When facing the defender at the beginning of his Outside Fake Move, the ballcarrier's stick will be exposed, but it is kept in close to his body. On the outside-fake step, turn the stick inward toward the body and turn the inside shoulder outward as if to cut outside. On the explosive step—the push-off by the outside foot—turn or rotate the upper body back inward and bring the stick back over the inside shoulder. This puts the offensive player in a good position to protect his stick in case the defender reacts quickly enough to slash or cross-check.

### Outside Fake Step

On giving the defensive man a small outside fake step be sure to plant the outside foot (right foot for a left-handed player) outside of the defender's outside foot, with a quick, hard step, making the defender think he is going to cut outside, then push off hard with this outside foot (right foot), and take a quick, large step with the left foot back inside of the floor. Stress stepping right and pushing left, off the same foot, at a 90-degree angle (V-cut pattern). As the ballcarrier cuts across the top, he should dip the inside shoulder to help "weasel" by the defender if there is any contact.

*Note: Great players just simply fake outside, cut inside across the top of the floor, and shoot quickly.*

### Variation of the V-Cut

A variation to this V-cut pattern is the Z-cut pattern where the ballcarrier plants his inside-fake foot first, then plants his outside foot as if he is going to cut outside. This time he keeps his inside-fake foot planted, keeps it on the floor, and does a crossover step with the outside foot by stepping over the inside foot to cut back into the middle. This is like a double-fake—fakes inside, fakes outside, then cuts back inside.

## 10. Inside Body Fake Move (Cut Outside)

### The Inside-Fake Step

The ballcarrier sets up the defender by giving him a small inside-fake step by planting the right foot, for a right-handed player, making

**Photo 42:** Inside Body Fake—fake inside step

the defender think he is going to cut across the top. The ballcarrier tries to plant the inside-fake step outside the defenders' inside foot but this is not a big concern. If he can do it, it is a good move. Then he pushes off hard with the inside fake foot (right foot), and takes a quick, large step with the outside foot (left foot) to the outside i.e., forming a V-cut pattern.

### Protect the Stick with the Body

As the ballcarrier cuts outside, he turns his inside shoulder outward and swings his stick across and to the outside of his body, away from his defender to protect his stick. The ballcarrier accomplishes this by either passing his stick to his right hand only—grabbing the stick about halfway up the shaft and resting the bottom half of the shaft on his forearm—and cradling the ball in the stick with one hand while still protecting the stick with his body. Or the ballcarrier can just swing his stick to the outside of his body with both his hands and hold it there while protecting the stick with his body. In this situation there is less cradling as the ballcarrier just holds his stick out to his side.

**Photo 43:** Inside Body Fake—push off hard with inside foot and take large step with outside foot and swing stick across body into an Undercut

### Using His Body on the Undercut

Once the ballcarrier gets his body beside his defender, he drops his inside shoulder and, using his inside arm and forearm to ward off or push his defender behind him, he basically "weasels" his way around the defender, until he is in front of him with the defender ending up on the ballcarrier's back. He still cradles the ball with one hand or both hands on the stick.

### If the Defender is Beat, Be Aware of Being Checked From Behind

Once in front of the defender the ballcarrier now switches the stick back to both hands in front of his body being aware that the defender is right behind him and is going to try to stick-check him from behind.

### Use the Body to Protect Stick on Shot

The ballcarrier has to use his body to protect his stick by holding it out in front of his body when shooting. If he brings the stick back over his shoulder to take his shot, he could be stick-checked by his defender.

### Variations of the V-Cut:

- A variation to the V-cut pattern is the Z-cut pattern, where the ballcarrier plants his outside-fake foot first, then plants his inside foot as if he is going to cut back into the middle. This time, however, he keeps his outside fake foot planted, and does a crossover step with the inside foot—stepping over the outside foot—and cuts to the outside. Again, this is like a double-fake—fakes outside, fakes inside, then cuts back outside.
- Another variation for both the Inside Body Fake and the Outside Body Fake is the Stutter Step to a fake. The ballcarrier does a Stutter Step, which is many short little steps in rapid succession, then a jab step or fake step with a foot one way then accelerate the other way. The ballcarrier tries to get the

defender on the back of his heels or moving backward with the Stutter Steps. The ballcarrier reacts to what the defense does. For example, if the defensive man commits in one direction, the ballcarrier goes in the opposite direction.

*Nick Trudeau, formerly of the Albany Attack of the NLL,* on one-on-one offensive moves. "I try to read the defender but have no pre-planned move, as I may try something I would never do in another situation. My best move is a stutter step into the middle. I make a hard cut to the outside to make it look like I'm going outside and then I make a hard cut into the middle. When taking a hit, I still try to get my shot off. My first thought is to keep shooting even to the point where I'll take a shot around someone."

## 11. Inside Pivot Move (Inside Cut Across the Top of the Floor)

**Executing the Inside Pivot Move When the Defender is Running Beside the Ballcarrier**
In this move, balance and footwork are very important. A player uses his feet more in this move to beat his defender than any other offensive move. The ballcarrier makes a full, 360-degree turn when executing the Pivot Move. He starts out facing the defender and after the pivot he ends up facing the net.

The left-shot ballcarrier fakes an outside Undercut with his outside foot, then plants his inside foot into the middle of his defender's feet and spins back into the defender. The ballcarrier spins onto the defender's stick with his back and continues around, all the time pivoting on his inside foot. The outside foot is swung around, planting it on the outside of the defender's inside foot, which will give him good offensive positioning. When the ballcarrier is pivoting with his back to the defender, he must protect his stick by tucking it in close to his body and cradling it. He should come out of the pivot in a good shooting position.

**Variation**: The ballcarrier fakes a drive to the outside, faking an Undercut, and pivots quickly on his inside foot, pivots around in front of his defender, preferably with no contact and cuts across the top.

**Executing the Inside Pivot Move When Running Straight at a Set Defender**
The ballcarrier plants his inside foot between his defender's feet and fairly close to the defender's body. On the plant, turn the body sideways, turn the stick inward, and close to his body. Pivot on the planted foot, while at the same time pushing off with the outside foot. He then swings the outside foot around the outside of the defender's inside foot. The ballcarrier can lean into his checker with his back as he executes this move.

The pivot is executed in a 360-degree turn. The ballcarrier goes as straight as possible when trying to beat his defender. If the ballcarrier goes in an arc on his Inside Pivot Move, he will give his defender time and space to recover his defensive positioning.

## 12. Outside Pivot Move (Outside Cut)

**Executing the Outside Pivot Move Coming Out of the Corner Area**
In this Outside Pivot Move, the ballcarrier must make it appear he is working hard to come out of the corner area of the arena to go across the top of the floor to get a good shot. He must run the defensive man hard up the sideboards, but making sure he drives him high enough to give himself room for the Outside Pivot.

On executing the Outside Pivot Move, plant inside foot in the middle of the defender's feet while swinging the outside foot backward, hooking on the defender's outside foot while maintaining contact with his back on the defender's stick during the pivot. As the ballcarrier finishes the 360-degree turn, he hooks his inside elbow on the defender's back for leverage to push the defender behind him and get him on his back. He then dips his inside shoulder to "weasel" past his defender. At the end of the pivot, now an Undercut move, keep the stick in the outside hand (right hand), holding it in the middle of the shaft, while maintaining contact with rest of the shaft on the forearm. The ballcarrier does this to protect the stick from the defender's stick check, while with this type of grip he can swing the stick out to cradle the ball in the stick. Once he gets his defender on his back, he must bring his stick back around in front of his body to protect it for a shot.

### Executing the Outside Pivot Move When Running Straight at a Set Defender

The ballcarrier executes the outside pivot when the defender is overplaying the ballcarrier to stop him from cutting into the middle of the floor. The ballcarrier makes almost the same move as above, i.e., the ballcarrier plants his outside foot, pivots on it, and rolls back around, swinging his inside foot backward around his defender.

## V. Thoughts for Beating a Defender

### One-on-One Qualities

Qualities, such as quickness, balance, power, speed, intelligence, aggressiveness, deception, and instinct are important traits to have to be one a good one-on-one player.

Great one-on-one players have confidence in their ability to beat a defender; they are not intimidated by who the defender is or his size. This is often taken as cockiness, but most cocky players are exceptional one-on-one players.

### One-On-One Players Must Use Their Assets

A great offensive player learns to use his assets to the best of his ability to beat a defender. If he has size, he learns to use it; if he has speed, he learns to use it; if he has quickness, he learns to use it. Each player must find his own way to

beat a defender (i.e., develop a favorite move and develop a variety of countermoves in case his best move does not work). Just don't become predictable.

### One-on-One Is Instinctive

One-on-one seems to be a "knack" players have, and the good ones do it instinctively, before thought takes command. In fact, great offensive players seem to be able to make something out of nothing.

### Two Reasons for Going One-on-One

An offensive player goes one-on-one either to score or to beat his opponent and draw a teammate's defender, and then pass off to his open teammate.

### One-on-One Players Must Have the Ability to Go Both Ways

Great offensive players have moves to go both ways, which becomes a big advantage as the defenders can't overplay their strong side. The ability to go both ways (two basic moves) is a must. The great players want their defenders to have no idea what they are going to do, which makes it hard to defend them. Great players face their defenders and beat their defenders with speed and a quick move going either way. They can make a move going across the top of the floor and if they are stopped they have a countermove to cut outside or vice versa. They try to read their defender and have no pre-planned move, as they might try something they would never do.

The one-on-one confrontation is like a chess game in which the offensive player is always trying to set up his defender. The offensive player wants to keep the defensive man wondering what he is going to do. So, he pretends to do one thing and then does something else. The whole idea is to get the defender to react to the offensive player instead of the offensive player reacting to the defender.

*Josh Sanderson of the Boston Blazers of the NLL* talks about four keys to beating a defender: 1) Use your speed. 2) Use your quickness. 3) Go inside first then outside; or outside, then go inside. One move opens up the other move. 4) Keep your stick in a shooting or a passing position while watching the play all the time.

*Gavin Prout of the Edmonton Rush of the NLL* talks about one-on-one offense:

1. For larger offensive players, try to use your size as an advantage; you want to make your move closer to the defender and shield your stick.
2. For smaller offensive players, use your quickness to your advantage. You want to make your moves farther away from your defender, farther than a stick length away, so it's harder to check.
3. Use a change of speed move by lulling your defender to sleep, then using a burst of speed to go around him.
4. Use faking and deception as part of your repertoire:
   - Make your first few steps the opposite way you want to go (i.e., if you want to go underneath, then make the first few steps across the top). Once you have your defender moving the same way you are, quickly change your direction and head hard to the net.
   - If you want to go into the middle, then make your first couple of steps look like you're running down the side to the net and quickly change your direction across the top once your defender starts moving down with you.
5. Only take a maximum of one or two steps, any more than that and all the other defenders will be focused on you and ready to help.

## One-on-One Players Must Have an Outside and Inside Game

Good one-on-one players look to go inside first then outside second, or look to shoot outside first then go inside second. The one opens up the other. Stress that after making an offensive move, either end up shooting planted or on the run, which is hard to do.

In today's game it seems players are scoring as much on the Undercut Move (cutting outside) as the Slide Move (cutting across the top).

To neutralize the defender, make him react to a move by getting him moving either backward or sideways. If an offensive player doesn't attack the defender, he will attack you.

## Remember: Be Quick, But Don't Hurry

When a player is quick, he has patience, which means he actually slows down or even pauses before he makes his move. He then all of a sudden accelerates or explodes and makes his move with a purpose. He moves rapidly, but not franticly, and he has a calmness about himself. A player gets best results when he plays in a relaxed manner. When a player hurries he becomes anxious, he plays out of control, he doesn't think, he panics, and he looks flustered and confused.

## The Quickness Principle

The small, quick offensive player would rather have a big defender checking him or a defender maybe a little bit bigger in size. The slower the defender the better it is. Quickness is the key for small players as they want to play against defenders they can beat with footwork. Since footwork comes into play more for smaller guys, they work on their first-step quickness.

### Remember: the Harder One Tries, the Tighter One Gets

Offensive players should play in a relaxed mode, with knees bent, so that they can: move quickly into an attack mode at the defender, go after any loose balls, or to get back on defense. The most common fault is trying too hard.

### One-on-One Player Must Have a Good Shot-Fake Move

A player has to make the shot-fake move look like the real thing, make it "believable." A bad shot-fake looks like a fake, a good shot-fake looks like the real thing. Great players in close on the goalie have a great "pump" shot-fake to freeze the goalie or make the goalie react to the fake before they shoot the real shot.

### One-on-One Player Must Be in a "Triple-Threat" Position

What makes Josh Sanderson of the Boston Blazers of the NLL so good is that he keeps his stick in a "triple-threat" position to go: one-on-one, pass the ball, or shoot the ball. As he goes one-on-one he is always looking at the net and watching the play to shoot or pass all the time. He does this by keeping his stick parallel to the floor and hands close together. A lot of players with the ball are just looking to pass all the time. Great players while going one-on-one keep their stick in the "triple-threat" position so they can shoot, pass, or go on-on-one.

### One-on-One Player Must Be an Offensive "Threat"

- He must look to go one-on-one first and look to pass second.
- He must start his offensive move from the Outside Lane rather than from the Middle Lane. This is especially true in minor/youth lacrosse.
- He must keep his balance by keeping a good wide stance when being cross-checked.

- He must have the ability to go one-on-one and hang on to the ball while being slashed, harassed, or cross-checked. A player has to protect the stick as opponents are stick-checking all the time, trying to steal the ball.
- He must always keep his head up, looking at the net and seeing any cutters going through the middle.
- He must keep his offensive moves simple. The less movement in his execution of offensive moves the better.
- He must be a scoring threat on offense to contribute to the team.
- He must be a player who can go one-on-one, shoot from the outside, pass as he is being cross-checked, and pass-and-cut quickly.

### Best Scoring Area is the Middle of the Floor

The best area to go one-on-one is from the ballcarrier's proper side of the floor in the Outside Lane. If he beats his defender, especially with an Inside Slide Move, he will be in the best shooting area—in the middle of the floor. Whereas, if he goes one-on-one near the center of the floor and beats his defender, he will probably end up on his wrong side of the floor and in a poorer shooting area.

### Move the Ball on Offense

A good ballcarrier does not hang onto the ball too long. The strategy of not moving the ball stops the offense from moving and gives the defense time to back each other up. If the ballcarrier can't beat his check with his initial one-on-one move, he should make a cross-floor pass to create an off-ball play with his teammate on his side of the floor. A good offensive player does not stand still, with or without the ball. If he keeps moving, he will be harder to hit, and he could wear out his defender. Players must also pass the ball around the outside of the defense. If they pass through the middle of the defense the ball will be intercepted unless a teammate is cutting toward them. A good offensive rule is "players cannot pass into the defense unless a teammate is cutting toward them, or unless nobody is guarding the receiver."

## The Best Time to Go One-on-One Is:

- When the defender is not in a good defensive stance to check, i.e., his knees are not bent.
- When the defender is out of position, i.e., playing the offensive player even or in a straight-up position, where he can go two ways, rather than playing him at an angle to force him one way.
- When the defender is still getting back on defense. Defenders are still looking for their checks and will not be in the best position to back up their defensive teammate.
- When the ballcarrier's teammates are moving around occupying their defensive men with the result of little or no backup.
- When the ballcarrier thinks he can beat his defender because of a mismatch, such as when the defender is smaller; when the offensive player knows he is quicker than the defender, or when the offensive player knows is going against a weak checker.
- When the defender is tired.
- When the defender is overly aggressive and tries to get the ball from the ballcarrier by checking his stick and thus overcommitting himself.
- When the defender rushes at the ballcarrier. To counter this move just fake him one way and go the other way or just sidestep him.
- When the defender reaches on his cross-check, i.e., checks air, and overcommits.
- When the defender slashes and over commits.
- When the defender reacts to the ballcarrier's offensive move and makes a mistake or overcommits.

Generally, in all these situations the ballcarrier "reads" the defender and reacts to his defensive mistake. Beating a man, often enough, is done instinctively—one doesn't think, he just does it.

## VI. Non-Ballcarrier Beating a Defender ("Give-and-Go" or "Go")

When moving without the ball, a player usually uses the same moves as the ballcarrier in beating a defender. It is important to always know where the ball is and to learn to work off picks.

### 1. Non-Ballcarriers Must Move on Offense

Non-ballcarriers must move or cut. If players stand and watch the ballcarrier, nothing will happen and the team ends up running a stagnant offense. Besides, if a non-ballcarrier moves with a purpose it's amazing how many times he ends up in the open.

### 2. The Give-and-Go Play

**Start the Give-and-Go Play by Making a Pass**
The ballcarrier can pass either across the floor or down the floor into the corner. These passes can initiate the Give-and-Go play. The offensive

**Photo 44:** Start the Give-and-Go play by making a pass

guideline is "If a player passes the ball, he must cut or move." On any pass to a stationary player, the passer must cut for the return pass unless it is a set play. This rule gets rid of any standing around and creates movement.

**Why Pass and Cut in the Give-and-Go Play?**
Players cut to get open for a pass and a shot. They either cut toward the net or toward the ballcarrier to receive a pass and hopefully get a good shot on net. It is just a matter of getting one step in front of the defender or just getting an inside position on the defender, i.e., between his defender and the ballcarrier.

**When to Cut in the Give-and-Go Play**
When the ballcarrier passes the ball, the defender has a tendency to relax as he thinks the play is now over and this is the time for the former ballcarrier to cut.

**How to Cut in the Give-and-Go Play**
a. Timing is important. Perfect coordination must occur between the passer and the cutter, i.e., the passer must release the ball just as the cutter makes his cut.
b. The cutter must use a degree of deception (fake), an element of surprise, and a move of quickness (first step), so that the defense will be a split second behind him. The cutter wants to get in front of his defender or at least get an inside position on the defender's body.
c. To time the pass and anticipate the passer (knowing when the cutter is cutting), the cutter must establish eye contact with the passer to let him know he is going to cut. All the cutting in the world will not help if the ballcarrier is not looking for the cutter.
d. When a player cuts he must keep going to the ball until he receives it. If he stops to catch the ball, he might get intercepted or stick checked.
e. If a cutter does not get the ball on a cut, he stops just past the Imaginary Center Line

**Photo 45:** The main cut in the Give-and-Go play—cut in front of checker

and returns back to his proper side of the floor to still be a threat.
f. Players have to cut through the center with authority and with the purpose of catching the ball. Some players cut just to "go through the motion" of cutting with no intentions of catching the ball.
g. The cutter must read the defender. If the defender plays the cutter low toward the net, then the cutter cuts in front of him. If the defender plays the cutter even or higher to take away the main front cut, then the cutter cuts backdoor or behind the defender.

**Being Checked on the Cut in the Give-and-Go Play**
When a player cuts he will either be one step ahead of his check or he will be cutting with his check right on him.
a. Always give a good stick target for the passer and concentrate on watching the ball all the way into the pocket, even though being hit.
b. When cutting, always expect to get hit so that when it comes it will not be a surprise.
c. On contact from the cross-check, the cutter should dip his inside shoulder, relax from the waist up, and lean his body weight into his checker's stick to equalize pressure and

stabilize his opponent's stick when catching the ball. The defender, from this body weight, will have a tough time pushing his stick forward on the cross-check to give the cutter a jarring cross-check. If a player stiffens up on contact, he will be holding his stick too tight to catch the ball.

### 3. "Go" or Cut Play

Again, the simplest way to beat a defender is to just face the defender and cut or step past the defender on his inside from the off-ball side for a pass. First-step quickness is important. So is deception before one cuts. This is accomplished by: faking one way and going the other way, knocking his defender's stick down, cross-checking the defender's body, or pushing off on the defender, or when the defender goes to cross-check the cutter, the cutter can turn his stick at a 90-degree angle to the defender's stick and push off without being cross-checked. (See Moves to Get Open—below)

### 4. Backdoor Cut

This cut is usually executed when the defender overplays the offensive player to stop the offensive player from cutting in front of him. To counter this defensive check the cutter cuts behind him.

### 5. 11 Moves for a Cutter to Get Open

All these moves are similar to a ballcarrier beating his defender.

### I. Inside Slide Move
Cutter takes a cross-check on the non-stick shoulder and slides their way past the defender for a pass into the middle.

### II. Outside Undercut Move
Cutter turns body sideways facing the end-boards and taking the cross-check on the stick-side shoulder, swinging the stick outside and keeping it there while "weasling" his way back inside of the defender and cutting backdoor for a pass.

### III. Fake Inside Slide Move to a Backdoor Cut
Cutter pretends to take a cross-check on the non-stick shoulder like he is going to cut across top and make an Inside Slide Move, then quickly cuts outside and cuts backdoor, running underneath and behind defender for pass.

### IV. Fake Outside Undercut Move to an Inside Slide Move
Cutter starts to turn his body facing end-boards as if to take a cross-check on the stick-side shoulder, then quickly cuts inside with an

**Photo 46:** If defender plays even with cutter

**Photo 47:** The Give-and-Go—cutter cuts backdoor

Inside Slide Move using a quick speed move and looking for pass.

### V. Inside Spin Move
Cutter fakes an Outside Undercut Move while being cross-checked, then spins back inside for pass.

### VI. Outside Spin Move
Cutter fakes an Inside Slide Move while being cross-checked, then spins or rolls back outside and Undercut backdoor for pass.

### VII. Outside Fake
Cutter fakes a cut to the outside, then cuts inside. Fake to get the defender off balance or to take a step in the direction of the fake and explode past the defender for the pass. The cutter wants the defender to think he is going one way while he goes the other way. Remind the players of the importance of the fake.

### VIII. Inside Fake
Cutter fakes a cut to the inside, then cuts outside and cuts backdoor or underneath and behind the defender for a pass.

### IX. Stutter Fake
Cutter stutter steps to an inside or outside fake.

### X. Inside Pivot Move or Outside Pivot Move
This is just a quick spin move by the cutter to end up either on the inside or the outside of the defender.

### XI. Change of Pace
The cutter starts with the ball and passes it. He then relaxes and moves lazily, walking or jogging toward the crease area, and then quickly breaks in front of his defender toward the ball.

## VII. Individual Offensive Drills

- Work a lot of one-on-one drills in your practice time. Players learn how to beat their defender and defenders learn how to stop their checks. Coach has to find out who can play defense.
- Start the one-on-one drills with the ballcarrier having a ball or the defender having it and passing it to the offensive player.

**Stress in One-on-One Offensive Drills:**
1. To keep the stick cocked as much as possible in the "triple-threat" position.
2. To always look to shoot.
3. Not to shoot from the wrong side of the floor, but to go back to his proper side of the floor and go one-on-one again.

**Defensive Progression in One-on-One Drills:**
1. Defender must hold his sweater.
2. Defender is allowed to push and shove with only his hands.
3. Defender holds a football blocking dummy to stop the ballcarrier.
4. Defender can use stick but only to lean on the ballcarrier to stop him, i.e., no cross-check.
5. Defender can tackle or grab the ballcarrier, but not wrap his arms right around his body.
6. Defender can only poke-check and jab with his stick at the ballcarrier.
7. Players play "live."

## Offensive Agility Drills

While jogging around the arena, do short, quick steps:
1. **Faking**
   Players run in a straight line and push with their right foot, then step with their left foot. Then they do the opposite, push with their left foot and step with their right foot. With this footwork they form V-cuts which are 90-degree change of direction moves.

2. **Hopping**

   Same as above, but while players hop on their right foot only, they push right and go left, then push left and go right. Now players do the same movement with the left foot only, then the progression on both feet together.

3. **Stutter Steps**

   Players running in a straight line do stutter steps which are little pitter-patter steps in rapid succession. Then they push right, go left, stutter steps again, then push left, go right.

4. **Inside Pivoting (Left-Shot)**

   Player running in a straight line, fake right with right foot, step inside with left foot, pivot on left, swing right foot around over left foot, a 360-degree spin, now facing in the same direction he started.

5. **Outside Pivoting (Left-Shot)**

   Player running in a straight line, fake left with left foot, step inside with right foot, pivot on right, swing left foot around over right foot, a 360-degree spin, now facing in same direction he started.

6. **Agility Run**

   Players cut in-and-out through six cones placed four to six feet apart, faking one way and going the other way. Find out the number of times they can run through the cones in one minute.

7. **Skipping (Preseason or for Warm-Ups Before Games)**

   Players go through a routine of skipping maneuvers. Time the skipping, starting from one minute and progressing up to five minutes.

8. **Bench Jumping (Preseason)**

   Players jump sideways over benches or cones with both feet together. Set a standard of 60 times in 30 seconds.

9. **Touch One Sideboard with Stick and Back to Other Sideboards**

   How many touches in one minute?

10. **Similar to Defensive Agility Square**

    Offensive player does it on his own or with a token defender. Player goes through this sequence: he cuts into the middle of floor, then he V-cuts back to his crease area, then he comes up and sets an imaginary cross pick, then he rolls to the net, and then "pops out" to wing area for pass and go one-on-one by cutting across the top of the floor (Inside) Slide Move or cutting outside into an Undercut Move.

## Ball-Handling Drills

Player does tricks with the ball in his stick.

### Drills to Teach Cradling the Ball

1. **One-on-Zero Stationary Cradling**

   Ballcarriers stand practicing cradling. Stress to players not to look at the ball, but to know where the ball is by feel and weight. Players use the "Small" Cradle when doing stationary passing, keep the stick horizontally over the shoulder.

2. **One-on-Zero Ballcarriers Jogging and Cradling**

   Players jog around the arena "cradling" a ball doing a "Medium" Cradle with the stick held horizontal in front of the body or held vertically at a 45-degree angle.

### Drills to Teach Protecting the Stick or Taking a Hit

1. **One-on-One Circle Drill**

   In this drill players learn to protect the ball in the stick. Checkers start the drill with their stick on the ballcarrier's body. On coach's command, the checkers try to stick-check the ballcarriers. The ballcarriers just pivot around in a circle cradling the ball and protecting their sticks. Stress to the ballcarriers to look over their shoulders to watch the checkers rather than watching the ball in their sticks; stress using the "Large" Cradle holding the stick in a vertical position as opposed to a horizontal one because it is easier to protect with the body; stress to players to be continuously cradling the stick. The stick is never "still" while the ball is in the stick. The ballcarrier who protects his stick the longest (i.e., does not drop the ball), is the winner and all the other ballcarriers must do a token sprint or push-up for losing.

2. **One-on-Two Circle Drill**
   Same drill as above, but two checkers try to take the ball off the ballcarrier's stick. The key here is to neutralize one of the checkers by leaning on his stick. Then, the ballcarrier just concentrates on the other checker.

3. **Tag Game**
   Everybody in the group (5–10 players) has a ball. The chaser is "it" and has no ball. The chaser chases any of the players and tries to dislodge the ball from a ballcarrier. If the chaser forces a ballcarrier to drop his ball, then that player is "it." If the ballcarrier steps out of bounds area, he is "it." Play the game in a restricted area.

4. **British Bulldog Game**
   Coach makes up two teams: one team is at center, the other team has balls at one side of the sideboards. On a call of "Bulldog" the ballcarriers run from one sideboard to the other sideboard. The defensive players at the center try to check as many ballcarriers as possible to dislodge the ball. Two possibilities are: if a ballcarrier loses his ball he becomes part of the defensive team and the last player with a ball is the winner; or if a ballcarrier loses his ball he sits out at the side.

5. **One-on-One Bump Drill**
   Players are paired up as a ballcarrier and a defensive player. The defensive player has no stick. The defender tries to jar the ball loose by pushing sharply with both hands on the ballcarrier's body. This drill teaches ballcarrier to relax with the ball when taking a cross-check; to take a wide stance when

taking a cross-check; and to lean into the direction the force comes from.

6. **One-on-One Equalizing Pressure Drill**
   a. The first progression, the ballcarrier cuts across the top while absorbing a straight push by the defender's hands on his upper arm.
   b. The second progression, the defender leans on his check, versus cross-checking, while at the same time the ballcarrier leans on the checker to counter the force and moves across the top trying to slide off the check for a shot. If he runs out of territory he rolls or spins back and still leans on the defender, but tries to cut around the defender on the outside.
   c. The third progression, the defender cross-checks as the ballcarrier cuts across the top, gradually increasing the intensity of the cross-checks, so the ballcarrier gets the feel of a hard check. Again stress that players should relax their body, lean into the check, and look at the net.

7. **One-on-One Charging Defender Drill**
   This drill teaches how not to take a hit. Ballcarriers have to learn not to panic when a defender charges them, but to see this as a defensive mistake and use it to their advantage. All an offensive player does is side step the defender by faking one way and going the other way. In this drill the defenders charge the ballcarrier with the ballcarrier practicing a side step.

8. **Gauntlet Drill**
   A straight line of defensive players are spaced out while the ballcarrier zig-zags around the defenders. The ballcarrier can work on staying balanced, using his quickness, turning his body sideways to protect the stick, keeping his head up to see the floor and his defender, and relaxing when taking a hit versus tensing up.

**Drills to Teach Individual Offensive Moves with the Ball**

*1. Four-on-One Man-in-Middle of Floor Drill*
The offensive player and the defender start the drill by standing in the middle of the floor. The defender plays behind the offensive man who uses his body to shield his stick and receive a pass from a Pointman at the top or from either Cornermen. The offensive man moves around and presents his stick as a target for one of the passers. Usually, the player is not allowed to stand in the middle of the floor on offense as he would clog up the middle. But this is a good drill for working on receiving a pass while being checked from behind.

*2. One-on-Zero Shooting Off an Offensive Move*
Coach forms two lines (left shots, right shots) with a cone in front of each line. The cone is placed just inside the Prime Scoring Area or inside the Outside Lane at about the 15-feet mark from the crease or slightly closer

depending on the age group. Everybody has a ball and the players in each line attack the cones straight on without touching the cones and using the offensive move the coach asks for. As players work on their offensive moves, stress deception, quickness, good footwork, and taking the shot a player would take in a game. *(See Diagram #15)*

Review of the 12 Offensive Moves:
a.  Undercut Move, cut to the outside and cut back inside for a shot
b.  Fake a shot into an Undercut Move, cut to the outside and cut back in for a shot
c.  Fake a Shot into an Inside Slide Move, cutting inside across the top of the floor for a shot
d.  Faking a shot while side stepping ("Drag") down the side and then cut into an Inside Slide Move across top of the floor for a shot
e.  Faking a shot while side stepping ("Drag") down the side into an Outside Spin-Around Move and cut to the outside and cut back in for a shot

---

**Diagram #15: Prime Scoring Area for a Left-Shot Player**

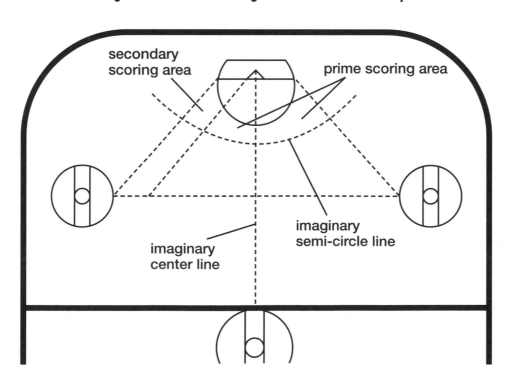

f.   Inside Slide Move or Bull Move, just cut across top of the floor for a shot

g.   Inside Spin-Around Move, cut inside across the top of the floor for a shot

h.   Outside Spin-Around Move, cut outside and back inside for a shot

i.   Outside Body Fake Move, cut inside across the top of the floor for a shot

j.   Inside Body Fake Move, cut outside and cut back inside for a shot

k.   Inside Pivot Move, cut inside across the top of the floor for a shot

l.   Outside Pivot Move, cut outside and cut back inside for a shot

### 3. One-on-One Progression to Practice Offensive Moves

Progression to practice offensive moves: neither player has a stick, only offensive player has a stick, both players have sticks.

a.   Partner practices one offensive move to beat his partner, defender plays token defense by just leaning on the ballcarrier, then they switch.

b.   Partner practices one offensive move to beat his partner, defender pushes and shoves, then they switch.

c.   Partner practices one offensive move to beat his partner, defender uses solid cross-checks and slashes then, they switch.

### 4. One-on-One Artificial Situation Set-up by the Defender

The defense sets up an artificial situation for the offense. The defense makes common mistakes and the offense reacts to them. This drill gives the offensive player confidence when he meets these situations in a game.

a.   Defender slashes at ballcarrier and when he overcommits, the ballcarrier makes his move.

b.   Defender tries to check ballcarrier's stick and when the defender overcommits,

(reaches, becomes off balance) the ballcarrier side steps him, protects his stick, and goes to the net.

c.   When the ballcarrier approaches the defender, the defender starts to move backward, and the ballcarrier fakes one way and goes in the opposite direction.

d.   Defender reaches on his cross-check and ends up touching air, not the ballcarrier, the ballcarrier side steps him and goes to the net.

e.   Defender rushes or charges the ballcarrier, the ballcarrier fakes one way and goes the other way.

f.   The defender plays the ballcarrier in a straight-up position, the ballcarrier now has two ways to go.

g.   Defender overplays the ballcarrier from cutting across the top, ballcarrier fakes inside then, cuts outside.

h.   Defender pokes or jabs his stick at ballcarrier's stick to dislodge the ball, ballcarrier turns his body to protect his stick and spins to the net.

i.   Defender uses his stick to execute the over-the-head check or does the wrap-around check to dislodge the ball, ballcarrier tucks his stick in close to body to protect it and goes to the net.

j.   Defender leans or pushes on ballcarrier with his stick to stop him from going to the net. Ballcarrier's options: 1. He rolls back and forth with his back and shoulders on the defender's stick to get a reaction. Once the defender commits in a certain direction to cut off the roll, the ballcarrier goes past him in the other direction. 2. He beats his defender by sliding past him off his stick while working on getting his shoulder and body on the inside of the checker's stick. 3. He just steps back to get away from the defender and shoots.

k.  Defender is standing still, flat-footed; ballcarrier beats him on a quick-step move.
l.  Defender is playing ballcarrier "tight," ballcarrier beats him by stepping by him quickly.
m.  Defender is playing off the ballcarrier. The ballcarrier's options are: 1. He can fake a long shot and go to the net. 2. With the space already created he just shoots and uses the defender as a screen.

## One-on-One Competitive Drills

### 1. One-on-One Offensive Player is Stationary and Starts His Move From a Cross-Floor Pass

Form two offensive lines with balls on opposite sides of the floor, left-shots and right-shots, and two defensives lines on opposite sides of the floor. The left-shot defender ends up checking the right-shot offensive player and so on. First ballcarrier in each line is covered by a defender. First offensive player in the opposite line doesn't have a ball, he receives a cross-floor pass then goes one-on-one (just like a real game). Then, the offensive player who just passed now receives a pass from the next offensive player in the opposite line and goes one-on-one.

### 2. One-on-One Offensive Player is Stationary and Starts His Move From a Down Pass

Have an offensive line in the corner of the floor, a defensive line in the same corner, and a single passer who is on the top-side area of the floor on the same side. The offensive player comes up-and-out (V-cut) the side to receive a pass from the passer and then goes one-on-one.

### 3. One-on-One Offensive Player Beats Defender by Turning Sideways to Receive Cross-Check

Form four lines on the floor: two defensive lines and two offensive lines. The one defensive line and the one offensive line are all right-shots on the left side of the floor; the other defensive line and offensive line are all left-

shots on the right side of the floor. The first left-shot defender throws a diagonal pass to the right-shot offensive player, runs out diagonally and touches his body with his stick, then the ballcarrier makes his offensive move. This drill reinforces that a defender has to pick up an opposite shot to himself, so that his stick can interfere with the ballcarrier's stick.

*Note: But be aware that in today's modern game coaches are more concerned with matching up size with size, speed with speed, versus matching up a right-hand-shot defender with a left-hand-shot offensive player.*

**Progression of One-on-One Drills:**
a.  Coach can run the drill in the Offensive Zone or the full-length of the floor.
b.  Defender can use no stick at first; then he can use a stick later to play defense.
c.  When the offensive player receives the ball he must wait for the defender to come out on him and touch his hands before he can go one-on-one.
d.  As soon as the offensive player receives the ball, he goes to the net and does not wait for the defender to touch him.
e.  Ballcarrier can only beat the defender by facing him. He cannot turn his back to the defender.
f.  Ballcarrier beats the defender (only after receiving) a cross-check.
g.  Ballcarrier beats the defender while the defender is "closing out."
h.  Ballcarrier must beat defender in five seconds.

**Start One-on-One Drills From Different Areas on the Floor:**
a.  From top-side area of floor (pointman's spot). Offensive player leans on defender and cuts across the top. He can cut outside or cut inside.
b.  From top-center area of floor. Offensive player takes defender to proper side of floor before he goes one-on-one.

Discourage ballcarrier from starting his one-on-one move in the middle of the floor as he could end up on the wrong side of the floor for the shot.

c. From mid-side area of floor (wing area) offensive player goes one-on-one.

d. From the corner area the offensive player can make one of two moves: cut across top or Undercut.

e. From a loose ball, then go one-on-one.

f. From top-side of floor and run down or side step down the sideboards and make his one-on-one move.

### 4. One-on-One Offensive Player Beats Defender by Facing Him

Run the drill from the four areas: top-side area of floor, top-center of floor, mid-side of floor (wing area), or corner area. Offensive player uses one of the four offensive moves:

a. Outside Body Fake Move (cut inside)

b. Inside Body Fake Move (cut outside)

c. Fake the shot, cut to outside, then back inside

d. Fake the shot, cut to middle of floor

### 5. One-on-One "Showdown" Game (Two Teams—Rights Versus Lefts)

Two teams are picked (or have the right-shots against the left-shots) for a one-on-one competition. Coach stresses offense and reinforces offensive players. If offense scores, team gets three points. If offense beats the defender and gets a good shot on net, but does not score, team gets two points. If offense cannot beat the defender or get a good shot on net, team gets zero points. Teams play to 15 points. Losers do push-ups or run sprints. To stress long-ball shot, give two points for a goal. To stress close-in shot, give two points for a goal.

a. Defender has the ball and rolls it out or passes it out to the offensive player.

b. Ballcarrier starts with a ball and on the run attacks defender.

c. Ballcarrier with a ball from a stationary position, top, side, or corner area, attacks the defender.

d. Stationary offensive player receives cross-floor pass, then goes one-on-one.

e. Offensive player cuts to the ball on the run across the top for a pass and shot.

f. Offensive player receives a down pass. Either in the corner area, or popping out to wing, player goes one-on-one.

### 6. Five-on-Five Scrimmage Where Players Can Only Go One-on-One

Players run a one-on-one offense (half-floor). Offense can pass ball around, then the ballcarrier must go one-on-one, defense cannot help and must stay with their check. Defense plays with their back to the ball.

## Drills for Non-Ballcarrier

### 1. Two-on-Zero Give-and-Go From Mid-Side Area Drill (Off-Ball Side)

Form two opposite lines in the cornerman's position (mid-side area), left-shots and right-shots, the cornerman passes the ball to other cornerman and cuts for return pass and shot.

**Variation:** Players can cut from the top-side of the floor, from the top-center of floor, or from the corner area of the floor. Stress cutting hard to the ball and passing hard to the cutter.

### 2. Two-on-Two Give-and-Go From Mid-Side Area of Floor Drill (Off-Ball Side)

This offensive drill is run with an offensive right-hand shot and an offensive left-hand shot in the cornerman's position.

**Defensive pressure:**

Start with one defender only on the cutter; then put a defender on both players.

**Defensive progression:**

a. Defense has no sticks (they can push with their hands).

b. Defense plays with their sticks held the wrong way.

c. Defense puts their sticks on the cutters, but they only ride with them.

d. Defense can push the cutters, but they cannot cross-check them.

e. Defense can cross-check and slash the cutters.

## 3. Two-on-One "Go" From Mid-Side Area of Floor Drill (Off-Ball Side)

Form two lines, offense and defense, in the mid-side area of the floor or in the cornerman's area. Offensive player who is guarded passes across to the lone passer in the mid-side area and then cuts for return pass in front of defender or behind the defender toward the passer.

## 4. Two-on-Zero "Give-and-Go From Top-Center of Floor Drill (Ball Side)

Form two lines in the pointman's position, left-shots and right-shots, the pointman passes the ball to either cornerman and cuts for return pass and shot.

## 5. Two-on-Zero "Give-and-Go From Mid-Side of Floor Drill (Ball Side)

Form two lines in the cornerman's position and creaseman's position on the same side of the floor. The cornerman passes the ball to the creaseman and cuts to net for return pass and shot.

## 6. Two-on-Zero "Give-and-Go From Corner Area of Floor Drill (Ball Side)

From the corner area of the floor, creaseman passes the ball up to cornerman on his side of floor and then cuts for return pass and shot.

## 7. Two-on-Zero "Circle" Drill

The cornerman passes the ball down to the creaseman who runs the ball out of the crease area for a shot while the cornerman interchanges into crease area.

## 8. Two-on-One "Go" From Top-Center of Floor Drill (Ball Side)

In this formation the players make no pass they just cut, "Go" play. Form two lines, offense and defense, on the same side of floor at top-center. Offensive player passes down to lone passer in the mid-side area and then cuts for return pass in front of defender down the middle of the floor. Then cuts down the middle behind the defender (Backdoor Cut).

## 9. Two-on-One "Go" From Corner of Floor Drill (Ball Side)

From the corner area of the floor, creaseman passes the ball up to the cornerman on his side of floor and then cuts in front of his defender for return pass and shot. Then he cuts behind defender for a return pass and shot (Backdoor Cut).

## 10. Two-on-Two Give-and-Go Live Defensive Drill (Off-Ball Side)

Two opposite defensive shots (left and right) check the two opposite offensive players. Stress to the offensive players to work on deception and quickness and that the cutters should try to get on the inside of their defenders.

The offensive passer's rule is to "pass early, not late, to the cutter."

The offensive cutter's rule is to "cut late, not early."

## 11. Two-on-Two Give-and-Go Game

Two teams of partners composed of a left-shot and a right-shot who must score off a Give-and-Go play. They play to four goals.

**Variation:** Both players are right-hand shots or both are left-hand shots. They work a Give-and-Go on the same side of the floor.

# Chapter 7

# Individual Defense and Drills

## I. Why Cross-Check and Slash?

- To prevent the ballcarrier from going to the net.
- To stop the ballcarrier from getting a good shot on net, or at least to interfere with his shot.
- To force the ballcarrier into errors through pressure, i.e., forcing a bad pass or "coughing up" the ball.
- To force the ballcarrier to go where the defender wants him to go, usually toward the sideboards.
- To force the ballcarrier to turn his back to the play.
- To worry the ballcarrier so that he becomes more concerned with protecting the ball than beating his man.
- To harass the ballcarrier so that he does not have time to see the plays developing on the floor.

## II. Cross-Check Technique

### 1. Floor Positioning on the Ballcarrier to Play Defense

Good floor positioning is half the battle in one-on-one defense, and saves a defender a lot of extra work. The other half of the battle is technically stopping the man with the ball.

**The Three Imaginary Lanes**

In teaching defensive floor positioning, draw three imaginary lanes down the floor—two Outside Lanes and a Middle Lane. The imaginary lines for the Outside Lanes are just outside the crease area. The defensive player's position on the "ball side" is in the Outside Lane and the defensive players positions on the "help-side" or "off-ball side" should be just inside the Outside Lane.

**Where to Pressure the Ballcarrier**

One of the big questions on defense is where to pick up the ball to pressure. The ballcarrier will be picked up and pressured when he is at the top of the floor in the Prime Scoring Area, when he is on the side of the floor in the Prime Scoring Area, or when he is in the corner of the Prime Scoring Area. So the best answer to the question is to pick up the ballcarrier when he enters the Prime Scoring Area. A defensive player has to know where that area is. Because so many great offensive players have the ability to "fire" the ball from farther out or even make great passing plays from a great distance, it is best to pick him up farther out than normal just to be on the safe side. *(See Diagram #15)*

### Position When the Ball is at the Top of the Offense

The main defensive position, of course, is the defender plays the ballcarrier in a "ball-you-net" position. In other words, the defender plays between the ballcarrier and the net to stop him from penetrating.

The other defensive position is "head-on-the-stick" position, which means the defender plays between his opponent's stick and the net forming an imaginary straight line with the stick, the defender, and the net. He forces or encourages the ballcarrier to go to the sideboards by either overplaying him half-a-man, overplaying him on his inside shoulder; or playing his "head-on-the-stick."

The last defensive position is picking up the ballcarrier on his stick side and playing this stick-on-stick position so he can't get a clear shot without some interference, and close enough so he can't use the defender as a screen shot. Basically the defender is telling the ballcarrier where to go.

So always maintain this position of overplaying the opponent's stick side. To get to this position, the defender angles out on the ballcarrier with his shoulders and hips at a 45-degree angle to the sideboards.

**Photo 48:** Floor positioning on the ballcarrier to play defense—stress force to outside, bent knees, head up, shoulders parallel to sideboards

### In This Overplay Position, the Defender Wants:

- To stop the ballcarrier from cutting across the top of the floor, i.e., try to take away his primary move.
- To force the ballcarrier to go only one way.
- To force the ballcarrier to the outside or to the sideboards, which become an extra defender.
- To force the ballcarrier outside, his teammates will know what direction he is forcing the ballcarrier and will get into a defensive position to help him if he needs it.

### Position When the Ball is Along the Mid-Side Area of the Floor

Here the defender wants to force the ballcarrier "down" into help rather than "up" away from help, keeping him in this side alley. He does this by putting his shoulders parallel to sideboards, still overplaying his check's stick. This position is called "Walling."

### Position When the Ball is in the Corner Area of the Arena

The defender wants to force the ball to the middle of the floor or "up" the floor again into help from the top defender rather than "down" where there is no help. Of course the defender tries to keep him in the side-alley by shuffling to prevent him from turning inside. But the defender definitely does not want to get beat on the outside, called the "Undercut," when the ball is in the corner area as the low help-side defender would have a tough time getting across to help.

## 2. Defensive Stance or Cross-Check Stance

Before a defender hits the ballcarrier he takes a position of "readiness," i.e., ready to move laterally or backward. This physical position is also called the "athletic stance" or the "fighter's stance." In this defensive stance:

**Photo 49:** Defensive stance or cross-check stance—holding the stick to cross-check

*Note: Never bend over at the waist, since this causes a player to become off-balance more easily; and never stand up straight, as a player has a higher center of gravity, making it harder for him to move quickly.*

## 3. Holding the Stick to Cross-Check

The cross-check grip is almost the same as in passing, except the hands are placed farther apart than normally, i.e., wider than the body width. The arms are cocked to give a player more power on the thrust-out of the stick in anticipation of cross-checking. The "open face" of the pocket should be facing backward or forward, whichever position puts the player's stick in a better and more natural position to pick up loose balls. All he has to do is turn the stick a quarter turn to scoop up the loose ball.

## 4. Defensive Footwork

Footwork is the key to being a good defender. He must keep his feet active and be ready to move his feet. The whole idea of playing good defense along the sideboards is to keep good feet position so the defender's hips and shoulders are parallel to the sideboards and between the ballcarrier and the net. The biggest thing with this foot positioning is the defender is trying to channel or force the ballcarrier to help, to a defensive teammate, or to the sideboards.

A good defender has to move his feet to cut off the ballcarrier going to the net whether he is cutting to the outside or cutting to the inside. Be aware of not using the stick to stop or delay a penetrating ballcarrier as the defender will be called for holding or grabbing.

There are three defensive steps a defender should be ready to use:

- The feet are staggered, with both feet facing in the same direction. Keep the feet a little wider than shoulder-width apart for a good, solid, wide base, and keep them active to be ready to move.
- Keep the weight on the balls of the feet and be bouncy so the defender doesn't get caught flat-footed.
- Keep the head up through the whole defensive process for balance and "explode the eyes," which means, before contact keep the eyes on top of the opponent's chest area or the top of his numbers, not on the ball. Looking at the numbers helps to keep the player's head up. If a player drops his eyes to look at the waist area, his head will drop and he will be off-balance. If a player looks at the ball, he is setting himself up to get beat with a fake shot.
- It is important to stay low, keep the rear down with the back slightly bent, and the knees bent (flexed). This position gives a player a lower center of gravity, providing better balance, making him able to make explosive moves, which enables him to move in any direction quickly, and creates a stronger base for power on his hit.

- **Retreat Step Versus the Outside Undercut Move**

  By overplaying the ballcarrier half-a-man at the top of the floor the defender is forcing him to the outside and the defender can now anticipate in which direction he is going to go which is to the outside and down the floor. To prevent the ballcarrier from beating him down the side, the defender must execute the Retreat Step.

  The defender takes a staggered stance with the inside foot forward and the outside foot back. This staggered stance allows the defender to push off with his front foot and step back with his back foot to go backward, which is usually the direction the ballcarrier is going to attack the net because of the way the defender is playing him, overplaying him half-a-man to force outside. Stress turning the knee of the inside foot inward and putting weight on the inside of the inside foot to push off with. Stress to keep both feet on the ground and shoulder width apart as the defender is in a position to move with balance, power, and quickness. Try not to pick up the feet, slide them, or cross them, as this will slow the defender down and could cause other footwork problems.

- **Drop Step to a Shuffle Step Versus an Inside Slide Move**

  If a ballcarrier fakes outside with the intention of cutting back inside across the top of the floor, the defender must have a countermove to change his direction. To execute the Drop Step the defender swings the front or inside foot backward so it is parallel to the outside foot.

  Then, he shuffle steps with short lateral side steps, pushing off the opposite foot in the direction he is going, to keep the ballcarrier from turning the corner and going to the net. He must keep his feet spread to provide a solid base, because if the feet come together he will lose his balance

and power; and if the feet cross, he may end up tripping himself or also losing his balance. When a player shuffles he must keep his head steady and not "bob" his head. He must keep his head up and directly in the middle of his shoulders.

- **The Attack Step**

  "Closing Out" occurs when a defender has to rush or run out to the ballcarrier to maintain pressure and to stop the ballcarrier from scoring. To execute the "Attack Step" the defender is usually Closing Out on the ballcarrier, which is usually his check. First he pushes with his back foot and runs out hard toward the ballcarrier, but with the last two steps he gets low and uses the Attack Step by pushing off with his back foot, the power source, and stepping with his front foot to be balanced and under control so he doesn't overcommit. Remember, he also comes out at an angle to force the ballcarrier to the boards. (See Chapter 7, Individual Defense)

## 5. Before Contact

- Stress to the defender to wait for the ballcarrier to come to him and not to make contact until he is an arm's length away. The biggest mistake for a defender is to lunge or reach at the ballcarrier on the cross-check. The result of charging the ballcarrier is that the defender overcommits and becomes off-balance with the ballcarrier just going around him.

- Stress to the defender to stay in a crouched position, possibly even getting lower than the ballcarrier. Never stand fully upright when cross-checking because the defender will have a harder time shuffling or moving laterally with his legs straight, plus he could be pushed or knocked off balance with this high center of gravity.

- Stress to the defender to watch the ballcarrier's chest rather than the ball. If the defender watches the ball, he will usually end up stick-checking and thereby setting himself up for a fake shot or overcommitting by going after the stick.

- Stress to the defender when getting ready to hit, not to tense the muscles completely since this will slow down the muscle movement. Instead relax the muscles to explode quickly on the hit.

## 6. Actual Contact with the Cross-Check

In today's game the defenders still cross-check to pressure the ballcarrier and to stop him from going to the net, but there is not as much cross-checking as there used to be. Now players like to slash on the hands and poke check the hands to stop the ballcarrier. (See in this section: On-the-Hands Defense.)

Stress on contact:

- **Keep the Head Up and Over the Groin Area**
  Cross-checking with the head forward puts the defender off-balance.
- **Be Stationary on the Hit**
  Most coaches believe a defender must be stationary on the hit. This gives the checker a solid base for a powerful hit outward, he will also be ready to move laterally if he needs to. If he is moving backward, and the ballcarrier cuts across the top, it is harder to recover, i.e., move sideways. The defender

**Photo 50:** Actual contact with the cross-check on the ballcarrier

cannot move in two directions at the same time, i.e., backward and sideways.

Then, there are some coaches who like their defenders to be moving backward because when the ballcarrier makes his offensive move they have more time and space to react to the move.

- **On the Hit Step Forward**
  On the cross-check, take a slight step with the forward foot on the hit so the body weight is going forward and thereby getting power behind the hit. Stress keeping the feet under the body when cross-checking or slashing for good balance.
- **Extend the Arms Upward and Outward**
  From the crouched position, extend the arms upward and outward on the hit. Many times if a player cross-checks straight out with the arms it means he is standing up. So hit up and under, but stay down on the hit. Remember, never overextend, lunge, or reach on the cross-check, as the head will follow and the player will become vulnerable and off-balance. The key is to wait for the offensive player to come to him. The defender may have to move out shuffling on the ballcarrier to maintain pressure, but wait for him to come to him—this is contradictory, defender goes after ballcarrier, but on the hit he waits for him to come to him.

  Make contact on the opponent's arm between his elbow and shoulder. The defender does not want a defender to cross-check too high up on the arm, as the stick may slide up the arm pad onto the neck with the result of a high-sticking penalty.
- **Keep the Ballcarrier Between Both Hands**
  On the cross-check, the defender should focus on keeping the ballcarrier in the middle of the stick, between both the hands. Keep the hands in a cross-check position even when an offensive person comes in-close to the body. In fact it is a good idea to use the upper body, with the elbows and

forearms bent out to the side to give more leverage and body width to help prevent or block the ballcarrier from getting by him.

- **Hit and Get Off the Ballcarrier**
Defender makes the hit short and hard, then recoils the stick back, ready to hit again. Fill the gap created by the hit with small steps, no space, and then continuously keep cross-checking. Once you hit the ballcarrier your feet end up parallel to each other. It helps a little bit to move the feet back into position, staggered stance, to get in a position to cross-check again. Also try to time the cross-check when your check is trying to get a pass off.

- **Do Not Let the Ballcarrier Lean on the Stick**
Stress to the defender not to let the ballcarrier lean on his stick. If the ballcarrier is allowed to lean on the defender's stick, usually with his back, the defender is setting himself up for a roll move. The ballcarrier will make him think he is going one way by faking or rolling in one direction and when the defender overreacts to this move he'll will go the other way. Also if the defender lets a ballcarrier lean on him with his non-stick shoulder when he is cross-checking the ballcarrier he will make an Inside Slide Move past the defender. When cross-checking, drive your opponent back with solid hits or solid pushes with constant pressure on the ballcarrier rather than just slashing.

   *Note: The same idea occurs when you try to push-check versus cross-checking. On a push-check the defender ends up leaning on the ballcarrier which could set him up for a fake and roll.*

- **Be Prepared to Get Screened or "Picked Off" as One Checks the Ballcarrier**
Defenders can either call a "switch" on a pick or the defender on the ballcarrier can fight through the pick. When checking the ballcarrier, always "bird watch," i.e., turning the head on a swivel to look and see if someone is coming to set a pick so you can anticipate a pick or screen being set. Defense is like dancing, continuous action while staying alert.

*Derek Suddons of the Edmonton Rush talks about individual defense:*

a. Awareness of what is happening before coming on the floor—"reading the play."
b. Get into your stance, be focused, and show confidence.
c. Know your opponents' tendencies.
d. Be aware of where your man is at all times for the full 30 seconds.
e. Proper floor positioning for the team defense.
f. Ball pressure is big.
g. Communication on the floor is important to get rid of any indecision.
h. When on the defensive help-side of the floor, be ready to help out a teammate, go after loose balls, and "read" broken plays.
i. "Box out" on an opponent's shot and "close out" on the ballcarrier.
j. Be ready for immediate transition to get the ball and get into the Offensive Zone.

## 7. "On-the-Hands" Defense or the "Slash" Technique

In today's game there is as much on-the-hands defense as cross-checking. This is where the

**Photo 51:** Grip and stance for on-the-hands defense or Slash Technique

defender's stick is very active by bothering, irritating, and pressuring the ballcarrier on his gloves and stick by poking, or slashing with two hands, at his hands, so that the latter has a hard time scoring, a hard time getting a good shot off, a hard time making a pass, and a hard time just hanging onto the ball. Coaches teach this on-the-hands defense because they have found a lot of the good offensive players did not like to be bothered on the hands when they had the ball. At one time the slash was used strictly to dislodge the ball from the stick or for intimidation purposes. It seems defenders now stick-check more on the ballcarrier and cross-check more on the off-ball offensive player to stop them from going to the net.

### Grip for On-the-Hands Defense

Defender grabs the stick with two hands close together near the butt of the stick so that they can get a good quick slash with the head of the stick. The hands are closer together to slash and poke the ballcarrier than in the cross-checking technique.

### Stance for On-the-Hands Defense

Stress keeping a good defensive position when pressuring on the hands: stay down or get lower than the ballcarrier; move the feet to shuffle sideways, keep the feet staggered, keep knees bent for balance, and overplay his stick side to take away his shooting lane. A defender in this defense should not step when he pokes, jabs, or slashes because he could become off-balance. The defender pokes, jabs, or slashes with two hands only on the ballcarrier's hands. He does not go after his opponent's stick.

### Pressure the Ballcarrier

The defensive philosophy of good teams is good pressure on the ball, i.e., on-the-hands defense, and it is this good defensive play on the ball that is the key to good team defense. At the beginning of the game, good defenders give a hard two-handed slash on the ballcarrier

just to let him know what kind of game he is going to be in. Remember, the defender puts pressure on the ballcarrier's hands to take away his ability to throw a nice pass, to take an open shot, to prevent him from going to the net, and to force turnovers. A defender definitely doesn't want the ballcarrier to be a "feeder" or "passer." So, do not wave the stick in front of the opponent's stick or go after the stick, stick-check, where the defender could set himself up for a fake shot or pass. Encourage the defenders to not even look at their opponent's stick as most offensive players are good at one-on-one and faking shots. The basic question is, "Are we pressuring the ballcarrier so he can't make that nice pass?" Although we want to bother all shooters, we do not want to be penalized by grabbing, slashing, or playing them illegally.

### Stop Penetration (No Inside Shots or "Layups")

Stop ballcarrier penetration by imagining a straight line from the ballcarrier, the defender, and the net. The defender has to guard the ballcarrier one yard on either side of him and keep the ball in front of him at all times. We use the linebacker analogy. That is, the defender should be in a position to tackle him head-on even if he has to move his feet to prevent a straight-line drive to the net. If the defender is beaten he must head for the net, never run beside the driver, and get in front of him to stop him or make him change direction. Anytime the ballcarrier penetrates the heart of the defense, everyone must collapse like an umbrella to force the ball out.

### Keep Short Gaps Between Defender and Shooter

The defender plays the shooter to maintain short gaps, a distance of one step plus the stick length between him and the shooter, so the shooter can't follow through on his shot and use him as a screen. Long gaps or big spaces between the ballcarrier and the defender, i.e., two steps away plus the stick length, will beat him in most games as the good shooter will have space to shoot around the defender as a screen. So when the defender hits or slashes he must fill the gap created by the slash with small steps, giving no space between the defender and the shooter.

## 8. Other Stick Checks

### a. The "Poke" Check Technique
Some defenders use longer sticks (43" to 44") to poke-check, and at the same time move backward to keep the ballcarrier out far enough away from him, so if he does make a one-on-one move the defender will have time to recover.

### b. The "Can-Opener" Check Technique
To execute the can-opener a left-shot defender must be checking a left-shot ballcarrier or right-shot defender checking a right-shot ballcarrier. The defender poke checks with the stick-hand and pushes on the opponent's body with the other hand on the defender's shoulder or side. Remember the good goal scorers don't like it when their hands are being bothered. The defender jabs the stick down into the opponent's chest area, (not at the chest area)

**Photo 52:** The Can-Opener Check Technique—defender gets stick in-between opponent and his stick

between the body and his stick, in an attempt to dislodge the ball by pulling down and back on his opponent's stick-arm.

If the left-shot defender is playing a right-shot ballcarrier, i.e., stick-on-stick position, and he overplays the opponent's stick side and hope he crosses his stick in front of his body with both hands on his way to an outside cut where the defender now has the opportunity to use this Can-Opener maneuver by still putting his free hand on the opponent's stick-side shoulder or back and sticking his stick down in between the opponent's stick and his chest and pulling back to dislodge the ball.

*Note: The CLA rule allows a defender to put a free hand on his opponent's body when checking him. But if he locks or holds a player in by using his free hand on the back it is a penalty. An example is when the defender puts one hand on the back and the stick in front, thus holding or locking a player into only one direction is a holding penalty. A big change in the modern game is this putting a hand on the ballcarrier's body. At one time the defender could not touch the ballcarrier's body, he had to keep both hands on his stick.*

### c. The "Wrap-Around" Check Technique
Here a defender swings his stick right around the ballcarrier's body, hoping to dislodge the ball out of the stick from the force of the swing on the stick. A defender can only use the wrap-around check if the opponent gets close enough. As one executes this move make sure he always keeps his body in front of the offensive player.

### d. The "Over-the-Head" Check Technique
This move is an attempt to check the ball from the ballcarrier by using an element of surprise. The defender goes over the ballcarrier's head and catches the ballcarrier's stick-arm with his stick and arm, causing him to drop the ball or knock it loose.

## III. Individual Defensive Strategies Playing the Ballcarrier

### Attitude to Play Defense

The main thing in playing defense is the defender must know that defense sets the tone of the game, so he must want to play it and play it hard. To play good defense a player must have a certain physical attitude: he must play with maximum intensity, he must be a relentless worker, he must be tenacious, he must love to hit, and he must be aggressive. He must have the mental attitude to be cocky and mouthy, to bother opponents after the play is over, to be a "pest" by irritating and "ticking opponents off."

### Concentration

A great defensive player must have good concentration 100 percent of the time and be mentally ready and alert to what is happening on the floor. By totally concentrating in the game a defensive player can anticipate plays better rather than just reacting to plays. He must be totally involved in the game, especially when his opponent doesn't have the ball. He cannot lose concentration for one minute by losing where the ball is, by losing his check, or getting picked off. It takes hard work to concentrate on his check, to know where the ball is, and to back up his teammate checking the ballcarrier.

### Physical Abilities of a Great Defensive Player:

- Have the proper defensive technique for stopping a ballcarrier either by cross-checking or slashing. Technique is more important than strength.
- Be physically ready to make contact.
- Have outstanding lateral and backward mobility.
- Must have good body balance.
- Must be able to take a good positioning on the ballcarrier. A good position saves

a defender a lot of work in stopping the ballcarrier.

*Brodie Merrill of the Edmonton Rush of the NLL* **explains his Five Keys to Playing Exceptional Defense:**

1. Footwork is the foundation of great defense. Defensemen must be able to stay with and react to the movements of the opposing attackmen. To use short, "choppy" steps are more effective, allowing you to plant and change direction quickly.

2. Body position is another important key. "The lower man always wins." In other words, a defenseman must play with a low base all over the floor. Your butt must be at least at a 90-degree angle, your shoulders should be back, your head up, your stick and hands should be out in front of your body so that your offensive check cannot create separation between you and him. "Lead with your stick and finish with body!"

3. A great defender must have a certain presence and display leadership on the floor. He must be able to communicate the different defensive "slide packages" and the opposition's team offensive concepts in a confident and deliberate manner.

4. Having great stick skills really separates you as a great defenseman. Defense is not just about defending anymore, it's about picking up ground balls, clearing the ball, and igniting the transition from defense to offense.

5. The last key is the ability to take the ball away from the ballcarrier. There will be times in the game where your team needs possession to stay in a game or even put the game away. The exceptional defensemen have learned the art of taking the ball off the ballcarrier in a safe, but effective manner; that is, without compromising other defensive disciplines, such as getting beaten.

## Picking Up a Check

On picking up a check a defender must point his stick at him and call out his number so there is no confusion on who is checking whom. This gets rid of any indecision and keeps the defenders mentally in the game. There are always easy goals scored because somebody did not call out his check.

Usually when picking up a check a left-hand shot picks up a right-hand shot and vice versa. This is so the defender ends up in a stick-on-stick position which makes it easier to interfere with the opponent's shot or pass. But in the modern game the trend is now that defenders pick up their checks by size-against-size, speed-against-speed, and quickness-against-quickness rather than the stick-on-stick position, which is not as high a priority as it once was.

## Analyzing His Opponent

On picking up his check, the defender should know how his opponent shoots, whether he shoots long overhand shots or sidearm shots, because he will take this into account on how he is going to play him.

A good defender reads and studies his opponent. He must outthink his offensive man by anticipating his move, by remembering his tendencies from previous games, by knowing his opponent, and by knowing his strengths and favorite moves. If the offensive player is a weaker ballhandler, the defender will try to force turnovers by jumping out on him and being aggressive by playing his stick.

The main questions he has to ask himself are:

- Does his opponent like to shoot far out or close in?
- Does his opponent like to Undercut or cut across the top?
- Does his opponent like to fake his shot and cut inside or outside?
- Does his opponent look to score or pass more?
- Does his opponent shoot long overhand shots or sidearm shots?
- Does his opponent shoot farther out than normal?
- Does his opponent rely on quickness or strength in beating a defender?
- Does his opponent handle the ball with poise and confidence or does he get "rattled" under pressure?

## Taking the "Monkey Off the Defender's Back"

The "monkey" is worrying about getting beat, so the defender plays cautious. Coaches take the "monkey off the checker's back" (worrying about getting beaten) by stating that they do not care if he is beaten, as long as he is pressuring the ball. Now, the defender will go all out and check the ballcarrier aggressively and not worry about getting beat as he's pressuring the ball because he knows his teammates will help him if beaten.

## Distance the Ballcarrier is From the Net

When checking a ballcarrier out of the scoring area, bother him by slashing at his hands or at the lower handle of the stick to interfere with the accuracy of his pass, but remain down in the defensive stance in case he decides to go one-on-one.

The farther the distance the ballcarrier is out from the net the better the slash is to use, but as the opponent gets in-closer to the net, start cross-checking and using the body to control him.

Some defenders, when the ballcarrier comes into the scoring area, like to give their opponent a slash on the initial contact, then, cross-check or poke-check. If the shooter shoots farther out than normal, the defender has to be ready to move out to pressure him, to take one-more-step-out than usual.

## Ballcarrier Running at the Defender

When going to hit a rushing ballcarrier coming into the scoring area the defender should lean forward slightly to absorb the force of the contact; or give him a little jab step to make him make his move prematurely and then he can read how he is going to defend him; or fake the hit and step away, causing the ballcarrier to lose his balance, then look to stick-check as the ballcarrier is trying to regain his balance.

If the ballcarrier is running toward the defender, but out of the scoring area, the defender must start moving as the ballcarrier approaches to pick up momentum to match the ballcarrier's speed, but when it is time to cross-check, the checker must make sure he is stationary on contact.

## "Closing Out"

"Closing out" occurs when a defender has to rush or run out to the ballcarrier to maintain pressure and/or to stop the ballcarrier from scoring. A defender "closes out" by running toward the ballcarrier, usually from a cross-floor pass or an "up" pass, to maintain defensive pressure and to stop the ballcarrier from going to the net. He closes out by sprinting hard then shuffling his last two steps in short, choppy steps, pushing off with his back foot and stepping with his front foot, called "attack steps." These attack steps put him under control, balanced, and in a good defensive stance when he makes contact. He also wants to get his body directly in front of the ballcarrier's stick, in an overplay position. And on approaching the ballcarrier must remember not to play his stick, but to play his hands, because the ballcarrier could wind-up for a fake shot and go around you.

## If the Defender is Beaten

If the ballcarrier beats the defender one-on-one, the defender shouldn't panic, but wait for the ballcarrier's stick to come back in order for him to shoot, then all that he has to do is knock the ballcarrier's stick down or up.

## The Big Hit

Stress to defenders that one big hit is not defense. A defender has to make two-to-three good cross-checks or slashes while moving down the sideboards or across the top of the floor to be able to play good defense.

## Playing Defense with a Shot-Clock

If the league has a 30-second shot-clock (NLL) then all the defender has to do is contain or just keep the ballcarrier in front of him for 15 seconds by not letting him get by. Most teams will take 10–15 seconds to get the ball up the floor or make an exchange of players, and that leaves another 15 seconds of playing defense. The best friend of the defender is the 30-second clock, which will give them the ball back if he plays good defense.

## Working with the Goalie

Defenders should talk to their goaltenders to find out where they want the shots to come from: close-in around the crease area or from farther out in front of the net. Then the defender can play their shooters accordingly. If a goalie is weak on long-shots, the defender plays out more; if the goalie is weak on close-in shots, the defender plays the shooter so he doesn't get beat in close.

## Defensive Reminders, or a "Don't" List

- Don't play the ballcarrier soft, make sure all shots are interfered with, pressured, or hurried.
- Be aware of overcommitting on a slash. If a defender slashes the ballcarrier, keep a good, balanced stance.
- Don't stick-check, i.e., try to steal the ball off the ballcarrier. It is extremely hard to get a ball off an offensive player and if a defender

does attempt this, he will more than likely get beaten.

- Don't get impatient and rush the ballcarrier. If a defender has to move out on a shooter, "close out," i.e., run at him and the last two steps are shuffle steps so he is down, balanced, and under control.
- Don't reach if a defender intends to cross-check, wait for him to get close enough to make good solid contact.
- Don't finish the check after the ballcarrier passes the ball. By doing this the defender takes himself out of the play and won't be able to help his teammates. For example, if the ballcarrier passes the ball rather than continue checking, the defender should drop to help out on the new ballcarrier. This "finishing your check" that has crept into the game, comes from hockey where players are taught to finish their check, but the better play is after your check has passed the ball to drop to help on the new defender on the ballcarrier, like in defensive basketball.

## IV. Individual Defensive Strategies Playing the Non-Ballcarrier

In today's game it seems most of the cross-checking occurs when the off-ball side defender makes a hard cross-check on a cutter to stop him from cutting and to make him pay the price; or when he helps out his teammate who is beaten by the ballcarrier by cross-checking him.

### 1. Defensive Communication on the Floor

The toughest thing to teach is to get players to talk on the floor. The rule, "players must talk on the floor during the game," helps to build team unity and to get rid of any indecision. A player should work on being the best defensive communicator on the floor. Here are a few things a defender can do and say to help his team:

- The defender playing the non-ballcarrier tells his teammate who is checking the ballcarrier, "You've got help."
- Besides calling out his check, the defender must know who has the ball and tell teammates where the ball is. It is amazing how many times teams get beaten on the "hidden ball trick," i.e., an opponent fakes giving the ball to his teammate while hanging onto it and having the opposition playing the player without the ball, thinking he has it.
- Defensive teams who are constantly warning and alerting each other before picks are set to play in a more unified way.
- Usually the back defenders do more talking, acting as defensive floor generals, because they can see better what is developing out in front.
- On a cutter, a defensive player has to call out "cutter" just to let the defender on the ballcarrier know to play him a little tougher so the ballcarrier can't pass to the cutter easily.

### 2. Some Defensive Definitions

**"One Pass Away"**
This refers to the offensive team moving the ball around the outside of the defense. One pass away is when the ballcarrier can make a pass to his teammate next to him either down the side of the floor, back to the top of the floor, or across the floor, but not to a cutting player.

**"Closed Stance" Position**
Means a defender is playing between his check and the ball with his back to the ball, in a "belly-to-belly" position, looking over his shoulder slightly to see the ball. When some defenders lose sight of the ball and want to search for it, they use their stick as a "feeler" to keep contact with their check by placing their stick over their check's stick, or just by touching their check's body with their stick to tell when their check cuts or moves.

### "Open Stance" Positioning

The defender plays his check facing down the floor to see both the ball and his check. In this position he can defend a pass to his check by intercepting any cross-floor passes, deny his check on a cut by cross-checking him, or help his teammate if the ballcarrier beats him.

### "Closing Out"

While the defender is playing in the "open stance" position between his check and the ballcarrier and the ballcarrier throws to his check, the defender must rush out hard or "close out" at his check to stop him from shooting or going one-on-one.

### "Denying" the Pass

Means a defender stops his check from receiving a pass by overplaying him on the ball side in a "closed stance" position—cross-checking, slashing his body, pushing the defender's body, and slashing his stick.

### "Backdoor" Cut

This occurs when the offensive player without the ball is being overplayed and prevented from cutting in front of his defender to receive a pass. He then cuts behind his defender to the net to get in the clear for a pass and shot.

## 3. Ball-Side Defensive Positioning

### Defending the Ballcarrier

When playing the ballcarrier, play him "ball-you-net" position; i.e., always play between the ballcarrier and the net.

### Defending the Non-Ballcarrier on the Ball Side of the Floor

When playing the non-ballcarrier on the ball side of the floor, the defender plays him "ball-you-man" in the "closed stance" position overplaying the passing lane so his check cannot receive a pass. He forces him to cut backdoor, which is a tough cut to make, and then swivels his head and switches his stick

to the inside to still deny this cut. Or he forces him out toward the sideboards, where he can receive a less threatening pass. He should look over his shoulder periodically at the ballcarrier in case his teammate needs help.

### Defender Helps to Stop Penetration on the Ball Side

The defensive rule on the ball side is that "no ballcarrier can penetrate between two defensive players." This gives the defender checking the ballcarrier great confidence because he knows if he gets beaten, there will be a teammate ready to help him out.

The only exception is when the helping defender is playing in the back defensive position or checking the offensive creaseman. Here he holds his position and lets the ballcarrier go to the net without helping his teammate. The reason is he does this is he doesn't want to give any inside shots close to the net. Again, this situation also depends on who is who. If the creaseman is a weak player and the penetrator is an all-star, then the defender might leave the crease to play the better player. Or if the situation is reversed he might stay playing the creaseman. The defender plays the offensive situation accordingly.

### Defender Helps Out on the Ball Side When the Ballcarrier Comes Out of the Corner Area and Cuts Inside

When the ballcarrier is in the corner area of the arena, the defender forces him up or into the middle of the floor where the defender knows he will get help from the top defender. The defender's help should come from the top ball side of the defense rather than from the lower off-ball side of the defense, which is harder to rotate from. If the help comes from the top of the defense, it is easier to slide down to help, but it could possibly give up a long shot which is better than a close-in shot. Again, this situation also depends on who is who.

The top defender plays the offensive situation accordingly.

## 4. Off-Ball or Help-Side Defensive Positioning

### Why Play Help Defense?

The defensive help concept is that "a good ballcarrier can beat a good defensive player in a one-on-one situation." Therefore, a defensive team stresses that teammates must be ready to help the checker on the ballcarrier. Teammates help out by cross-checking the ballcarrier, not stick-checking the ballcarrier.

### Best Help-Side Defensive Position

To play the non-ballcarrier on the off-ball side the best position to play him is the "ball-you-man" position. That is the defender plays between his check and the ballcarrier to deny him a pass. He can play him in a "closed" or "open" stance, depending on his team's defensive philosophy.

1.  **"Closed" Stance Off-Ball Positioning**
    Depending on the defensive philosophy the defender plays his check on the off-ball side in a "closed" stance, with his back to the ball, or a belly-to-belly position, to stop him from getting the ball. He stays between his check and the ballcarrier and makes body contact, stick contact, or cross-checks him on any cut to the ball, while looking over his shoulder or turning his head to peripherally see the ball.

2.  **"Open" Stance Off-Ball Positioning**
    Depending on the defensive philosophy the defender plays his check on the off-ball side of the floor in an "open" stance, or facing down the floor position to see both the ball and his check. In this position, by seeing both the ball and his check, he can either defend a pass to his check by intercepting any cross-floor passes, denying his check on a cut, or help his teammate if the ballcarrier beats him. If his offensive check cuts to the ballcarrier for a pass, the defender cross-

checks him or overplays him to stop him from receiving a pass. It is important in this stance that the defender keeps his check in front of him to always know where he is.

### Forming an Imaginary Triangle When Playing in an "Open" Stance Position on the Off-Ball Side

The defender on the off-ball side of the floor forms a flat triangle with himself, the ball, and his check. To form this flat triangle a defender plays one step off the passing lane, which is an imaginary line between the passer and receiver, and sags toward the Middle Lane. To help him maintain this proper flat triangle positioning, he holds the stick with one hand and points the head of the stick at his check and points his free hand at the ballcarrier. He is still in a good position to help a teammate if beaten by the ballcarrier or intercept any passes thrown to his check. The defender must remember to always keep the check in front of him, not beside or behind him.

### Defender Helps Out From the Off-Ball Side When the Ballcarrier Comes Out of the Corner Area and Cuts Outside (Undercut)

When the ballcarrier is in the corner area of the arena, the ball-side defender tries to force him into the middle of the floor toward defensive help, but sometimes that doesn't work. If the ballcarrier beats the defender to the outside, Undercut and back around the crease the bottom help-side defender has to come from the opposite side of the floor from the bottom of the defense. This is a hard slide to make and usually ends up with the off-ball help defender arriving late. This is why the bottom defender forces the ballcarrier in the corner up or into the middle of the floor where help comes easier from the ball-side top defender.

### Some Ideas in Playing Help-Side Defense:

*   Some defensive teams believe that when the bottom defender is in the corner area of the defense, he should not look to help at all on

the ballcarrier. They believe if the defender goes to help, they give up a good close-in shot.

- The top defenders may watch the defender on the ballcarrier ready to help him if he needs it, but the bottom defenders never slide or help from the crease area.
- A defensive rule is a defender does not leave a great offensive player to help, even if his teammate is beaten.
- A defender who just locks onto his own check (an average player) and only worries about one guy is selfish. Defense is supposed to be a group of five people working together.
- Since a defender plays with his back to the ball and plays his check's stick to deny a pass to him, if the defender's check still receives a pass, he is not doing his job. If the defender doesn't deny the pass what is the sense of playing belly-to-belly defense?
- If the ball is passed down over a defender's head, he must "drop to the level of the ball" and adjust to be in a good defensive position to help.
- A good rule to reinforce helping out is, "no ballcarrier should go between two defenders."
- Another defensive rule is, "the farther your check is from the ball, the farther you can be from your check."
- The defense moves and adjusts its position every time the ball moves. The defensive players must be constantly changing their angle and floor position as the ball is passed and while the ball is in the air. On movement of the ball, if the defense can move before the offense can move in regards to the new position of the ball, the defense will be in good shape.
- If there is pressure on the ball, the defenders can sag more off their checks, thus becoming more ready to help on the ballcarrier.
- If there is no pressure on the ball, the defenders play closer to their checks and become more man-oriented.

- Don't let a non-ballcarrier lean on the defender's stick as he can equalize pressure with the defender giving him the ability to catch the ball while being checked.
- If the defender's check does not have the ball, he must still keep his eyes and stick on his opponent, glancing every now and then at the ball to know where it is in case he has to slide to help a teammate with the ballcarrier.
- Never let a player cut through the middle while leaning on a defender's stick, as an offensive player can lean on the defender's body and still catch a pass. If an offensive player on his cut is covered by the defender pushing him and his stick is open, players are still good enough to catch the ball with a check right on him.
- Never allow an offensive player to cut through the middle wide open. Always deny the ball to the non-ballcarrier on the cut by staying between him and the ball, not between him and the net; protecting the net is playing cautious.
- A simple yet important rule is, "once a player picks up his check he has to stay with him." During a game it's amazing how many players lose their checks for some reason or other.
- Do not look to intercept a pass to your check. If you miss the interception, your check can cut to the net for an open pass-and-shot play.
- One of the most important rules is, "an off-ball defender must have his head on a swivel, turning it back and forth, to know what is going on in case he has to help the defender on the ballcarrier."

## 5. Why Deny the Pass? To Force the Ballcarrier to Go One-on-One

The defense wants the offense to go one-on-one (defense forcing) rather than the offense moving the ball around quickly (defense chasing). When the offense enter the Offensive Zone, to force this one-on-one situation, the defenders checking the non-ballcarriers overplay the passing lanes in a "closed" stance so that the ballcarrier cannot pass to his teammates. This maneuver also gives the checker time to put pressure on the ballcarrier. Once the checker has pressure on the ballcarrier, his teammates can drop off the passing lanes slightly or totally sag into the middle of the floor to be ready to help him on the ballcarrier if he needs it.

### 6. Defending the Give-and-Go

If the ballcarrier is in the scoring area and passes across the floor, the defender stays in a "closed" stance position and steps to the ball in the direction of the pass and also steps up into the cutting lane to defend the Give-and-Go play, i.e., turning his back to the ball, pushing and bumping the cutter and playing his stick. On the cut, the defender must always assume a pass is coming, so he plays him tough by staying in a "closed stance" to deny him the ball with body-to-body contact, cross-checking contact, or stick-contact. Now and then, he might look over his shoulder to see if his teammate needs help with the ballcarrier.

Because the cutter will have such a hard time trying to cut in front of the defender when moving to the ball, he might end up trying to cut behind the defender; i.e., going Backdoor to get in the clear. On this Backdoor Cut the defender will keep his back to the ball, swivel his head, and play his opponent's stick strong.

### 7. Defending the "Go" Play or the Off-Ball Cutter Play

If an offensive player just cuts from the off-ball side of the floor, the defender should already be in a "closed" stance position to deny a pass to his check and still be ready to help by looking over his shoulder. On the cut, the defender must always assume a pass is coming, so he plays him tough by staying in his "closed" stance to deny the cutter the ball. The defender

makes body-to-body contact or stick contact and tries to force him to go "Backdoor."

### 8. Defending the Backdoor Cut

If the opponent cuts Backdoor, then the defender should play him in a "closed" stance (face guard him), by turning his back to the ball, and running with him, playing his stick on his opponent's stick for a split second to take away the initial cut. This is one of the few times, on the Backdoor Cut, that the defender totally loses sight of the ball while on defense.

## V. Team Footwork and Defensive Stance Drills

Some tips on defensive drills:

- Build up the defense first through drills. The game starts with the defensive end.
- Defense is something a coach can teach players, whereas offensive skills are sometimes just the result of a player's natural talent. Therefore, any player can be a great defensive player if he wants to be.
- To teach defense, the coach should control what the offense does in the drill.
- In the beginning of defensive drills, the defense should always win. As the defensive players' skills improve, create drills that give defenders a tougher time than in an actual game situation.
- Coach should make a list of the toughest defensive drills he has.
- If the players are enjoying everything the coach is asking them to do, then maybe the drills are too easy.
- The defensive drills the players hate, the coach does.
- The battle cry in practice: "Nobody scores on me, even in practice."
- Teach players how to defend by spending three-quarters of the practice time on defense. If the players can guard, they can win.
- Make players talk in defensive drills.

## 1. Defensive Agility Footwork Drill

To improve footwork the majority of the defensive footwork drills deal with lateral motion, changing directions, and quickness.

a. **Running Backward Down the Length of the Floor**

b. **Carioca**

Move sideways to the right down the length of the floor while facing the sideboards. Step over the right foot with the left foot and then step behind the right foot with the left foot while maintaining the upper body facing in the same direction all the time. Then, repeat the process in the other direction stepping with the right foot.

c. **Step Over**

While running forward in a straight line, step in front of each foot.

d **Front Crossover**

While moving sideways, one foot steps over in front of the other foot continuously.

e. **Back Crossover**

While moving sideways, one foot steps behind the other foot continuously.

f. **Quarter Jump Turns**

Turn body 90 degrees then turn body 180 degrees.

## 2. Defensive Stance Drill

a. **Teach the Defensive Stance**

Spread team around the floor and teach the defensive stance. Players stay in a defensive stance position for a designated time (30–60 seconds).

b. **Defensive Lane Slide Drill**

Players slide or shuffle between two cones placed 10 feet apart while the coach counts the number of slides in 30 seconds. The coach will eventually figure out the standard in 30 seconds. (back and forth = 1) For example, players try to do 10 shuffles in 30 seconds.

Coach stresses that both feet must come outside the 10' lane to count as one while players stay in good defensive stance.

c. **Single-Line Defensive Slide Drill**

The whole team is in front of net. All players in a single line slide up to coach at the Defensive Line, and then slide over to the sideboards, then slide across floor to other sideboard. Players have to learn to cut around and through teammates while playing defense and still keep their eye on the ball.

Coach, at the Defensive Line with a ball, can toss the ball to anyone, and the player who catches the ball passes it back. Coach passes the ball to stress to everyone to keep their eye on the ball by turning their head and still sliding.

d. **Two Lines, "Closed" Stance to "Open" Stance—Defensive Footwork Drill**

Form two defensive lines on both sides of the floor lined up along and inside of their respective Outside Lane. Two coaches in top-right-side area and top-left-side area pass a ball back and forth. The two lines of players shuffle in and out, as if putting pressure on the ball in a "closed" stance, then sliding back into the Middle Lane in an "open" stance to take help position. In this drill, stress talking to the ball to encourage talking on the floor ("I've got ball"). Eyes are always on the ball, move as ball moves, and learn the "dance" of defense.

e. **Running the Width of the Floor**

Have the team line up along the sideboard and run back and forth from one sideboard to the other sideboard. Record how many sprints the team can run in one minute. They must touch the sideboards with their sticks.

f. **Teach the Attack Step, Retreat Step, and Drop (Swing) Step to a Shuffle Step**

Attack Step for "closing out," retreat step to stop penetration down the side of the floor, and a drop (swing) step to a shuffle step to stop penetration across the floor.

### 3. Wave Drill

This quickness drill is where the whole team reacts to the hand motion of the coach.

- If the coach points straight out to his side, team shuffles or step-and-slide sideways for two steps. Ballcarrier is cutting across the top.
- If he points to the sideboards at an angle, players drop step and shuffle sideways for two steps. Ballcarrier cuts to the sideboard trying to beat defender.
- If coach points straight back to the end-board, players do a retreat step and shuffle down two steps. Ballcarrier is trying to Undercut and go behind defender.
- If coach points behind himself (backward), the players do a two-step attack step. Ballcarrier is hesitant with the ball or a weak ball-handler.
- If coach points straight back and then points straight across the floor, the players drop step with outside foot and shuffle down the floor two steps, then they drop step with inside foot and shuffle across the floor two more steps.

Stress bent knees and proper defensive stance. Do this drill for five minutes—work one minute, rest, work one minute, rest, etc.

### 4. Shadow Drill

These are drills of "first steps." Defender works on quickness and body balance. Partners just mirror each other for 10 seconds. Defensive partners react to the offensive partner.

a. Ballcarrier cuts to the outside, defender pushes off with front inside foot to cut off the ballcarrier (retreat step).
b. Ballcarrier cuts to inside, defender with first step cuts off the ballcarrier by taking a drop (swing) step and then shuffles sideways across the top of the floor keeping the ballcarrier from going to the net.
c. Defender makes no contact, ballcarrier moves side-to-side facing the defender and defender stays with this sideways motion. The offensive player cannot beat the defender.
d. Ballcarrier moves side-to-side facing the defender and defender tries to stay with this sideway motion and still make contact. Ballcarrier just works him, but is not allowed to beat him.

### 5. Defensive Square Drill

In this drill the goal is for the players to always stay in a defensive stance. It is a drill to increase and test lateral motion and quickness. Complete the square with four cones to mark a square the distance one would use in a game. Use both sides of the floor at the same time. Players can go in a clockwise direction or a counter-clockwise direction. The objective is how long it takes to do the square four times or how many times in 20 seconds.

a. Start in the top left side corner of the square. Go in a counter-clockwise direction, shuffle down in defensive stance (face sideboards), stop, do a Drop Step and open up and shuffle across, stop, then run up, "closing out," shuffle last two steps, stop. Then shuffle back across to original position.
b. Face toward the far end of the floor all the time. Start in top left side corner of the square and run backward, then shuffle across between bottom cones, then run upward to top cone, and then shuffle across between the top two cones.
c. Face toward the far end of the floor all the time. Go in a reversal direction or clockwise direction, start and shuffle across, stop and run backward, turn and shuffle across, and then sprint up and "close out."
d. Start in middle of the four cones, run to a corner, slide back to middle, go to another corner and slide back. Do all four corners.

## VI. Individual Defensive Drills— Against the Ballcarrier

First priority on defense is to teach players to stop the ballcarrier.

### One-on-One Defensive Progression for All the Following Drills:

1. No-stick drill for defender. Defender holds the front of his sweater. He uses his forearm, upper arms, and body to make contact with the ballcarrier to stop them from scoring.
2. No-stick drill for defender. Defender allowed to push and to shove with his hands, clutch and grab, but not put his arms totally around ballcarrier.
3. Defender holds the football, hand-held blocking dummy to stop the ballcarrier.
4. Defender, with his stick, tries to stop ballcarrier, who attacks the defender to score.
5. Defender is timed to see how long he can stop the ballcarrier from going to the net (hold for 5–10 seconds).

### One-on-One From Four Different Areas of the Floor for All the Following Drills:

1. One-on-one defender defends ballcarrier from the mid-side area of the floor (wing area).
2. One-on-one defender defends the ballcarrier from the corner area of the floor. Defender tries to force ballcarrier to middle, not to outside for Undercut.
3. One-on-one defender defends the ballcarrier from the top-side area (pointman's spot).
4. One-on-one defender defends the ballcarrier from the top-center area of floor (pointman's spot or "X" spot).
5. One-on-one defender defends the ballcarrier running down the side of the floor.

### How to Start the One-on-One Drill:

1. Ballcarrier has the ball.
2. Ballcarrier receives a pass from the opposite side of the floor.
3. Ballcarrier receives the pass from the defender who is in the middle of the floor and waits for defender to touch him with his stick to start the drill.
4. Ballcarrier receives the pass from the defender who is in the middle of the floor, but doesn't wait for him to touch him, but just goes directly to the net.

### Set Up Drill For One-on-One:

1. Two lines: an offensive line and a defensive line. Here anybody can be any type of shot when checking.
2. Four lines: on one side of floor an offensive line and a defensive line, and on the other side the same set-up. Here left-shot defender will check a right-shot offensive player and vice versa.
3. Three lines: an offensive line, a defensive line, and a passing line. The drill starts from a pass. The rotation for the three players is: defender goes to offense, offense goes to passer, and passer goes to defense.

### 1. One-on-One Defending the Ballcarrier From Top-Side of Floor Drill (No Pass)

Form two lines, offense and defense. Defender must stop the offensive player if he does stop him, he can rotate to the offensive line. If he doesn't stop the ballcarrier, he stays in the defensive line. Points are only given for defensive stops, players play to four stops.

### 2. One-on-One Defending the Ballcarrier From Top-Center Area of Floor Drill (No Pass)

Defender contains or stops penetration by trying to veer or force the ballcarrier wide to the sideboard. Do not let him penetrate straight down the middle of the floor. See how long a defender can stay on defense. (10–15 seconds).

### 3. One-on-One Defending Ballcarrier From Mid-Side Area of Floor Drill (No Pass)

Ballcarrier starts drill with a ball, defender tries to keep the ballcarrier in the alley. In other words, no penetration into the middle of the floor. Allow ballcarrier 5–10 seconds to beat their defender.

### 4. One-on-One Defending Ballcarrier From Corner Area of Floor Drill (No Pass)

Defender tries to force the ballcarrier into the middle, not Undercutting to the net, but be ready to cut him off from even going into the middle of the floor. Give him something then take it away, beat him to the spot. First defensive move is backward to force him upward, then his next move is upward to cut him off. See how many times he can turn the ballcarrier. If beaten into middle, run and cut him off from going into the middle and force him back to the sideboards.

### 5. One-on-One "Live" From Four Different Areas of the Floor Drill (Pass From Defender)

Defender in middle of floor passes ball to player in wing. He touches the ballcarrier with his stick on the hip, who then goes one-on-one. If offense scores they get a point. Play to nine points.

**Variation:** Defender passes ball to wing player, then "closes out." Here he doesn't touch the ballcarrier. The ballcarrier can go to the net as soon as he gets the ball.

### 6. One-on-One Using Cones Drill

Put cones on the side of the floor (10' apart) where the ballcarrier will go one-on-one, but must stay between the cones. This drill is good for offense and defense, as one has to stop a player in a restricted space and a player has to beat a defender in a restricted space.

### 7. One-on-One Stationary Game

Defender flips the ball to the offense from one of the four areas. If the ballcarrier scores from one-on-one, he keeps the ball. On a missed shot opponent gets ball. Game is played to seven points.

### 8. One-on-One "Steal the Ball" Drill

Sometimes during a game a team needs to get the ball. In this drill the defender practices getting the ball off the ballcarrier. The defender has to be deceptive playing cat-and-mouse with the ballcarrier faking to get the ball one way and going the other way. The defender can slash, poke, jab, and wrap-around to knock the ball out of the ballcarrier's stick. The defenders only get a point if they steal the ball.

### 9. One-on-One Grab-Him Drill

Defender tries to grab ballcarrier as he goes to the net. Defender cannot wrap his arms completely around the ballcarrier.

### 10. One-on-One Team Against Team "Stops" Drill

Five players play as a team against five players as another team. One player from each team goes one-on-one. To encourage physical and aggressive defense let the defenders be physical (bump, push) and do not call penalties unless they are blatant. To stress defense each team gets a point on defense for stopping the offense. The first team to seven points wins. The winning team gets a drink or rest while the losing team runs sprints or does suicides.

### 11. One-on-One Four-Corner Drill (With One Defender)

There are offensive players in all four corners of the offense. One defender will check all four offensive players one-on-one, going from one offensive player to another.

## 12. One-on-One Four-Corner Drill (With Four Defenders)

There are four offensive players and four defenders at each corner. Each defender will check his offensive player, while the other defenders will play his checks accordingly, faking a defensive slide as if to help. In this drill the checker and ballcarrier have a more realistic look when defending and beating their check.

## 13. Three-Man Weave to a One-on-One Defensive Drill

Start the drill with three players at center and weave the ball. The middle man passes to the wing and goes behind him and takes a defensive help-side position, wing man who receives the first pass passes to the opposite wing, then follows his pass and takes a defensive stance on the ball. These two players go one-on-one. The defender tries to keep the wing offensive player in the "alley" forcing him low. If offensive man cuts into middle of the floor the "help-defender" slides and helps his teammate.

**Variation:** The three players weave, but this time put an extra offensive player in the opposite corner. Run the same drill, middle man on weave drop down and take "help-side" position, now playing the offensive player in the corner. If the ballcarrier drives into the middle he looks to pass to his teammate in the corner if the "help-defender" comes over to help. The drill could turn into a two-on-two situation.

## 14. Two-on-One "Closing Out" to Defend a Shooter Drill

Whole team forms two offensive lines on opposite sides of the floor and one defensive line in the middle of the floor, guarding one of the offensive players. The two offensive players are spaced 15' apart, the unguarded passer passes to the other offensive player, while the off-ball defender "closes out" hard on this

ballcarrier. Coach wants the new ballcarrier to fake a shot, go one-on-one, or just shoot. If the offensive player fakes a shot, he can cut outside to try to beat the defender (Undercut) or cut inside.

Stress to the defensive players when the offensive player winds-up like he is going to shoot (fake shot), do not play his stick, but play his hands. Good pressure on his hands, yet no stick checking.

## 15. Two-on-One Stopping Penetration Drill

Ball-side defender plays off his check, the creaseman, on the same side of the floor as the ball-carrying cornerman, to be in a position to stop penetration. When the ball-side defender comes up to stop penetration, the ballcarrier makes a pass to the creaseman on his side of floor. The defender must now recover back to his original check. The question is, "Does the ball-side defender stop penetration and give up a pass to the creaseman or stay with his check on the crease?"

## 16. One-on-One "Battle" Drill

This is a one-on-one checking drill using sticks. There are two offensive lines and two defensive lines. The defenders can check the ballcarrier by going right-shot on left-shot, by going big on big, by going speed on speed, or by just having defenders mixed up and check anybody.

Usually the coaches have the left-shots stay on one side of the floor and rotate from offense to defense while the right-shots do the same thing on the other side of the floor. Coach can make it a game with right-shots versus left-shots.

**The Set-Up of the Drill:**
The drill has six lines: form two lines on both the top-side areas of the floor, form two lines on both the mid-side areas of the floor, form four lines on the same side of the floor in the mid-side and corner areas of the floor.

**To Start the Drill:**

a. The offensive player receives a "diagonal" pass from the defender in the opposite side of the floor to the mid-side area, then attacks the net.

b. The offensive player receives a "cross-floor" pass from the defender in the opposite side of the floor to the top-side area, then attacks the net.

c. The offensive player in the mid-side area receives an "up" pass from the defender, who is on the same side of the floor, from the corner area, then attacks the net.

d. The offensive player in the corner area receives a "down" pass from the defender from the same side of the floor from the mid-side area, then attacks the net.

Alternate the drill. Start on one side, then work the other side.

**After Receiving the Pass:**

a. The offensive player waits for defender to touch his body, then he goes one-on-one.

b. The offensive player attacks the net and does not wait for the defender to get set.

### 17. Two-on-One—Fight Through Pick Set by Second Offensive Player Drill

Defender in this drill learns to fight through picks while checking the ballcarrier. When the pick is set on the defender checking the ballcarrier, the defender must step back and through the screen, called "through," and then "fire out" to fill the gap to maintain pressure on the ballcarrier. Or the defender can step up and over the screen, called "over the top," to close the gap and maintain pressure on the ballcarrier.

### 18. One-on-One "Showdown" Game

This drill is a one-on-one competition between two teams: lefts versus rights, defensive group versus offensive group, or picked teams. There are only two lines: the offensive line and the defensive line. To stress the defensive aspect, the defensive player gets a point for stopping the offense from scoring. The first team to 10 points wins.

### 19. One-on-One Box-Out Drill

Shooter shoots wide of the net and hits the end-boards and then tries to get his own rebound and score. The defender has to "box out" by facing the offensive player and cross-checking or interfering with him to stop him from getting the rebound. Then he goes after the rebound.

### 20. One-on-One Zig-Zag Defensive Drill (Between Cones) (Half-Floor)

Start the one-on-one drill in front of net area and two players go to the Defensive Zone Line with the offensive player trying to stay between the cones the width of the crease. The defensive player tries to stop the ballcarrier from going around him. He can make body contact, slash, cross-check, push, but he cannot wrap his arms around ballcarrier.

### 21. One-on-One Zig-Zag Drill (Full-Floor)

Defender tries to keep his "head on the ball," ballcarrier only runs token speed full-length of the floor.

### 22. One-on-One Zig-Zag Drill (Full Floor)

Defender tries to stop the ballcarrier from going into middle for the full length of the floor.

## VII. Individual Defensive Drills—Defending Against the Non-Ballcarrier

### 1. Two-on-One Defending the Give-and-Go Drill (Off-Ball Side)

Here, an offensive player has the ball, is closely guarded, and passes it across the floor to a open teammate. He then cuts in front of or behind the defender for a return pass. The defender works on denying the cutter to the ball.

## 2. Two-on-One Defending the "Go" Drill (Off-Ball Side)

Here, the non-ballcarrier is on the opposite side of the floor from the ballcarrier and a cross-floor pass away. Again, the defender tries to deny the off-ball cutter from going Backdoor to the net or cutting across the top of the floor for a pass. Defender makes him pop out of the scoring area.

## 3. Two-on-Two Defending Give-and-Go Drill (Off-Ball Side)

This defensive drill is run with an offensive right-hand shot and an offensive left-hand shot in the cornerman's positions.

**Numbers:**
Start with just one defender on the cutter; then just one defender on the passer; then two defenders on each offensive player. Defenders play the cutter tough or they play the passer tough.

**Defensive progression:**
a. Defender has no stick (they can push with their hands).
b. Defender plays with his stick held the wrong way.
c. Defender puts his stick on the cutter, but he only rides with him.
d. Defender pushes the cutter, but he cannot cross-check him.
e. Defender can cross-check or slash the cutter.

The cutter works on different ways of beating his defender with the defender playing token defense.

## 4. Two-on-Two Give-and-Go Live Defensive Drill (Off-Ball Side)

The two defensive players check the two offensive players who are on opposite sides of the floor. Stress to the offensive players to work on deception and quickness and that the cutters should try to get on the inside of their defenders. The defenders play in a "closed stance" to deny the cutter and the defender on the passer pressures him with his stick.

**Remember:** The offensive passer's rule is to "pass early, not late, to the cutter" and the offensive cutter's rule is to "cut late, not early."

## 5. Two-on-Two Give-and-Go Game (Off-Ball Side)

Two teams of partners composed of a left- and a right-shot offensive player on the opposite side of the floor. They try to score only off a Give-and-Go. The defenders play accordingly trying to stop them from scoring on a Give-and-Go. They play to four goals.

## 6. Two-on-One Defending "Go" Drill From Top-Center Area of Floor (Ball Side)

Form two lines, offense and defense, on the same side of floor at top-center area. Offensive player passes down to lone passer in the mid-side area and then cuts for return pass in front of defender down the middle of the floor or behind the defender down the middle.

## 7. Two-on-One Defending "Go" Drill From Corner of Floor (Ball Side)

From the corner area of the floor, ballcarrier passes up to the passer on his side of the floor and, then cuts in front of his defender or behind his defender for a return pass and shot. The defender playing belly-to-belly denies him from getting the ball, but will let him get the ball out of the scoring area beside the sideboards.

**Variation:** Now and then run two left-hand shots or two right-hand shots together and run the Give-and-Go or the "Go" play on the same side of the floor.

## 8. Three-on-One "Closing Out" Defensive Drill

Two offensive lines—one is in the mid-side area and the other line is across the floor in the other mid-side area. The coach is in the top-center area of the floor with a bucket of balls.

Defensive player is in the middle of floor—the drill is to simulate being in the "help" defensive position, i.e., where the defender's man doesn't have a ball. So, in essence the defender is responsible for guarding both offensive players, because he doesn't know who will end up with the ball. This drill is also an exaggeration of the "help" position, so a defender learns about "closing out" quickly.

When the coach passes the ball to one of the offensive players in the mid-side area, the defensive player's job: is to sprint out hard, then "close out" quickly, and guard the ballcarrier who is going to try and score on him.

So, the defender has got to: contest or force the shot, contain or stop the ballcarrier, then, block out the shooter on a shot and rebound the ball if it goes off the boards or off the goalie. When the defender does all that, the possession is done.

If the defender doesn't do all those things he has to stay and play defense again. Then coach passes the ball again to either line in the mid-side areas and the defender has got to go out and defend the offensive player again. If he doesn't defend the first or second time, he will be dead tired by the third time. If the defender stops the ballcarrier in the first or second time he is not punished. If he doesn't stop the ballcarrier the third time, he has to run sprints.

# Chapter 8

# Shooting

## I. Terminology for Shooters

**Short Side**—the goalie's "near side" or the shooter's "short side" is the side of the net closest to the shooter.

**Long Side**—the goalie's "far side" or the shooter's "long side" is the side of the net farthest from the shooter.

## II. Overhand Long-Ball Shooting Technique

What makes this shooting technique so simple is that a player imitates the same motion as in overhand passing. Shooting is the most important skill, passing is second. The reason the long overhand shot is one of the best shots in lacrosse is because the shooter can pick the top corner or pull it down as a low bounce shot all in one motion. If a player can shoot the overhand shot, directly over his shoulder, he has more options, especially from the outside. Besides, the long low shot or long low bounce shot are still the best shots to take.

**Checklist for Overhand Long-Ball Shooting**
- Stance for Overhand Long Shot
- Grip of Stick for Overhand Shot
- Shooting Position of Stick for Overhand Long Shot

**Photo 53:** Front view of cocked position or "winding up" of the overhand shot—stick parallel to floor

**Photo 54:** Front view of follow-through of the overhand shot

- Cocked Position or "Winding Up" for Overhand Long Shot
- Shooting Motion or Release of Ball for Overhand Long Shot
- Follow-Through for Overhand Long Shot

## 1. Stance for Overhand Long Shot

- The side of the shooter's body faces the net at a 45-degree angle.
- Keeping the knees bent and taking a wide stance will give a shooter good body balance and better power into his shot.
- The feet should be ready to shoot, which means the front foot (foot opposite side of the stick) is at a 45-degree angle to the net, and the back foot is parallel to the net, with most of the body weight on it.

## 2. Grip of Stick for Overhand Shot

- Hold the stick with the fingers, but loosely to get the "feel." This grip creates "soft hands." The thumbs are usually placed along the shaft, but some players like to wrap the thumbs around the shaft. It seems to be a matter of personal preference as to which feels best.
- The top-hand arm is the "power and guide" arm in the shot and the bottom-hand arm is the "stabilizer." Both arms are flexed at the beginning of the shot.
- For experienced players, the positions of the hands do not change for passing and shooting. The top hand is just below the mid-point (halfway) of the shaft and the bottom hand is placed at the butt of the stick. Some overhand shooters like to slide their top hand down closer to the bottom hand to get the hands closer together, approximately four inches apart, for a better "whip" motion in their shot. By bringing the hands closer together, a player gets more momentum into his shot because he can drop his stick farther behind his body. The farther the head has to rotate forward the more "whip" he gets into his shot. He may,

however, lose some control over his stick if he brings his hands too close together on the overhand shot.

## 3. Shooting Position of Stick for Overhand Shot

- The stick can be held in one of three positions: straight up and down (in-close shot), straight back at a 45-degree angle to the floor (mid-range shot), or parallel to the floor ("winding up" for a long-shot), depending on the type of shooter he is, where he is on the floor when he shoots, and how much time he has to get his shot away.
- Some shooters hold their stick in a vertical cradling position and move it from side-to-side to fake a shot and cut outside or just shoot. Other great shooters hold their sticks level to the floor while looking to shoot, pass, or go one-on-one (the "triple-threat" position).
- The height at which the stick is held varies with shooters. Overhand-shooting players who hold their sticks vertical at a 45-degree angle like to hold the stick high, i.e., with the top hand level with the head and behind their head. Other shooters like to hold the stick a little lower, with the top hand parallel to the chin. But whatever the preference, a shooter should hold his stick at the same level for every overhand shot. Some players have a tendency to hold the stick high for high shots and low over the shoulder for low shots which allows the goalie to predict the shot.

## 4. Cocked Position or "Winding Up" for Overhand Long Shot

- The shooter cocks the stick, moving it farther back by extending the top-arm fully or partially behind the body, with the bottom hand remaining flexed, and flexing both of the wrists backward. Moving the stick backward and holding the stick horizontally will help get more momentum

**Photo 55:** Side view of cocked position or "winding up" of the overhand shot—stick parallel to floor

into the shot and therefore a more powerful shot.

- At the same time, the shooter steps four inches with his front foot to give himself a transfer of weight and a good wide base for power. While the stick is cocked, the shooter turns his body slightly with his back almost facing the net.
- The shooter should not have too much tension during the cocking stage. If the shooter does, his shot will not be effortless or efficient.
- A player winds up for a long shot only if he has time and space to shoot. If he doesn't have time and space, he has to shoot a quick release with little or no wind up which seems to be more common in today's game because of the tight checking and for the element of surprise against the big goalies.
- The stick can be over the shooting shoulder for an overhand shot or to the side of the shooting shoulder for a sidearm shot or a combination sidearm-overhand shot. Some players in today's game like to use an overhand with a slight sidearm shot (three-quarter shot).
- The stick is now held horizontally or at a slight 45-degree angle to the floor, and over

the stick shoulder. The butt of the stick is now pointing at the target.

*Note: When an overhand shooter has a deeper pocket, he has to drop his stick back farther behind his body to get more "whip" (power) and a higher trajectory into his shot, because the ball may "hook" or shoot low from this deep pocket.*

- Good players adjust their stick's pocket so the ball goes to the same spot—the "shooting pocket"—every time.
- Players might do a small cradle just before shooting to check, by the weight of the ball, that it is still in the shooting pocket.
- Although shooters try to catch and shoot from the same spot in the pocket, they sometimes catch the ball in the middle or at the throat end of the pocket by mistake and, therefore have to do a small cradle or drop the head of the stick below the butt end to roll the ball into the "shooting pocket" just before shooting.

**Remember:** the "shooting pocket" is usually at the tip of the stick on the edge of the bottom (last) shooting string.

## 5. Shooting Motion or Release of Ball for Overhand Long Shot

- It is important to begin the shot with the body weight on the planted back foot. As the shooter takes another small step

**Photo 56:** Side view of shooting motion or release of ball of the overhand shot—from behind head

(4") with his front foot, the body weight is transferred to this foot. This transfer of weight and wider stance helps to put more power into the shot.

- To get power, synchronization, and rhythm in the shot, shooters almost automatically take a slight hop-step into their shot preceding the wind up to enhance its power. In doing the hop-step their back foot steps behind the front foot, then, they step with front foot. Shooters use their legs by putting weight on the back foot, doing the hop-step, then stepping with the front foot giving them a wide stance and a transfer of weight onto the front foot. This slight hopping motion with the rear foot helps to put rhythm into the shot and gets everything into sync.

- Pull the stick from behind the shoulder by extending the top-hand arm forward and snapping both wrists forward. Remember to keep the bottom-hand arm flexed even though the shooter snaps the wrists forward, and stress sliding the top hand down on shooting the ball.

- The quicker and stronger the swinging motion of the stick, the more momentum it will pick up, and thus a more powerful shot. The speed of the "head" is important. Also stress being a "wrist" shooter rather than a "pusher." A "pusher" is a player who has a tendency to hold the stick too high on the shaft with the top-hand and extends both his arms to release the ball.

- The shooter's body starts with the side of the body facing the net at a 45-degree angle and ends up with the body square to the net. The hips and shoulders have rotated on the shot to put more power into the shot.

- Start the shot with a relaxed grip as the passing or shooting motion does not require a fast start, but it does require a smooth effortless start. But the shooter does need that firm grip at the end of the shot. A shooter cannot be tight when he starts his

swing because he will never be smooth on the release.

- Early release of the ball, when it is still behind the body, produces a high and level trajectory. This early release is exaggerated more when a shooter wishes to compensate for a "hook." A later release of the ball, when the ball is beside or in front of the body, produces a low trajectory. This is a very common mistake for beginning players.

**Remember**: To shoot or release the ball from behind the head.

## 6. Follow-Through for Overhand Long Shot

- A shooter will end up with a full extension of his top-hand arm, and with the butt of his stick touching his top-hand arm's elbow. In actuality, the shooter may not be touching his elbow, but the elbow is a good reference point to encourage a pure overhand shot.

- Release the ball when it is behind the head, but continue on the follow-through after the ball has gone. Speed and power of the shot picks up as the player moves his stick through the full range of motion. Stress to players to shoot relaxed and effortlessly.

- The head of the stick ends up pointing at the target, as if the shooter were following the ball into the net with his stick. Coach

**Photo 57:** Side view of follow-through of the overhand shot

encourages shooters to "freeze" or hold their follow-through to see if their stick is pointing at the target.

- Body weight ends up on the front foot after the step.
- To get the full weight of the body behind the shot, make sure the shooter's shoulders and hips end up facing square to the net.

## III. Types of Long Shots

### Overhand Long Shot (Straight or Bounce Shot—Stationary or on the Run)

Here, the ball comes high above the shooter's head at a downward trajectory at the goalie, giving the shooter many targets to aim at—top corners, sides, glove or stick hand, between legs, bottom corners, bounce high, or bounce low. The overhand shooter also has the option of releasing the ball early for a straight shot, or releasing it late for a bounce shot.

### Long Overhand Bounce Shot

This is a very deceptive shot for a goalie because the ball comes down then ricochets off the floor going up. There are different levels of bounce shots: the short bounce shot hits the floor close to the feet and to the side of the goalie, deflecting up around the ankles; the medium bounce shot hits the floor about one to two feet out and to the side of the goalie, ricocheting up around the goalie's hips area; the long-high bounce shot hits the floor at the top of the crease area ricocheting into the top corner. Basically, the farther out the ball hits the floor from the goal line, the higher it goes. A player must be sure to pick a corner when using a bounce shot. Just to bounce the ball toward the net can be the most ineffective and easiest shot for a goalie to stop with the result of the shot leading to a fast-break situation.

It is easier to hit the far-side of the net with the bounce shot. The near-side "bouncer" is more difficult but if executed properly it is very deceptive.

### Long Sidearm Shot

The player slides the top-hand down beside the bottom-hand to get a better whip action with his stick. Some sidearm shooter's hands do not move much, whether passing or shooting. Again it is preference where the sidearm shooter's hand end up. He starts the shot with the head of the stick at waist level and because they usually have deeper pockets they bring their stick back farther behind the body to get more "whip" into their shot. The sidearm shot can be very deceptive because the stick extends three feet from the body. With his arms fully extended out to the side, the shooter has the advantage of aiming for the far-side of the net or around the goalie. Depending on the release, the ball can go up, level, or down, but usually the ball is released on a level trajectory. On the follow-through the stick comes around the body like a baseball swing, so with a late release the player has the option of bringing his shot back to the near-side of the net which is a very tough shot to make.

A similar shot that is close to the sidearm shot is the three-quarter overhand shot. Here the shooter does almost the same motions as the sidearm shot except it is halfway between the overhand and sidearm shots. This has become pretty common in today's game.

**Photo 58:** Three-quarter overhand shot

### Long Underhand Shot

The player starts this shot with the head of the stick near the bottom (level) of the floor. Again, the player slides the top hand up beside the bottom hand to create the whip action. Remember the stick is inverted upside down. The underhand shot can also be deceptive because usually the shot is low and parallel to the floor, but the follow-through is like a golf swing and with a late release the player can make the ball rise up to the top corner which is a hard shot for a goalie to judge and stop. Underhand shooters have very hard and "heavy" shots.

**Photo 59:** The underhand shot—the beginning

**Photo 60:** The underhand shot—the ending

## IV. Knowing What a Good Shot Is

### Players Should Know What a Good Shot Percentage Is

Players have to understand what a good shot is. Good shot selection helps to obtain a high percentage, which is one of the most important statistics in lacrosse. The team shooting objective for each game should be around 20 percent (one out of five shots) or approximately 12 goals on 60 shots. If a team doesn't obtain this stat, then the coach has to analyze why the team didn't obtain it.

*Note: In the game of lacrosse, the ball is played in the air, so shots are not usually deflected or screened. Therefore, it is extremely important to stress high percentage shooting. Although, players are now shooting more screen shots around defenders if the defenders are not out pressuring them.*

### Location on the Floor Leads to a Good Shot

As the angle of the shot is important, the shooter should know the best position on the floor to score from called the "Prime Scoring Area." During practices, it is a good idea to measure and mark the high percentage spots on the floor with an "X." *(See Diagram 15 pg. 81)*

Remember for a left-hand shot he will be shooting from the right-side of the floor to about the center area of the floor. One of the best spots to shoot from is in the "dead center" of the floor. Once players get past the Imaginary Center Line they have to shoot against the grain which is hard to do.

### Being in One's Proper Distance Leads to a Good Shot

The shooter should shoot in his range, but he should find his range in practice, not during the game. For most long-ball shooters, around the Imaginary Semi-Circle Line (15') is a good distance for a shot. After beating his defender, the tendency for the ballcarrier is he wants to beat one more defender to get in closer to the net for a better shot and ends up getting double-teamed by the defense. Players must understand that they do not have to be right at the crease for a good shot.

## No Defensive Pressure Leads to a Good Shot

If a shooter is wide open, that is, not closely guarded or having a defender's stick in front of his stick bothering his shot, he will get a better shot off. A good shooter will use the defender as a screen, if the defender gives him a "long gap" or plays off of him, he will then shoot quickly around him.

## Discipline Shooting Leads to a Good Shot

The shooter must use good judgment in taking his shots. He should "pick" the open spots at the net on his shot rather than "bomb" his shot, i.e., just shooting at the net at nothing in particular. Players who lack "shooting discipline" make bad decisions and take bad shots where they have nothing to shoot at and still shoot the ball rather than pass to a teammate for a better shot.

## Knowing the Goalie Leads to a Good Shot

The shooter should know how the goalie plays angles, if he reacts to stick fakes, and how he plays different shots.

## Good Shot Distribution Leads to Good Shots

It is also important that each player knows his role on the team. Coach should try to put two long-ball shooters on a line complemented by two inside shooters. To get a good idea of who the good long-ball shooters are on the team, just rate the players by their shooting percentage at the shooting board in practice. A challenge for a coach in a game is to get the ball to the player who has the "hot stick."

## Who Shoots on the Team Leads to Good Shots

Offense is not a game of equality. The coach does not believe in equal opportunity on offense. Players must know their roles (passer, scorer, picker, screener, loose-ball player). If a player wants to shoot in a game, he must prove it in practice by shooting at least 20 percent (one out of five shots). Coach's philosophy is to score first and keep on scoring, so the coach must base his offensive attack around shooters who can shoot 20 percent. Players have to learn that when they are open they have to take the shot. Players are also encouraged to shoot around screens, using the defender as a screen when there is a good gap or space.

# V. Shooting Progression

## First Progression is to Use Good Shooting Technique

To begin with, a shooter has to have a good shooting form or the right mechanics. He gets this by practicing shadow shooting with no ball. When he starts to practice form shooting with the ball, he shouldn't worry about putting the ball in the net as much as having the right form. Remember that shooters are made, not born. Attention to detail and feedback is important here for the shooter, as there is a right way and a wrong way to shoot. But as a coach, do not force every player to shoot the same way; if he can score, don't mess with him.

## Second Progression is Working on Accuracy—the Most Important Thing

- Once a player has the proper form, then he starts to work on his accuracy over power or speed at first. Accuracy is the most important part of shooting. The shooter has to practice "picking" or placing his shot at the open spot rather than just shooting at the net, i.e., "bombing" his shot. When good players shoot, they force the goalie to make a great save. They don't shoot right at the goalie, as that doesn't force the goalie to do anything to make a save. Great shooters don't just shoot the ball straight and hard, they "think" their way around a goalie.

- Players must understand that long shots do not have to be hard to go in; accuracy and deception are far more important.
- The shooter has to learn to pause for a split-second, if he has the time, after he gets the ball so he does not rush his shot. This slight hesitation move will give him time to take a quick look to pick his spot and then shoot.
- Occasionally, a shooter may not have time to look at his target, or just knows by instinct that his checker is right behind him, but he knows by intuition that he has an opening. Most times he usually "picks" an open spot on the net, but sometimes he just shoots at no spot. As soon as the ball hits his pocket, he shoots. This quick release before the goalie is set is called a "quick-stick" and is a much underrated shot. The quick-stick is used effectively more in today's game for the element of surprise and particularly against goalies that do not move very well laterally or quickly because of all their padding. So it is certainly best to shoot quickly when the goalie is not expecting it or knowing he is out of position.

  **Remember**: "Power is nothing without control."

*Josh Sanderson of the Boston Blazers of the NLL* uses what he calls a "memory shot," i.e., knowing what he is going to do before he does it. This could be an "instinct shot" or a fake shot where he sets up the goalie with a fake shot and reacts to the goalie's mistake.

## Third Progression is Power

1. Once a shooter gets accuracy, he must then work on the hardness or speed of his shot. He must learn to "explode" into his shot. Shooters should not have to snap the wrist

harder the farther back they go, they should keep the same wrist and stick movement through all different distances. Remember, if a player is trying to shoot farther out from his range, he ends up forcing his shot, and strength now becomes a factor and technique goes out the door.

2. The shooter gets power into his shot by:
   - The position of the ball in the pocket is so important in getting power into one's shot. So shooting the ball from the tip of the stick will give a shooter more power into his shot. The "shooting pocket" is when the ball is sitting on the last or bottom shooting string rather than in the middle of the pocket.
   - Using his legs, i.e., taking a wide stance and moving his body weight from his back foot to his front foot to get his body weight behind his shot. This transfer of weight is one of the most effective ways of generating power into his shot.
   - "Cocking the stick" farther back to put more swing or momentum into his shot for power. The top-hand arm takes the stick straight back and then pulls it straight forward for this momentum.
   - Grasping the stick with his hands slightly closer together than the passing position creates more momentum into his shot and thus more power.
   - Pulling the stick straight forward with the top-hand arm and snapping the cocked wrists forward gives more whip and stick speed and as a consequence generates more power in his shot. Here, the bottom-hand holds the stick tighter and, thereby becomes more involved in the shot.
   - The hips start out at a 45-degree angle to the net, then, on the shot, they end up rotating along with the shoulders facing the net.
   - Having a good follow-through of the stick after the ball leaves the pocket gives

power and is executed by extending fully the top-hand arm with the tip of the stick facing the target.

- A player has to have something behind his shot, but he shouldn't bomb it. To get this power into their shot some players need a wind up, because they don't have a heavy shot. So, instead they hold the stick at a 45-degree angle to the floor and out to the side of their body for a three-quarter shot, or they hold their stick over their shoulder parallel to the floor for a wind up into their overhand shot. Both these positions will give the shooter more power into his shot. Ideally, the best thing a shooter can have is a hard shot and the ability to put it where he wants it.

**Recall:** To get power on the overhand shot stress: "winding up" to shoot, stick level to floor, release the ball when it is behind one's head, and do a "little cock" or twist of wrists before release.

## Fourth Progression is Being Ready to Shoot for a Quick Release

1. Quick release for long-ball shooter:
   - Being physically and mentally prepared to shoot the long-ball before receiving the pass is very important.
   - Before catching the ball, the experienced long-ball shooter should be ready to shoot the ball before he gets it. He does this by putting his stick's target back behind his body with both arms extended backward in a "cocked position" ready to shoot. Feet are shoulder width (wide base) apart for a good solid base, in case of contact, and the shooting foot is ready to step into the shot.
   - Only experienced players should think about their shots before catching the ball. Beginners should concentrate on catching the ball first, then think of shooting.
   - When the shooter is completely open

and has time to shoot, he can take the stick back to "cock" it, turn the body at a 45-degree angle to the net, take a hop-step, and then step with the front foot into the shot

2. Quick release for in-close or mid-range shot:
   - Being ready to shoot the "quick-stick" shot, the shooter must have his stick up and ready to shoot for a quicker release by holding the stick beside or in front of his body as the shorter release means a quicker release.
   - For mid-range shots, it is important to have the stick "up and ready" to catch and shoot. When in the scoring area, always keep the stick up, not down, at the side of the body. Not only should the stick be ready to shoot the ball, but the feet should be ready to shoot with the back foot planted and weight on it and the lead (front) foot out in front.
   - Getting into a good scoring position before receiving the ball saves time on getting his shot off.
   - The mid-range shooter can shoot without cocking the stick or taking a step when cutting across the top, one step ahead of his check or when he does not have much time to shoot. More players in the NLL are "cocking" or "winding up" less and just holding their stick beside their head to catch and shoot all in one motion. So learn to take "quick shots," not too much of a wind up, and just shoot wherever you catch the ball in the pocket. The reason for this is to get the shot off quicker, giving the goalie less chance of moving and stopping their shot.

## Fifth Progression is Getting the "Feel" of the Shot

The feel of a good shot is important because the feeling of a good shot makes one feel confident. When a shooter has the "feel," everything is done without thinking, the mind is free of thought, and the shot is effortless. To get in this "groove," master the mechanics, trust one's instincts, feel the swing without thinking, and get into the proper state of mind. He should "be one with the ball" and "become the stick." A shooter should never fear failure, never have tight muscles, never lose his concentration, and always focus on the "present" moment.

## Sixth Progression is to Concentrate on the Target

On a straight shot, a shooter must learn to concentrate on the target or the open spot all the way through the shot, that is, before, during, and after the shot, yet not telegraph his shot. He must see the whole net using his peripheral vision, yet not look directly at where he is going to shoot because some goalies watch the eyes of the shooter. *(See Diagram #16)*

## Seventh Progression is Working on the Fake-Shot—a Move of Deception

When stick-faking, the shooter tries to dictate the shot rather than letting the goalie determine it, because some goalies like to give the shooter a spot to shoot at, then take it away.

So, when shooting, the shooter should have a preconceived idea before he shoots, if he has the time, he should fake the shot to try to move the goalie, to get a reaction from him, or at least to "freeze" him, i.e., the goalie will tighten up because he thinks a shot is coming. Usually, the stick-fake is the bad angle, setting the goalie up, and the shot is the good angle. The key in stick-faking is to be deceptive: faking with the body and shoulders; faking with the stick; and faking with the eyes, not the head. A good faker should do something out of the ordinary that a goalie would seldom think of.

### 1. Long-Ball Overhand Fake-Shot
*A. The Stick-Fake*
One type of stick-fake is from a hard overhand stick-fake back into an overhand shot. A player "fakes" his overhand shot by starting the forward motion of his stick as if he is really going to shoot, then he "checks" or stops his shot by rotating in strongly with his top-hand wrist and rotating in lightly with his bottom-hand wrist. Basically, the top hand grips the stick fairly tight for control and the bottom hand holds the stick loosely so that the stick can rotate easily in the grip. This turning inward motion of the wrist with his top-hand turns the

### Diagram #16: Near Side/Far Side of Net

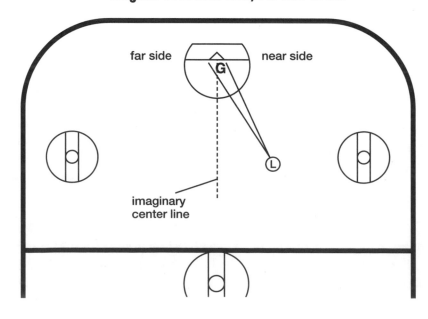

stick clockwise, keeping the ball in the netting. It is important this motion is done quickly and hard to make it look real. The shooter must "sell the product." Speed and fluidity are very important in stick-faking. (See section below on Strategies for Close-In Fake Shots.)

**Variation:** Some players like to stick-fake using the bottom-hand as the power hand. The bottom-hand wrist turns inward rotating the stick counter-clockwise. The stick just turns in the top-hand grip.

*B. The Hesitation Move*
To counter a goalie watching his eyes, a shooter can look at the far corner and pretend to shoot at that corner by holding the open "face" of the stick toward the far corner. This is not a fake-shot motion, but more of a hesitation move. As he brings the stick off his shoulder, he hesitates slightly, then turns the stick inward and in one continuous motion continues with his stick shooting at the near corner.

*C. The Body Fake*
To complement the stick-fake, the shooter can make the goalie think he is going to shoot at the goalie's short-side by dropping his front shoulder, making it look like he is going to shoot at the near-corner, but instead of pulling his stick across his body he continues the stick straight ahead and shoots at the far-side of the net.

*D. Eye Fake*
When stick-faking, the shooter should always look at the corner at which he is faking, since some goalies watch the shooter's eyes to anticipate the shot. For example, to counter a goalie watching his eyes, a shooter can look at the far-corner and fake a shot at that corner then shoot at the near-corner.

**2. Long-Ball Sidearm Fake-Shot**
From a hard sidearm stick-fake into a fluid, quick overhand shot, or from a hard sidearm stick-fake into a sidearm shot. This sidearm

stick-fake is the same wrist motion as the overhand stick-fake. The shooter must make sure on "checking the shot" or stopping his shot by turning his top-hand wrist up strongly. (See section below on Strategies for Close-In Fake Shots.)

## Overhand Long-Ball Shooting Strategy

**Strategy of Taking Comfort Shot**
A player can use a variety of shots in a game, overhand, underhand, and sidearm, but usually he uses the shot he feels most comfortable with through practice.

**Strategy of Mixing Up the Shot Placements**
Mixing up the shot placement is very important when shooting. The shooter wants to keep the goalie wondering where he is going to place his shot: at the corners, off the hips, under the glove hand, between the legs, or off the ankles. He can make it a straight shot or a bounce shot. Bounce shots are a much underrated and a very difficult shot for a goalie to stop. If a shooter sees no open top spots, he can bounce the ball down by the side of the goalie's foot.

**Strategy of Just Picking an Open Spot and Shooting**
Even though some goalies, especially reflex goalies, like to give the short-side, when the overhand long-ball shooter cuts across the top, he should still look to shoot for the far corner of the net most of the time. Most shooters believe they can shoot faster than a goalie can move, so just pick an open spot and shoot. So, don't think "shot," think "score."

Sidearm shooters, when cutting across, should also look to shoot for the far-top corner. The top-corner near-side is a very difficult shot for a sidearm shooter.

**Remember:** A lot of times what a shooter's eyes do not see the "open" spot, his stick's head can "see" (for lack of a better word), especially if the stick is held high above the head or out to the side and in front of the body.

*Josh Sanderson of the Boston Blazers of the NLL:* His favorite spot is the far-top corner, but he will go somewhere else if he has to. He shoots to his strength. He doesn't try to shoot to the goalie's strength too much and he tries not to let the goalie get into his head. He shoots his shot to beat the goalie where he knows his personal strength is.

### Strategy of Placement of Long Shots
- Long shot for far top corner
- Long shot for near top corner
- Long bounce shot for far top corner
- Long bounce shot for near corner
- Long low shot for far corner
- Long low shot for near corner

*Note: Great shooters look to shoot all the time!*

### Strategy of Knowing the Goalie's Weaknesses and His Favorite Moves

It is also important to know the goalie's weaknesses, his favorite moves, and whether he is an angle goalie or a reflex goalie.
- Some goalies like to bait a shooter into shooting at an open spot and then taking it away by stepping in front of the open spot on the shot, so to counter this move just fake to that open corner and pick the opposite corner.
- Some goalies are weak on long low shots, so take long top-corner shots or shoot under the glove hand, or waist down.
- Some goalies drop or do a "butterfly" on a lot of long shots, so shoot the overhand shot for the top corner, or take a long bounce shot to the top corner, or down around his feet.
- Some goalies are good covering the upper part of the net, so fake high and bounce low, or shoot a long underhand shot on the stick side, or take a long bounce shot to top corner.
- Some goalies are weak between their legs, so look to shoot long bounce between his legs.
- Some goalies are "jumpers," in other words,

they jump up or "go" for fakes, so close in the shooter should make sure he gives the goalie one or two good fakes when cutting across in front of the net.
- Some big goalies just fill the net without moving, they don't move at all on fakes, so a shooter should fake at him, knowing he is not going to react, and then shoot around him, or get him moving sideways and shoot near-side. Whatever a shooter does, he shouldn't just shoot at the goalie. It happens a lot.
- Some goalies cover the whole top of the net close in, so fake high, then bounce or shoot low.

### Know the Strategy of Reflex Goalies
- Most reflex goalies will give the shooter the short-side of the net because it is usually the shorter distance to move to cover that open spot.
- A shooter should have a counter to this "give-and-take-away" move by the reflex goalie. For example, if a goalie gives a left-hand shooter his left side of the net (short-side) to shoot at, the shooter, while winding up, will look at the short-side, slightly drop his right shoulder, and hesitate a split-second with his stick. These moves will give the goalie the impression that the shooter is going to come across his body with his stick and throw the ball into the short-side. As the goalie starts to move across to cover the short-side of the net, instead of pulling the stick across his body the shooter will continue the stick straight ahead from the shoulder position and pick the far-side of the net.

### Strategy of Stick-Faking to Get a Reaction
- On long shots, a player can play "cat-and-mouse" with the goalie, i.e., create a stick-faking action to get a reaction from the goalie. A shooter should always be thinking ahead of the goalie or trying to anticipate

what the goalie is thinking. It is important that a player remembers where he took his last shot and use this information to set up the goalie on his next shot with stick-fakes and shooting motions.

- For example, if a shooter scored on a long short-side shot, the goalie thinks he will try it again. However, this time, before shooting, the shooter hesitates a spit-second with his stick and drops his shoulder slightly making the goalie think he is going to shoot again for the short-side (he stick-fakes to the short-side). As the goalie moves across to cover the short-side, the shooter continues his stick straight ahead for the long-side.

**Strategy of Knowing the Prime Scoring Area**

Players should shoot from their "Prime Scoring Area" 90 percent of the time. But sometimes a player is caught in a situation where he is on his wrong side of the floor with the ball. If he is still in the "Secondary Scoring Area," he should shoot the ball if he has an opening or thinks he can set up the goalie. *(See Diagram #15)*

Once a player passes the Imaginary Center Line, the most natural spot to shoot at is the

new far-side of the net, i.e., shooting across both the shooter's body and the goalie's body. A goalie will often give this new far-side to a player shooting from his wrong side. A slight shoulder drop or fake shot will give the goalie the impression the shooter is going to shoot to this new far-side, and he may move back across to cover the new far-side. At this time the shooter comes straight through with his stick and shoots the ball at this new near-side. *(See Diagram #17)*

*Note: It is better for younger players to hang onto the ball once they have passed the Imaginary Center Line rather than shooting. They can just reset the offense and work for a better shot.*

**Strategy of a Shooter Hiding His Shot**

Some shooters like to hide the stick from the goalie. This is done by turning the body sideways to the goalie and holding the stick behind the shoulder to block his view. They believe the goalie is like a batter in baseball: the later a batter sees the ball coming at him, the harder it is for him to react and hit it. Without the goalie seeing the ball early, a shooter might get a goalie guessing where he

**Diagram #17: New Near Side, New Far Side of Net**

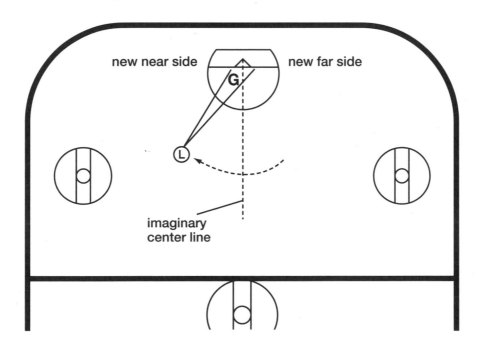

might place his shot and that's what a shooter wants.

*John Tavares of the Buffalo Bandits of the NLL,* one of the greatest goal-scorers in lacrosse, on his wind up to shoot, he keeps his stick hidden behind his body so the goalie can't see the ball. He tries to hide the ball a little bit more so he brings his stick back more.

*Josh Sanderson of the Boston Blazers of the NLL* also keeps the ball hidden behind him when he is ready to shoot or pass.

### Strategy of Scoring on the Breakaway Shot

- On a breakaway, shooters, as they approach the goalie, break their wrists, not to fake, but to "cradle" the ball while the stick is vertical to get a "feel" of the ball.
- Breakaway shooters should run down the off-center of the floor, not down the middle or straight at the goalie, then cut across slightly to move the goalie sideways.
- Here a shooter decides to shoot or fake depending on how the goalie is playing his position.
- Some players like to keep the stick out from the body and high and just shoot.
- Others, when they get a breakaway, like to wait to get close in on the goalie. Most goalies expect at least one fake in this type of a situation. This is all the more reason for the shooter to just pick a spot and shoot.

*Dan Stroup, formerly of the Toronto Rock, of the NLL* when he shoots close in he holds his stick way out in front of his body for the far-corner shot and if that open spot is not there, he shoots back inside to the near-corner.

### Strategy When in a Shooting "Slump"

Some tips to help shooters in a slump: they have to learn to laugh and just relax, not force their shots. Go back to basics and practice, practice, practice!

**Remember:** In shooting, there is always room for improvement, because no one can score 100 percent of the time, although a player must have the confidence that he will score most of the time.

### Being Aware of Problems in Shooting

If a player can make shots in practice, what's the problem with making them in a game if it's the same shot?

- Problem of not believing in himself.
- Problem of telegraphing the shot. Shooter is looking directly at where he is going to shoot.
- Problem of taking bad shots—bad angle, nothing to shoot at, shooting on wrong side of the floor, being pressured, by being cross-checked or hand-checked, by a defender.
- Problem of rushing, hurrying, or forcing his shot. Shooter needs discipline. If it is not a good shot, then he shouldn't shoot (patience).
- Problem of bombing his shot, just winding up and shooting at no particular spot.
- Problem of the shooter being inaccurate, he can't hit the spot.
- Problem of lack of concentration, shooter does not focus on the open spot.

*Gavin Prout of the Edmonton Rush of the NLL* talks about his strategy when shooting:

- Gavin feels deception is the key to shooting. Body positioning can make the goalie think you are shooting one way when you are actually shooting the other way. "As a right-handed shooter, if I drop my left shoulder the goalie may think I am going to shoot at the near-side of the net, whereas I will shoot at the far-side."
- Stick positioning is important. You can use your own body as a screen by hiding your stick behind your body and making it harder for the goalie to see the ball on the actual release. You can also take screen shots by using your defender as a screen by shooting around him.
- When on the crease, you should use a quick hard fake and then shoot the ball to where

the goalie isn't. A quick fake will usually freeze the goalie or make him jump out of position to give you more of the net to shoot at. One fake is more than enough to set up the goalie.

- See the net behind the goalie when shooting, not the goaltender. If you focus on the goaltender as your target, you are more apt to shoot at him rather than the netting.
- Always know where the net is, even when your back is to it. This will allow the shooter to shoot quicker, not having to turn and find the net and then look for an opening. You can catch the goalie "off guard" by knowing where the net is before you even look at it.
- Use the length of the stick to shoot around the goalie. The stick can "see" around a goaltender better than your eyes can. You can use the full length of your stick to reach around the goalie's body and place it in the empty net.
- Use your defender as a screen on outside shots. Most of the defenders don't take the proper angle to take away your shooting lane. As the defender is running out at you, use him as a screen and shoot around him.
- "Some goalies read my eyes, so as a shooter, I try not to look and focus at the spot I want to shoot at. By not looking at the spot, the goalie cannot anticipate where I am going shooting at."
- "As a shooter, I do not want to shoot at the same spot too many times in a row and become predictable, and that's the last thing I want to do, become predictable."

## VI. Practicing to be a Long-Ball Shooter

### Great Shooters Practice the Long-Ball Shot

Great shooters are made, not born. A player must practice shooting on his own. The three keys to becoming a great shooter are: Practice! Practice! Practice! Most great shooters are made or developed through shooting practice. Some players are "natural" goal scorers, yet they still have to practice. Confidence with the stick results from repetition of shots in an arena or against a wall (200 shots per day). It helps a player's confidence if he shoots at specific targets, such as spots on the wall or a net drawn on the wall.

When practicing one's shooting technique remember to shoot relaxed, not forcing the shot; to shoot at game speed (not slow); to shoot from the distance in a game (not in close); and to shoot from the spot you would normally shoot from in a game.

### Great Shooters Know How to Fix Their Sticks *(See Chapter 1, pg. 12)*

A good carpenter cannot do a good job unless he has the right tools and looks after them. Similarly, a good lacrosse player cannot become a great shooter unless he looks after his stick. A player should always be adjusting and playing with his shooting strings and netting, but only when he can't get a feel for his stick or when the flight of the ball doesn't feel right.

There are three philosophies of fixing a stick that "hooks" during a game:

- **Fixing a Stick That Hooks by Changing His Mechanics**
  Most players do stick maintenance before a practice or before a game to get it working right. In a game, if a player knows his stick is "hooking" or shooting low, he can adapt by adjusting his release of the ball, by releasing the ball farther back behind his body. At least he will know what it is doing wrong and how to compensate for it. If he changes the stick during the game, he will not know what the stick is going to do.
- **Fixing a Stick That Hooks In-Between Periods**
  Other players feel a player should never use his stick in a game if it is "hooking." If a player has to compensate for a "hook" in his stick by changing his mechanics, he will

be in trouble. A player then repairs the stick either during the game or between periods where adjustments can be made and the stick practiced with, before going back into the game. Another possibility is to have a back-up stick already broken in on the bench to use until the player's number one stick is fixed.

- **Fixing a Stick That Hooks During the Game**

  Some players make the adjustment during the game by fixing the shooting string or netting on the spot. They check the release of the ball by holding the stick in a horizontal position and pulling the stick toward themselves, spinning the ball out of the pocket to see if it rolls out properly.

  *Note: Great shooters know how to take a stick apart and restring it. Players who have a great love for the game take the time to find out how the tool they use works.*

## Great Shooters Work on the "Feel" of a Good Long-Ball Shot

- Practice shooting with no ball and eyes closed.
- Practice shooting the ball with eyes closed. Memorize the "feel" of the ball in the stick as you shoot.
- Practice shooting, concentrating on the "feel" of a good shot rather than just hitting the target. Shooting is muscle memory and eye-hand coordination. Coaches want players to develop the proper "feeling" of a great shot.

## Great Shooters Work on a Progression for Long-Ball Shooting

- Develop good "form" first. The coach has to give feedback regarding form.
- Develop accuracy next. Placement of the shot is more important than power in the shot. If the shot is released and correctly placed, no goalie will stop it. Shooters feel

they can shoot faster than a goalie can move. A good shot is not an accident. A player hits the spot on purpose by using good form and practice.

- Work on speed or power third. Too much emphasis is put on power when a combination of power, quickness, and accuracy is needed. Shoot it right, shoot it hard with accuracy, and shoot the same way, every time. Work on consistency through repetition.
- Work on quickness of shot, "quick-stick," by keeping the stick up beside the head, ready to shoot so a shooter can just catch and shoot all in one motion.
- Work on getting the "feel" for a great shot.
- Work on seeing the whole net, yet concentrating on the target.
- Finally, work on deception and faking.

## Great Shooters Practice Long-Ball Shooting at an Empty Net

- The most important thing in practicing shooting into an empty net is scoring, i.e., hitting the spot one aims for. This positive reinforcement of scoring gives the player good feelings and tremendous confidence from seeing the ball being retained by the netting and hearing the "thud" on the twine.
- A player should pick only one corner and shoot at it until he can hit it consistently. Practicing this way tells the player a few things. First, that his stick is working properly, and second, that he can hit what he is aiming at. Being satisfied the ball is going where he wants it to go gives a player the confidence that if the goalie gives him that opening in a game he can score. Then, the player progresses to shooting at another corner.
- Start shooting in close and work out. Practice like a golfer, start with the short-game and then increase in distance. If the

shooter misses the spot he was aiming for he steps in, if the shooter makes the shot he was aiming for he steps back.

- Players must practice the type of shots they will take in a game. Try to stay within one's own abilities whether it is faking, shooting long, or shooting close in. If a player tries something different, especially in a game, he will most likely botch it.

- Shooter practices his shot at game speed, from his game spots, and with game moves. The shooter can place "Xs" on the floor, so he knows exactly where to shoot from.

- When practicing shooting, follow the rule of "don't make the same mistake twice in a row." For example, a player aiming for the top corner should not miss it two times in a row without making a mental adjustment. If he shoots high the first time, he should adjust his shot so that he either hits the corner or at least his shot is lower.

- When practicing, keep a record of the number of shots taken and scored. A good game shooting objective is 20 percent, i.e., score one out of five shots attempted, but in a practice, shooting against a goalie, the objective should be slightly higher, (40 percent, or two out of five). Shooting against the shooting board or an empty net, the objective should be 60 percent, or three out of five.

- A player, when practicing shooting on his own, must discipline himself. If he makes his shooting objective he rewards himself by maybe taking a water-break. If he does not make his shooting objective he punishes himself by running sprints or doing push-ups.

- When correcting his shot, use the principle of "simple and straight" and eliminate any excess motion.

- Make sure when "cocking" the stick to shoot that the butt points at the target, and the stick is held horizontally over the stick shoulder.

- Make sure on the follow-through that the butt of the stick ends up touching the top-hand arm elbow or in the vicinity, and the head of the stick ends up pointing at the target.

- Sometimes the best helper in correcting a player's shot is his own goalie, because he sees his teammate shoot more than anyone.

## Great Shooters Practice Long-Ball Shooting at the "Shooting Board"

The shooting board is a shooter's laboratory. This is where great shooters are made.

The shooting board is a 4' x 4' or 4'6" x 4' wooden or fiberglass board cut out diagonally at the four corners. The corners, at the beginning, should be cut out fairly large so the players can score easily, gaining lots of confidence. The players should take a high repetition of shots to help acquire this confidence.

**Variety of cuts:** Cut out on the mid-side of the board for hip shots, or cut out bigger corners at the top corners for bounce shots.

The coach can use the board to teach shooting. The player stands where he likes to shoot from and receives cross-floor passes from his passing partner and shoots at the cut-out corners. The reason a coach likes using the shooting board is players can shoot the ball as hard as they can and as many times as they can without hurting a goalie, which happens in shooting drills.

## Some Competitions to Put Pressure on the Shooter Shooting at the "Shooting Board" Are:

- *A "Ladder"*
  Charting all players to see what their shooting percentage is. A player should average around 25 percent (five made shots out of 20 taken). Keep a "ladder" with a list of the players' names and a list of the players' percentages. Have a rule that a player can't shoot in a game unless he shoots 25 percent against the shooting board.

- *In a Row*
  Seeing how many goals a player can get in a row. Chart the results to create a healthy competition on the team, or use candy as an incentive. If a player scores two in a row, he gets two candies; if a player scores three in a row, he gets three candies, etc. Or have it that a player can't leave practice until he scores two in a row.

- *"Bump" Shooting Drill*
  The whole team lines up, and the rule is the player must score before the player behind him scores. If player misses on his first shot, he must pursue the rebound and take a close-in shot. If he still misses, he must keep on shooting close-in shots until he scores. If the player behind in the line scores, before the first player does, the first player is out of the drill.

- *Timed Shooting*
  Chart the number of goals a player can score in 30 seconds, or 60 seconds.

- *Shooting on the Move*
  The player shoots on the move. Two passers pass to the shooter for 60 seconds. The shooter must be in constant motion, so the drill also becomes a conditioner.

- *Out-of-Range Shooting*
  Practicing out-of-range shooting requires the player to shoot out farther than he normally would.

- *Variety of Shots*
  Have players to take a variety of shots—overhand, sidearm, underhand, etc., and to shoot with a purpose.

## VII. Close-In Shooting and Types of Close-In Shots

- The player who plays around the crease area executes close-in shots rather than long shots. These are short-distance shots that are made with little wind up or no wind up at all, called "quick-stick," and in a lot of traffic. This close-in shooter, also known as a creaseman, grips his stick differently than the long-ball shooter.

- The top hand grips the stick fairly tight with the fingers, while the bottom hand holds the stick loosely, so that the stick can rotate easily with all the faking he will do. This grip allows for an increased range of motion, during stick-handling close in.

- The creaseman relies heavily on his finesse, fluidity, accuracy, quickness in his feet and stick, and in his ability to manipulate the goalie around the net. With close-in shooting, the shooter does not need power as much as accuracy and quickness of the shot. Therefore, he does not need to "cock" his stick or step into his shot.

The close-in shooter has two main weapons: he can just pick and shoot for the open spot, or he can stick-fake the goalie trying to get a reaction from him.

**CLA Rule Regarding in the Crease**—a player can fake in-and-out as much as he wants over the crease semi-circle line, it's his body that cannot touch the crease line, especially his feet. The shooting player may not step on the goal crease, but his stick may enter the goal crease in the act of shooting or faking. It is important to know that sticks can break the plane of the semi-circle crease.

The same rule applies in the NLL that the body of the player may not touch the floor in the crease prior to the ball entering the goal. A player can break the crease plane on a shot with his stick as long as he does not touch the crease line on the floor. The difference from the CLA is a player can reach in the crease to pick up or knock the ball into the net.

*Note: Creasemen, because they are closest to the net, have to go after any rebounds off the goalie or off the boards.*

## I. Strategies for Close-In Straight-Shots

### Close-In Shooter Must Work on Getting His Shot Away Quickly

Players can stick-fake close in on the goalie, only if they have time and space. A lot of times a player does not stick-fake close in to the net because he has no time, i.e., he's expecting a hit from a defender, the goalie may be out of position for a split-second, or because there is an opening and he just shoots it.

### Close-In Shooter Catches Ball in Middle of Pocket

When shooters are close in, some players feel it is better to catch the ball in the middle of the pocket rather than the tip, because it is easier to place the ball and it is quicker to get their shot away.

### Close-In Shooter Must Protect His Stick

A close-in shooter must keep his stick in close to his body to protect it, because when around the net the defender is also close, ready to check his stick or his body. But whenever the defender is not a defensive threat, the stick can be extended from the body to move around, over, or under the goalie, or to quick-stick a pass.

### Close-In Use the Three-Foot Advantage of the Stick

The head of the stick moves more quickly than the goalie and gives a shooter a 42" advantage. So, a shooter should have in his repertoire a strategy of two moves: while keeping the stick head still, moving the stick from an inside-out position, i.e., from a vertical to a horizontal shooting position, or moving the stick from an outside-inside position, i.e., from a horizontal to a vertical shooting position. Players should mix up these stick moves, so that goalies cannot categorize them, and thereby anticipate these moves.

### Straight Close-In Shot to the Far-Side of the Net

- A shooter can set the goalie up for a far-side shot by keeping the hands and stick in an overhand position, in close to the body to begin with, and at the last possible moment before shooting, he extends his arms and moves his stick out in a sidearm position and shoots around the goalie putting the ball into the far-corner. The shooter should avoid showing the sidearm shot until the last second. The three possible moves are: from an overhand position to a sidearm shot, from an overhand position to an overhand shot, and from a sidearm position to a sidearm shot. This far-corner shooting move is done about 80 percent of the time.

- If the situation permits, some players extend the stick out as far as they can and put the ball into the far-side, or they just take a big step in front of the net. That step, plus the reach of the arms and the stick itself, gives the shooter extra distance to shoot around the goalie.

- A shooter must out-think and "out-quick" goalies that rely heavily on angles. Because they have slow lateral movement, the shooter should come around the goalie on his shot as both he and his stick can move more quickly laterally. Again, he can reach around the goalie with his stick or take one step out in front of the net and shoot around him.

    **Remember:** A shooter should start with the stick close into the body so when he is shooting he can reach over or around the goalie.

- Against large goalies it is even better to run across in front of the net any time a shooter can, rather than running down the side of the floor. Many shooters reduce their scoring opportunity by running down the side of the net. Cutting across the top going from the near-side to the far-side of the net gives a shooter more shooting options and takes away the large goalie's asset of playing angles and works on the goalie's liability, his inability to move laterally quickly.

- The one problem in cutting across in front of the net is the shooter puts himself in a position of taking a hit by a defender. That's why some players hesitate about cutting across in front of the net, because of the chances of being hit. To protect oneself from a solid hit from behind, the close-in shooter should bend down low so that the hit will ride up his back and not take direct hit on his back.

### Straight Close-In Shot to the Near Side of the Net

- A shooter can start with his stick in close to his body and if he sees an opening at the near-side of the net he just shoots from this overhand position.
- The shooter can make the goalie think he is shooting to the far-side by holding the stick out from his body, either in an overhand or sidearm position, then quickly and in one continuous motion bring it back in close to his body to take an overhand shot to the near-side. The two possible moves are: from an overhand position into an overhand shot, or from a sidearm position into an overhand shot.
- The shooter can step with his inside foot, i.e., left foot or back foot for a left-handed shot, out in front of the net with his stick held out to the side and hesitate a shot to the far- side (not a fake) to move the goalie or at least "freeze" him, then bring his stick back to the near-side. A slight hesitation makes all the difference when in close. Patience is a very difficult skill to teach. If the goalie moves to the far-side, fluidity and speed are essential in shooting back to the near-side.
- If cutting across in front of net, the general rule is to put the ball back where the shooter came from, i.e., near-side. But now with the larger nets players should think about going

to the far-side of the net 80 percent of the time.

*Note: A good move for a close-in shooter is to look at one corner and take a straight shot at the other corner.*

### The Quick-Stick Shot

The quick-stick shot is a quick catch-and-shoot shot with no wind-up at all. The quick-stick shot occurs when the shooter is wide open at the side of the net for a crease-to-crease pass, from a diagonal pass, or when cutting in front of the net wide open. If the shooter plays in tight around the net he won't need much of a wind up. He just uses his wrists.

**Variation:** Put the stick above the head with the arms extended upward, and on catching the ball the shooter shoots downward without bringing his stick back. This shot is more of an element of surprise as the goalie expects the shooter to bring the stick down or take it back to shoot.

### Placement of Straight Close-In Shots

Shoot for far-top corner
Shoot for near-top corner
Shoot down around ankles (far or near side, straight or bounce)
Shoot medium shot around the hips or glove hand
Shoot between the legs
Shoot bounce shot for far-top corner
Shoot bounce shot for near corner

- Between-the-legs shot works best against goalies that have a tendency to lift their sticks. But usually this shot is a "cop out" for shooters who just throw the ball low between the legs and hope for the best because of defensive pressure or lack of imagination or concentration.
- Most shooters have a natural tendency to shoot for the far-side of the net, but they should be aware of where the glove-hand side of the goalie is also. Shooting under the

glove hand, whether a bounce or a straight shot, is a very good strategy requiring the goalie to make a difficult body, stick, or leg save.

- Some players like to shoot low most times around the hip because of poor lateral movement of the goalie, thereby exaggerating their follow-through to make sure the ball goes low. Shooters aim low because even if the goalie gets a piece of the ball it could still go in. In fact, some players try to bounce their shots off the goalie's body. By shooting low to the hips they can only miss the net one way, to the side. Whereas, if a shooter shoots for the top corner he has two possible ways to miss the net, over the top and to the side.

## 2. Strategies for Close-In Fake-Shots

### The Fake

To execute a great fake a shooter should think in his mind that he is going to shoot, make it look real, then "check" or stop himself from shooting. On the fake, the shooter has to turn both wrists in to "check" the ball from falling out. The top hand can be higher on the grip when faking or the top hand can grip just below the mid-shaft for quicker and more fakes. Shooter can fake with the bottom hand or the top hand it is a matter of preference. On the fake make it one quick hard fake, not too many fakes and not too fancy.

### Have a Patented Move

Every shooter should have a patented move (his best shot, his favorite corner) that he can always depend on under pressure. Although he should use the move he feels most confident with most of the time, he should mix up his fakes, since good goalies categorize shooters: favorite fake, favorite spot, favorite side.

The shooter should remember what shot or stick-fake he used the last time and if the goalie

stopped or came close to stopping the shot. If the goalie did stop the shot, the shooter should set the goalie up the next time.

### Techniques of Close-In Fake-Shots

One technique of faking is using only the wrists (no arm action) on the fake. The other technique of faking is using two different methods, such as an overhand fake to a sidearm shot, where the shooter would fake with both, wrists and arms. If in-close cutting across in front of the net, a shooter can fake short-side and then shoot far-side, or he can fake far-side and shoot short-side, or fake high and shoot low or bounce.

### From a Hard Overhand Fake to an Overhand Shot—Near Side

a. From a hard overhand stick-fake to the near-side of the net back into an overhand shot to the near-side. The shooter puts the ball back to where he just faked usually because the goalie didn't move or commit to the first fake.

b. From a hard overhand stick-fake to the near side of the net into an overhand shot to the far-side. Goalie reacted or committed to near-side fake leaving far-side of net open.

**Photo 61:** Close-In Fake-Shot—a hard overhand fake to near side (goalie reacted to fake)

**Photo 62:** Close-In Fake-Shot—to an overhand shot far-side (far-side of net open)

c. From a hard overhand stick-fake to the far-side of the net, back into an overhand shot to the near-side. Once the shooter scores on the far side, that opens up the near side all night.

d. When in-close shooting with the big nets, fake high with an overhand shot, then shoot low or bounce with an overhand shot.

*Note: Using the in-close overhand shot gives the shooter lots of options.*

### From a Hard Overhand Fake to a Sidearm Shot—Far Side

From a hard overhand stick-fake to the near-side into a fluid sidearm shot to the far-side. This is one of the most common and one of the best fakes a shooter uses.

**Variation:** Make a quick-stick fake to near-side, bring stick across body, then step over to the outside and step back in for a far-corner shot. The player just drops the ball over the shoulder of the goalie for the far-top corner.

### From a Hard Sidearm Fake to an Overhand Shot—Near Side

From a hard sidearm stick-fake to the far-side into a fluid, quick overhand shot to the near-side. The far sidearm stick-fake greatly influences the goalie who knows that a sidearm shot can, in most cases, only go to the far-side of the net, therefore he leaves more room on the near-side in anticipation of a far-side sidearm shot. The shooter then brings the stick back quickly across his body to the near side.

*Gary Gait, formerly of the Philadelphia Wings, of the NLL* liked to fake to the far-side of the net and come back to the near- side.

**Photo 63:** Close-in Fake-Shot—From a hard overhand fake near side (goalie reacted to fake)

**Photo 64:** Close-in Fake-Shot—To a sidearm shot—far side (far-side of net open)

**Photo 65:** Close-In Fake-Shot—From a hard sidearm fake to far side (goalie reacts or commits to far-side of net)

**Photo 66:** Close-In Fake-Shot—To an overhand shot near side (near side is open)

### From a Hard Sidearm Fake to a Sidearm Shot—Far Side

From a hard sidearm stick-fake to the far-side into a sidearm shot to the far-side. The shooter puts the ball back to where he just faked because the goalie didn't move or commit to the first fake.

### Know the Style of the Goalie

A close-in shooter should know what style the goalie is and where his stick is. The shooter has to know which arm the goalie is going to lift. If the shooter is left-handed he wants the right-handed goalie to lift his stick up with his right hand to create a low opening on the far-side. If the shooter fakes his shot to the far-top corner the goalie will then lift his stick arm up. Now the shooter is looking at a 50 percent advantage to the far-side, as he can shoot a low bounce shot or if the goalie keeps his stick down then the shooter can shoot at the far-top corner.

### "Reading" What the Goalie Does on the Fake

There are "standard fakes," but sometimes there are shots called "automatics" if a shooter shoots without thinking or "reading" what the goalie does on the fake. The ability to judge whether or not a goalie has moved for a stick-fake requires patience, experience, and a split-second response. Here are some reactions by the goalie to fakes.

### If the Goalie Reacts or Commits to the Stick-Fake at One Corner, Then the Shooter Shoots at the Opposite Corner

a. The shooter looks and stick-fakes at the far-top corner. If the goalie reacts, he then brings his stick back and shoots to the near-side-low, waist high, or to the top-corner. Most goalies know the shooter wants to shoot to the far-side, his most natural side, so for the shooter to fake to the far-side and then come back to the near-side can be very deceptive.

b. The shooter looks and stick-fakes at the near corner, the goalie's short-side. If the goalie reacts to the fake, the shooter then reaches around him and shoots to the far-corner.

c. The shooter stick-fakes high. If the goalie reacts to the fake by raising his upper body or stick, the shooter then shoots low.

**If the Goalie Does Not React or Commit to the Stick-Fake at a Corner, Then the Shooter Shoots at the Same Corner at Which He Just Faked**

General rule is on a fake shot, if the goalie doesn't move, the shooter shoots at the corner he just faked at.

a. The shooter looks and stick-fakes at the far-corner. If the goalie does not react to the fake, the shooter shoots at the far-corner.

b. The shooter looks and stick-fakes at the near-corner. If the goalie does not react to the fake, the shooter shoots at the near-corner.

c. The shooter stick-fakes high. If the goalie does not react to the high fake, the shooter shoots high. In all these fakes the shooter puts the ball back to where he just faked.

*Note: Usually when a shooter fakes at a big goalie, he anticipates he will not move, so he just fakes at him to freeze him, then picks a spot and shoots. It's a good idea also for the shooter to look at the corner he is not going to shoot at. Another good idea against big goalies is don't fake, just pick and shoot because he relies on angles a lot.*

**Hesitation Move for a Close-In Shot**

All these shooting moves can also be made from a "hesitation move" or a "freeze" move. The shooter just holds his stick, he doesn't turn the "stick-head" as on a fake, but keeps the stick-head still or hesitates. He can look at the far-corner, dip his inside shoulder like he is going to shoot at the far-corner, flinch his body, fake his head, or take a step toward the far-side of the net. He does one or all these moves to get the goalie to tighten up or to make him think he is going to shoot to the far-corner. Then, in one continuous motion he brings the stick back around to shoot at the near-corner.

**Two Stick-Fakes**

Some players like to use two stick-fakes, but they must assess the situation to see if they have time. Don't stick-fake twice just for the sake of faking twice. Have a reason for stick-faking, primarily to get a reaction from the goalie. Don't be predictable, be deceptive.

**Faking Twice in a Row at the Same Corner**

The close-in shooter looks at the corner he is not going to shoot at, stick-fakes once at that corner, then stick-fakes a second time at the same corner, then comes back and puts the ball in the other corner.

**Faking Once at One Corner and Then Faking at the Other Corner, and End Up Shooting at the First Corner He Faked**

The close-in shooter looks at the corner he is going to shoot at, stick-fakes at that corner, then stick-fakes at the other corner, and then comes back to the original corner he first faked at and puts the ball in.

• For example, the close-in shooter looks at the near-corner, which he is going to end up shooting at, and stick-fakes at the near-corner, then he stick-fakes to the far-corner and then brings his stick back to the near-side corner for a shot.

• Or the close-in shooter stick-fakes to the far-side corner, then stick-fakes to the near-side corner and then he shoots at the far-side corner.

## 3. Behind-the-Back Shot or Over-the-Shoulder Shot

This shot can be used when the goalie comes with the shooter across the net and takes away the opening on the shooter's stick side (far-side) leaving the near-side vacant, i.e., the side that the shooter just came from. Once he has passed the mid-point of the net and sees he has nothing to shoot at the far-side he thinks of the over-the-shoulder shot.

The shooter executes this over-the-shoulder shot by moving the stick out to the side and slightly behind his body. The shooter flexes his

**Photo 67:** Behind-the-back shot or over-the-shoulder shot—goalie has taken away far-side of net as player cuts across (shooter shoots to near-side)

top-hand arm, bringing the stick over his stick shoulder and behind his head and back.

For the average player this shot is really one of desperation where there is no time on the shot clock if it is used in the league. If the shot clock has time left, often it is better to just keep control of the ball for a higher percentage shot. The "behind-the-back" shot is a hope shot unless a shooter practices it a lot and becomes good at it.

# VIII. Shooting Drills
## Long-Ball Shooting Drills

### One-on-Zero Long-Ball Shooting Drills
#### 1. One-on-Zero Long-Ball Shooting Off a One-on-One Move Drill (No Pass)
In this drill all the players have a ball and form two lines, left-shot line and right-shot line. In rapid succession all the players in one line make an offensive move, around a cone placed just inside the Prime Scoring Area. Players can make these one-on-one moves from the four areas—from top-side, from mid-side, from top-center, from corner area. Through these drills coach wants to find out who are his long-ball shooters.

Here is a list of all the one-on-one moves:
a. Undercut Move (cut outside—taking a hit while running—coach holds a blocking dummy to hit the players with)
b. Fake shot to an Undercut Move (cut outside) then back inside
c. Fake shot to an Inside Slide Move (cut to middle of floor)
d. Fake shot while side stepping (dragging) down the side into an Inside Slide Move cutting across the top (cut inside)
e. Faking a shot while side stepping down the side into an Outside Spin-Around Move (cut outside)
f. Inside Slide Move or "Bull" Move across the top (cut inside—coach holds blocking dummy and hit players)
g. Inside Spin-Around Move (cut inside) (Counter to No. I—do it while running down the sidelines)
h. Outside Spin-Around Move (cut outside) (Counter to No. VI—do it while running across top)
i. Outside Body Fake (fake outside, cut inside—no contact—running)
j. Inside Body Fake (fake inside, cut outside—no contact—running)
k. Inside Pivot Move (cut inside—taking a hit while jogging)
l. Outside Pivot Move (cut outside—taking a hit while jogging) *(See Diagram #18)*

#### 2. One-on-Zero Single-Line Breakaway Drill (No Pass)
In this drill everybody has a ball, the team forms a single line at center floor, and then runs down the middle of the floor shooting at the goalie. If anybody scores, he yells out "goal." This is a good drill for the "offensive" or "transition" defenders, who could also end up on a breakaway running down the middle of the floor. The coach can control the tempo of the drill with either:
a. "Rapid Fire" Shooting Drill where there is no pause between shots. (A) Players

**Diagram #18: Two-Line, No Pass, Cornerman Shooting Drill**

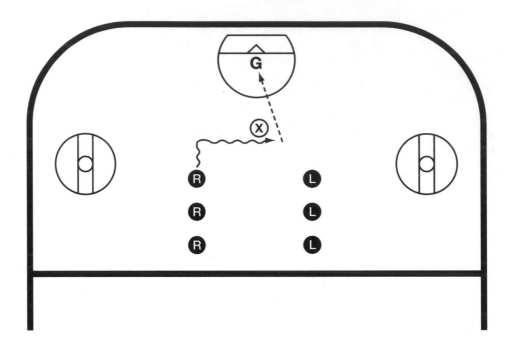

can shoot a straight long shot for the far corner only. Here there is no fake and no space between players, (B) they can shoot for the near corner, (C) or just wave their stick around all the way down the floor and shoot. Here there is still no shot-fake.

b. "Controlled" Shooting Drill where there is more time between shots so players have the time to fake or just shoot.

**Variations:**
- Two lines—left-shots and right-shots—run down their proper side of the floor and shoot.
- Two lines run down their proper side of the floor and use a fake shot. They can fake as many times as they want and then shoot.

### 3. Semi-Circle Drill Long-Ball Shooting (No Pass)
Players with a ball form three semi-circular groups about 15 feet out from the crease, behind each other. Players in the first semi-circle line shoot continuously in succession around the horn, starting at one of the ends. Then the players in the second and third line do

the same thing. After the players shoot, they get out of the way and go to the back of the line. The next time, the players shoot alternating from side-to-side in the semi-circle. Lastly, the players in the second line shoot around the players in the first line and use them as screens. Coach can vary the tempo of all these drills so that the players can shoot in "rapid fire" or in a "controlled" manner and he can have the three lines compete against each other.

### 4. Follow-the-Leader Drill (No Pass)
Teams form a single line at the top-center of the floor. Coach put the players in groups of five. The first group runs in a single file following the front player who is the leader. He can vary from where the shots are taken, either cutting across the top, down the side, or down the center of the floor. Groups compete against each other for most goals scored.

### 5. One-on-Zero Two Lines Shooting Off a Loose Ball Drill (No Pass)
Coach forms a line on each side of the floor and alternates the players from each line. The first

player in one line goes after the loose ball that the coach either places or rolls (in the middle of the floor, off the end-boards, or in the corner) picks it up and comes out looking to shoot long from the mid-side area high spot.

### 6. One-on-Zero Two Lines Cutting Across Top Shooting Drill (No Pass)

The coach puts a cone in the top-center (middle) of the floor about 15 feet from the crease. All the left-shots each with a ball cut around the cone, taking long shots in succession, then all the right-shots go. Players can shoot planted around the cone, or shoot just past the cone on the run cutting across the top. (See Diagram #18)

**Variations:**

- Alternate the lines with left-shots, then right-shots. Make the drill into a game with right- versus left-shots.
- Coach can place two cones on the side of the floor in different spots rather than in the middle of the floor. Players form two lines on each side of the floor of lefts- and right-shots.
  a. Players start from top-side area (pointman's spot), cut across, plant and shoot.
  b. Players start from mid-side area (cornerman's spot or wing area), cut across, and shoot on the run.
  c. Players start from mid-side area, fake a shot, pull the stick across the body, and shoot running down the side of the floor.
  d. Players start from the top-side area facing an imaginary defender. Shooter uses no offensive move, he just winds-up and hop-steps into his shot.
  e. Players start from the corner area (creaseman's spot), cut up and across the top, and shoot.

These shooting drills should be competitive and highly repetitive.

### 7. Two-on-Zero Cornerman Cutting Shooting Drills (Off a Pass)

Stress in all these drills to cut hard to the ball and to pass the ball hard to the cutter.

**a. Two-on-Zero Give-and-Go Shooting From Mid-Side Area of Floor (Opposite Sides)**

Players work on their Give-and-Go technique. The coach puts two cones in the Prime Scoring Area of the floor. Everybody has a ball except for one player at the front of one of the lines. Players work on passing and cutting for the return pass and shot. The first player in one line throws a cross-floor pass to the first player in the other line who has put his ball down beside himself. The passer then puts an offensive move on the cone and cuts to the ball for a return pass and shot. The cutter yells "ball." The passer must hit the cutter early enough so he has lots of time to make a good judgment on his shot. Then the former passer picks up his ball and passes to the next player in the line opposite him, so he can work on his Give-and-Go move. The players alternate from side-to-side until the coach stops the drill or until one side scores so many goals. (See Diagram #19)

**b. Two-on-One Give-and-Go Shooting Drill (Opposite Sides)**

This drill is similar to the one above. From the mid-side or top-side area of the floor the ballcarrier who is covered passes across to the passer and cuts in front of the defender (who plays token defense), and receives pass back and shoots. Then the next player does the same thing from the same line.

The next progression is that the ballcarrier who is covered passes across to the passer in the other line and cuts this time behind the defender (Backdoor Cut).

Stress to the cutter: To fake a cut the opposite way he wants to cut; to cut with his stick up and ready, and to catch the ball before he reaches the center line of the floor.

**Diagram #19: Two-Line, "Give-and-Go" Pass, Cornerman Shooting Drill**

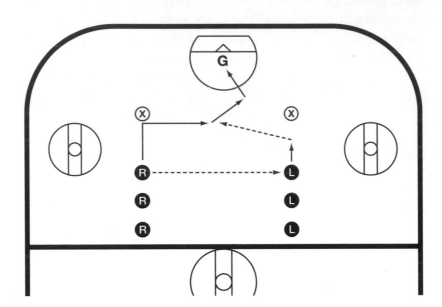

**c. Two-on-Zero "Go" Shooting Drill From Mid-Side Area of Floor (Opposite Sides)**

In this drill the players work on their cut or "Go" move. Again form two lines on opposite sides of the floor in the mid-side area. Everybody has a ball except for one player at the front of one of the lines. Players alternate sides on their cut. They just cut and shoot. Can run the drill also from the top-center area where the players just cut at an angle to the far-side of the net for a short pass and shot.

**d. Two-on-One "Go" Shooting Drill (Opposite Sides)**

In this drill, one passer has all the balls. There are two lines: an offensive and defensive line. Run the drill from the mid-side area, the corner area, or the top-side area. The offensive player who is covered cuts first in front of his defender (who plays token defense) and receives a cross-floor pass for a shot. Then the next offensive player cuts in front of his defender.

The next progression is the offensive players cut behind the defender (Backdoor Cut) and receives a cross-floor pass for a shot.

**e. Two-on-Zero "Merry-Go-Round" Shooting Drill (Opposite Sides)**

This is a two-line passing drill, but the left-shots shoot continuously with the right-shots just feeding the cutters. Then the players reverse roles. The cutters learn to move without the ball, cut quickly and hard, and cut with their sticks ready to catch and shoot. The two lines can compete against each other on which team scores the most goals or on who has the best shooting percentage, i.e., the number of goals/ number of shots. Players can cut from the four areas of the floor: top-center area, top-side area, mid-side area, and corner area of the floor.

**8. Two-on-Zero Stationary Long-Ball Shooting Drill (Off a Pass)**

This drill consists of a shooter, two passers, and a bucket of balls beside each passer. The passers feed the shooter as fast as they can. The shooter shoots for one minute from his favorite spot and the coach records the number of goals/ number of shots. Can put a goalie in net or use the "Shooting Board." *(See Diagram #20)*

### Diagram #20: Cornerman Stationary Shooting Drill

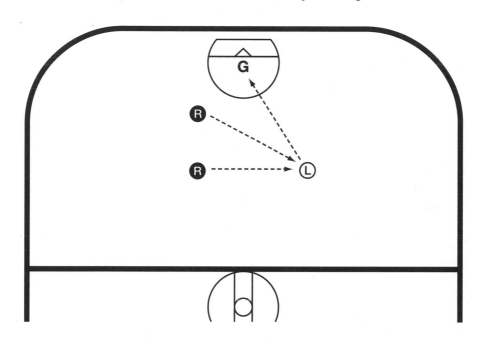

#### 9. One-on-Zero On-the-Move Long-Ball Shooting Drill (Off a Pass)

This drill consists of a shooter, two passers, and a bucket of balls beside each passer. The passers on different sides of the floor feed the shooter as fast as they can. The shooter shoots for one minute, cutting toward the one passer before V-cutting back to receive a pass from the passer on his side of the floor. The coach records the number of goals/number of shots. Can put a goalie in net or use the "Shooting Board."

*(See Diagram #21)*

### Diagram #21: On-the-Move Shooting Drill

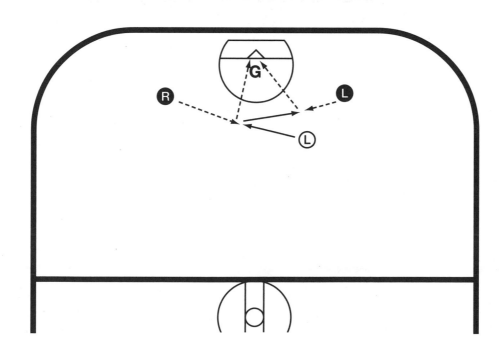

**Variation:** The two passers are on the same side of the floor on the opposite side of the floor from the shooter. The shooter moves up the side of the floor to receive a pass for a long-ball shot and then runs back down the side of the floor for a close-in shot.

*(See Diagram #22)*

### 10. Three "Closers Out, One Shooter Shooting Drill (Off a Pass)

This drill consists of one shooter and three passers. The shooter is stationary. Three players, one at a time, pass the ball out to the shooter from the middle of the floor and then "close out" trying to interfere with his shot.

a. Shooter shoots with the passer trying to interfere with shot.

b. Shooter fakes a shot and steps to the side for a shot.

c. Passer "closes out," overplaying the right side, shooter goes left.

d. Passer "closes out," overplaying the left side, shooter goes right.

### Team Long-Ball Shooting Drills

### 1. Four-Corner Shooting Drill—Stationary (Balls with Cornerman—Same and Opposite Sides)

The team forms a square or four corners where they would start their offensive plays in the corner areas (creasemen's spot) and in the mid-side areas (cornermen's spot).

a. Balls with cornerman pass to crease on same side of floor for close-in shot. Allow one to two fakes on the goalie. Work both sides of floor, alternate sides, and switch lines on same side.

b. Balls with cornerman passes down to creaseman on same side of floor who passes back out to cornerman for a long shot.

c. Balls with cornerman who make diagonal pass to opposite crease for close-in shot.

d. Balls with cornerman makes cross-floor pass to opposite cornerman for long shot.

---

### Diagram #22: On-the-Move Shooting Drill

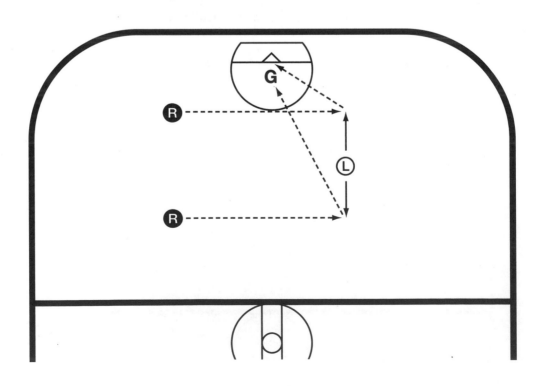

*2. Four-Corner Shooting Drill—Off-Ball-Side Cutting (Balls with Cornerman)*
Start drill in mid-side area or the cornerman's area.

a. Cornerman makes a diagonal pass to the opposite creaseman cutting ("Go") into the middle for close-in or long shot ("X" Drill). *(See Diagram #23)*

b. Cornerman makes cross-floor pass to other cornerman who makes diagonal pass to opposite crease cutting ("Go") into middle for pass ("X" Drill). *(See Diagram #24)*

---

**Diagram #23: Four-Corner Shooting Drill—One Pass**

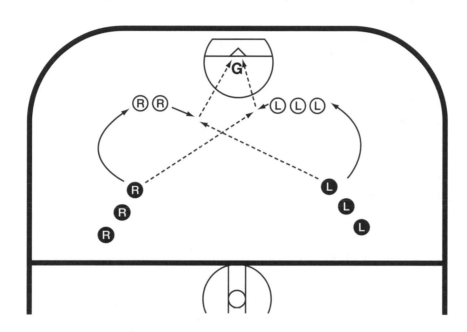

---

**Diagram #24: Four-Corner Shooting Drill—Two Pass**

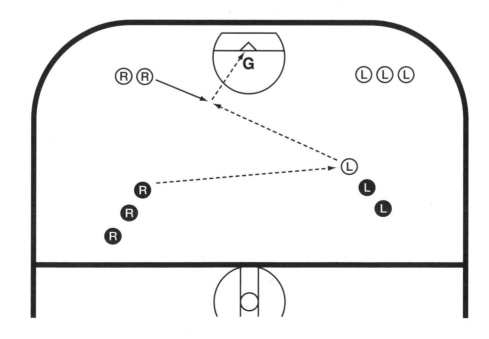

c. Cornerman makes cross-floor pass to opposite cornerman cutting ("Go") into middle for a long shot. Option: creaseman can replace the cutter on his side for return pass and then pass to a new cutter (cornerman).

d. Cornerman makes a cross-floor pass to opposite cornerman, who passes down to creaseman on same side who makes diagonal pass to off-ball cornerman cutting ("Go") and shot. *(See Diagram #25)*

e. Cornermen makes cross-floor pass to other cornerman then cuts (Give-and-Go) for return pass and shot. Option: Put a token defensive player on both sides to cut around or to cut behind (backdoor).

f. Cornerman passes down to his crease then interchanges with him while the off-ball players also interchange, but the off-ball crease cuts ("Go") after the interchange for a cross-floor pass and shot.

g. Cornerman makes cross-floor pass to player coming off an interchange on the off-ball side for quick shot ("Go"). Option: After he passes he interchanges with the creaseman on his side.

### 3. Four-Corner Shooting Drill—Off-Ball-Side Cutting (Balls with Creasemen—Opposite Sides)

a. Creaseman make a diagonal pass to opposite cornerman cutting ("Go") into middle for pass and shot. ("X" Drill) *(See Diagram #26)*

b. Creaseman passes up to cornerman, who makes a diagonal pass to off-ball creaseman cutting ("Go") into middle for shot. ("X" Drill) *(See Diagram #27)*

c. Creaseman passes up to cornerman and he passes across floor to other cornerman, who passes to off-ball creaseman cutting ("Go") into middle for shot. ("X" Drill) *(See Diagram #28)*

d. Creaseman interchanges with cornerman on both sides of floor, and as the ball-carrying creaseman comes up he makes a cross-floor

**Diagram #25: Four-Corner Shooting Drill—Three Pass**

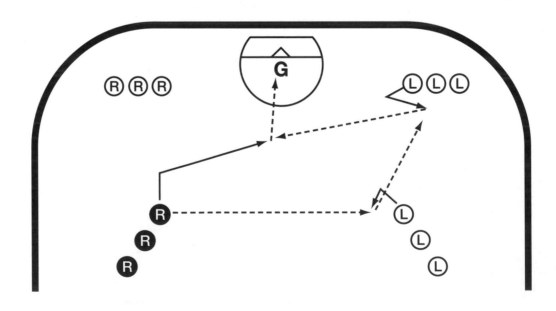

**Diagram #26: Four-Corner Shooting Drill—One Pass**

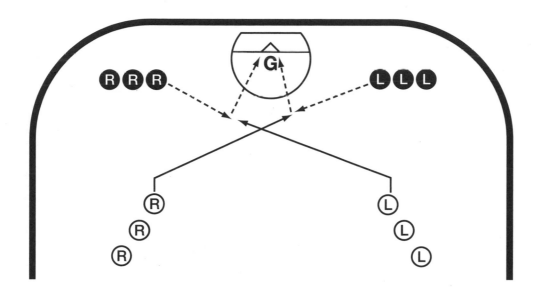

**Diagram #27: Four-Corner Shooting Drill—Two Pass**

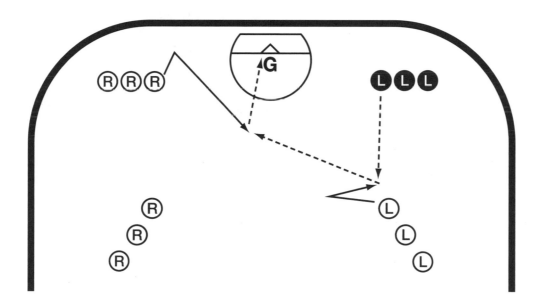

pass to the opposite creaseman cutting ("Go") into middle.

e. Creaseman passes up to cornerman, who passes across and opposite cornerman passes down to crease on his side ("around the horn") who makes a cross-floor pass to

the original creaseman who cuts ("Go") into middle for shot.

f. Creaseman passes up to cornerman who passes to other cornerman and the former cornerman gets return pass on cut (Give-and-Go) for shot.

---

**Diagram #28: Four-Corner Shooting Drill—Three Pass**

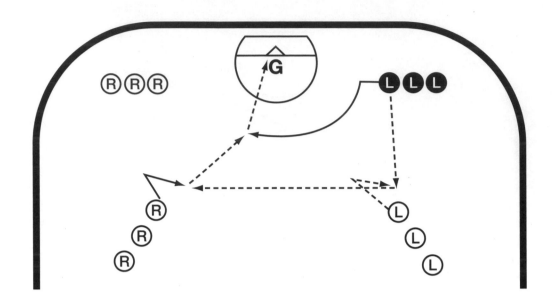

**4. Four-Corner Shooting Drill—On-Ball-Side Cutting (Same Side)**

a. From the mid-side area, left-shot cornerman passes to left-shot creaseman on same side of floor and cuts into the middle (Give-and-

Go) for return pass and shot. Rights do the same. *(See Diagram #29)*

b. From the top-side area, left-shot pointman passes to left-shot cornerman and cuts down the middle ("Give-and-go down

**Diagram #29: Four-Corner Shooting Drill—On-Ball-Side Cutting—"Give-and-Go"**

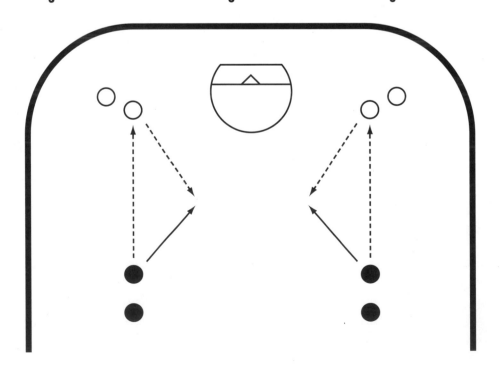

**Diagram #30: "Give-and-Go"**

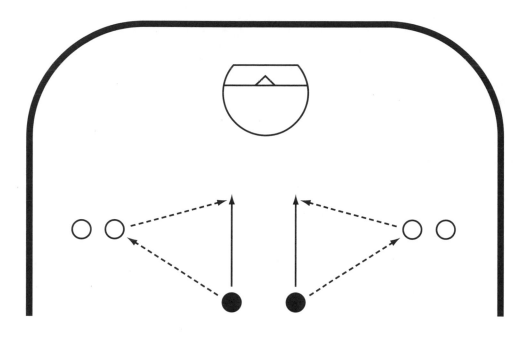

the center") for return pass and shot. *(See Diagram #30)*

c. Creaseman who is covered (defender plays token defense) passes up to cornerman, in

the mid-side area on his side of the floor and cuts in front of the defender (Give-and-Go) and receives pass back. *(See Diagram #31)*

**Diagram #31: "Give-and-Go"**

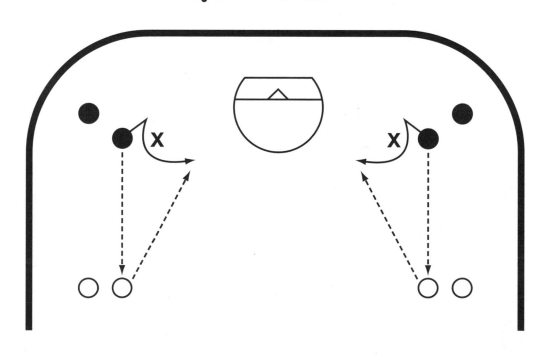

d. Creaseman who is covered (defender plays token defense) passes up to cornerman in the mid-side area on his side of the floor and cuts behind (backdoor) the defender (Give-and-Go) and receives return pass back. *(See Diagram #32)*

e. "Rotate"—cornerman runs the ball down to the corner area while the creaseman on his side of the floor runs inside to the top area for a return pass and shot. *(See Diagram #33)*

f. Players "interchange" positions. Cornerman passes down to the creaseman on his side of the floor and looks for a return pass on his cut to the inside of the floor. The creaseman could pass or go off the cutter's tail for one-on-one or shot. *(See Diagram #34)*

**Diagram #32: "Backdoor" Cut**

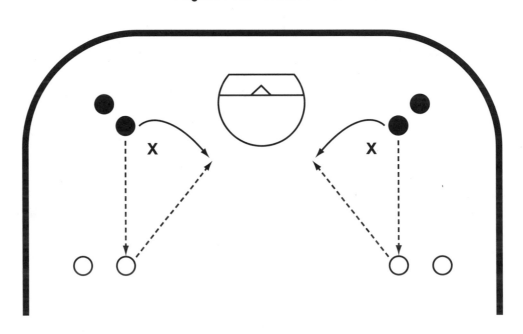

**Diagram #33: "Rotate"**

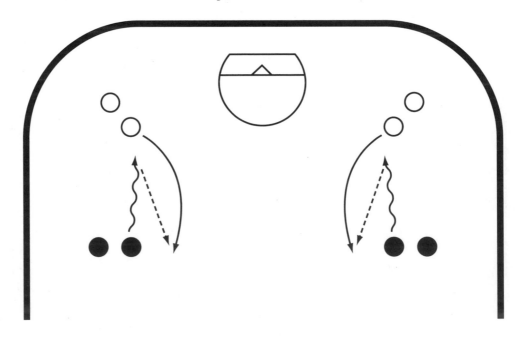

**Diagram #34: "Interchange"**

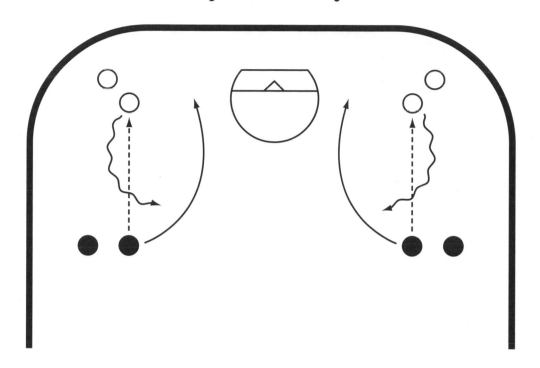

### 5. Four-Corner Shooting Drill—On-Ball-Side Picks (Same-Side)

Coach can run these drills from top-side, mid-side, or top-center area of the floor. Balls can start with the cornerman, who has the option of passing down, or the creaseman who has option of passing back up.

Stress when players have the ball they are looking to shoot—sticks are level and behind the head while doing small cradles as they figure out what they are going to do. Stress to picker when he rolls that he holds his stick in front for a target.

a. Cornerman receives an on-ball "Cross" pick-and-roll in the mid-side area by crease and takes a shot. (A) Stress when coming off the "Cross" pick ballcarrier looks to shoot right away or go one-on-one rather than looking to pass. (B) The second option is the ballcarrier passes to the picker rolling down the side for a short "rainbow" pass or underhand pass. (C) Countermove to the "Cross" pick when the ballcarrier's check backs off to play the picker and the switcher

fires out on the top-side of the pick to play the ballcarrier, he goes the opposite way, Backdoor Cut, or Undercut to the sideboard. *(See Diagram #35)*

b. Cornerman receives an on-ball "Up" pick-and-roll in the mid-side area by the creaseman and makes an Undercut. (A) First option for ballcarrier is Undercut to the net. (B) The second option is the ballcarrier passes to the picker rolling into the middle of the floor with a short "rainbow" pass or underhand pass. Ballcarrier while cutting outside can lean on his check and flip an underhand pass to the picker rolling to the net. (C) Third option after the ballcarrier Undercuts outside, picker pops back for a one-hand flip-back pass. (D) Fourth option is a countermove if the ballcarrier's check backs off to play the picker and if the switcher starts to fire out to the boards side, ballcarrier goes the opposite way, Backdoor Cut across the top for a shot. *(See Diagram #36)*

### Diagram #35: Four-Corner Shooting Drill—On-Ball-Side Picks

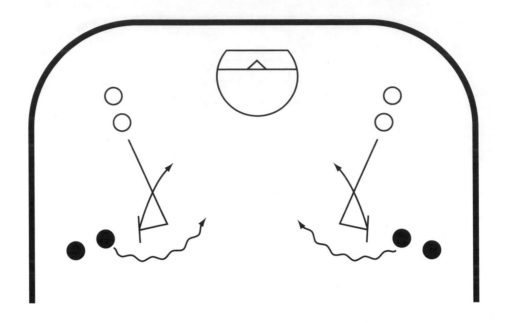

### Diagram #36: "Up" Pick-and-Roll

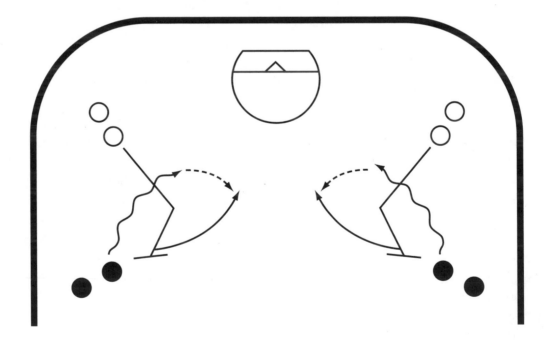

c. Cornerman receives an on-ball "Up" fake pick or "Slip" and passes to picker. Ballcarrier just faces the play, he doesn't use the "Up" pick and just throws a "rainbow" pass to the picker who faked an "Up" pick and rolls to the net. Option: Both players can meet at the same time to create confusion, one up one down, and throw a short pass. *(See Diagram #37)*

### Diagram #37: "Fake" or "Slip" "Up" Pick-and-Roll

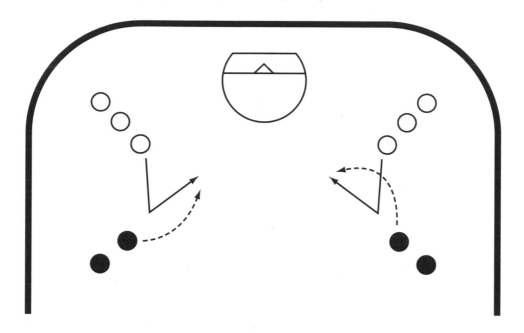

d. Cornerman makes a down pass and sets an on-ball "Down" pick-and-roll at mid-side area for crease. (A) Creaseman pops up and receives a down pass and a "Down" pick by cornerman for a long shot. (B) Second option

is picker rolls to the net for a pass. *(See Diagram #38)*

e. Cornerman passes down and sets an on-ball "Down" screen at mid-side area for the creaseman. Cornerman passes down and

### Diagram #38: "Down" Pick-and-Roll

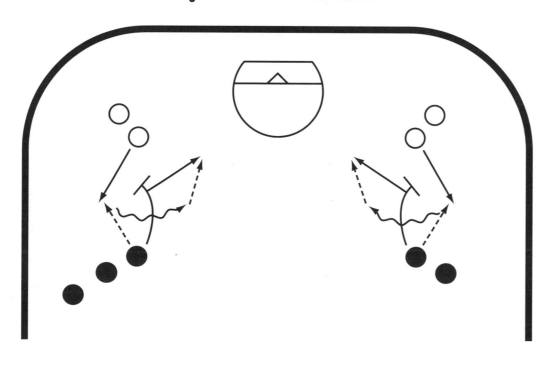

goes to set a "Down" screen. He must get on the inside of his defender by cutting slowly down the side. The creaseman cuts off the screen for a shot. Screener pops back after cutter passes him for defensive safety. *(See Diagram #39)*

f.   Creaseman sets an on-ball "Up" screen for an Undercut by ballcarrier. Screener gets on lower side or below his defender so the defenders can't switch. *(See Diagram #40)*

**Diagram #39: "Down" Screen**

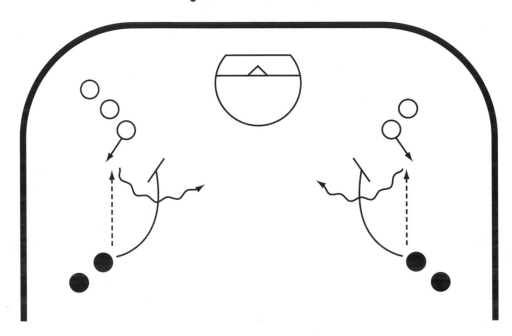

**Diagram #40: "Up" Screen**

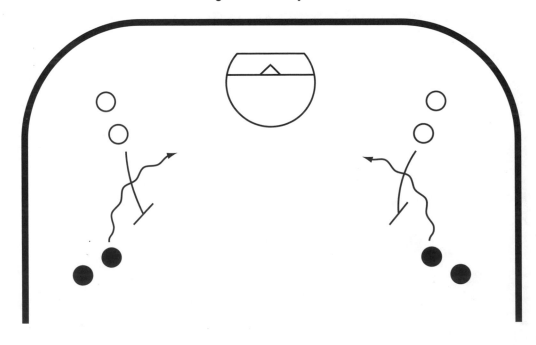

## 6. Four-Corner Shooting Drill—Off-Ball-Side Picks (Opposite Sides)

Balls can start with cornerman who throws a cross-floor pass to other cornerman and receives pick by creaseman.

a. Cornerman waits for off-ball "Up" pick-and-roll by creaseman and passes to picker the first option. The second option is to pass to the cutter (cornerman) going backdoor. Another option is the creaseman sets a "Fake Up" pick-and-roll and ballcarrier passes to the picker (creaseman). *(See Diagram #41)*

b. Cornerman waits for off-ball "Cross" pick-and-roll by creaseman and passes to cutter (off-ball cornerman) the first option. Second option is the picker rolls and follows the cutter for a pass. Another option is the picker pops up, after cutter goes by him, and receives the pass. *(See Diagram #42)*

### Diagram #41: "Up" Pick-and-Roll

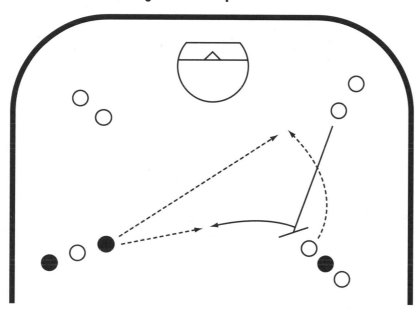

### Diagram #42

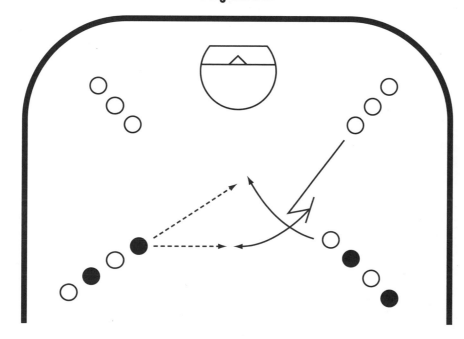

c. Cornerman waits for off-ball "Down" pick-and-roll by off-ball cornerman and passes to cutter (creaseman). Or top-side ballcarrier passes across and sets an imaginary off-ball "Down" pick for the creaseman on his side, who comes off the pick for pass and shot.

Players switch positions on own sides. *(See Diagram #43)*

d. Cornerman waits for off-ball "Down" screen to pass to the cutter (creaseman). *(See Diagram #44)*

### Diagram #43: "Down" Pick-and-Roll

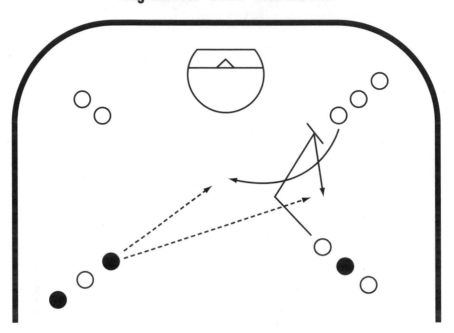

### Diagram #44: "Down" Screen

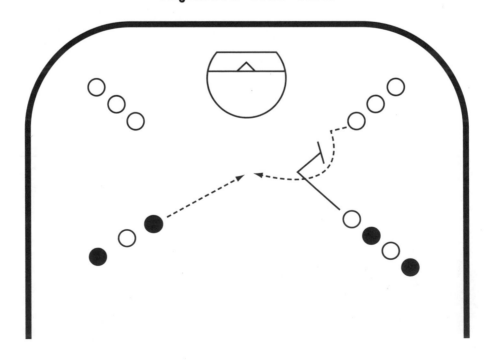

e. Cornerman waits for off-ball "Up" screen to pass to cutter (cornerman) going backdoor. *(See Diagram #45)*

### 7. *Shooting Games*
**a. "Showdown" Game**
This drill involves the whole team. Each player shoots until he scores. If the goalie stops him, the shooter goes after the rebound. The player has 30 seconds to score or he has to get back in the line and go again.

**b. Shooting Game "21"**
Coach makes up two teams—left-shots versus right-shots, or mixed teams. The first team to 21 points wins. The losing team runs. Players can use any type of shot. Shooter gets one point if he scores on a close-in shot; two points if he scores on a long shot; and three points if he scores on a long bounce shot.

**Variation in scoring:**
I.   Can only score with a close-in shot. One point if shooter scores. No long shots.

II.  Can only score with a close-in shot, but must fake first. Shooter gets one point if he scores. No long shots.
III. Can only score on a long shot. Shooter gets one point if he scores.
IV.  Can only score on a long bounce shot. Shooter gets one point if he scores.
V.   "Garbage shots only"—Shooter cannot score on a normal shot he must shoot a sidearm, underhand, behind-the-back, fake like crazy shots.

**c. Breakaway Shooting Game "15" Points**
Coach makes up two teams—left-shots versus the right-shots or mixed teams. The first team to 15 points wins. The losing team runs. Ballcarrier runs full-floor or from center. Good drill for offensive or transition defensemen.
I.   Shoots close-in straight shot only.
II.  Shoots close-in shot, but must fake first.
III. Shoots long-shot on the run only.
IV.  Shoots long-shot, but stopping in cornerman's spot.

---

**Diagram #45: "Up" Screen**

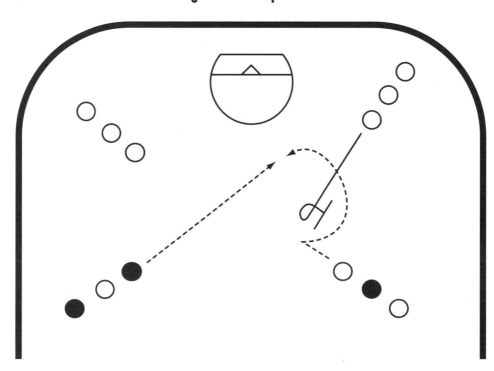

**Fast-Break Shooting Drills**

*A. One-on-Zero Single-Line Breakaway Drill*

I. Players run down the middle and take a straight long shot.

II. Players run down the middle and shoot at far corner (no fake, no space).

III. Players run down the middle and shoot at near corner (no fake, no space).

IV. Players run down the middle and wave stick around all the way down the floor (no fake) and shoot.

V. Players form two lines. They run down their proper side of the floor and shoot (one at a time) or fake a shot or they can fake as many times as they want and then shoot.

*B. One-on-Zero Fast-Break Cornermen Long-Ball Shooting Drill*

Two lines, right- and left-shots. Ballcarrier runs the length of floor to the cornerman's spot and stops (plants) and shoots. Option: Run two-on-zero to cornermen spots, one pass and shoot.

*C. One-on-Zero Fast-Break Creaseman Shooting Drill*

Two lines, right- and left-shots. Ballcarrier runs to the creaseman's spot and shoots.

*D. Two-on-Zero Fast-Break Creasemen Shooting Drill (Off a Pass)*

Two lines, right- and left-shots. From center, creasemen run down passing ball back and forth until someone scores. They can even plant themselves at the crease and still pass back and forth until they get an open shot. Good drill to improve quick passing back and forth.

**Long-Ball Shooting at the Shooting Board**

*Competition amongst players:*

a. Record number of goals out of 25 shots— chart made and missed shots—slower drill, work on form also.

b. Two passers one shooter—record number of goals in one minute.

c. Keep ladder of shooting percent by players (cannot shoot in game unless shoot 25 percent).

d. Out of your range shooting.

e. Two in a row, then three in a row.

f. "Bump" drill—whole team lines up, player must score before the player behind him scores. If player behind scores before the first player, the first player is out of the drill.

*Practicing shooting off a cross-floor pass at shooting board:*

a. Stationary shooting

b. Shooting off an offensive move

c. Quick stick shooting—no wind up, no step—use arms only

d. Shooting on the move—two passers, one shooter

e. Two shooters, two passers

f. Fake first to freeze defender, step around imaginary defender, cut across, and shoot.

g. Fake first to freeze defender or make him play your stick, pull stick across body, step-in and shoot.

h. Three players in single line cut into middle of floor, "circling," receive pass and shoot planted—rotate them around in a circle.

i. Shooting board for bounce shots at one end and shooting board for corner shots at the other end. Two lines at both ends of the floor (left and rights). Use both ends of the floor. Player shoots at one end, then runs down to other end and shoots. Use four cones or four blocking dummies.

**Close-In Shooting Drills**

- Most creasemen shooting drills work on speed and fluidity in faking, i.e., work on the ability to keep the ball in the stick as the speed of the fake is increased.

- Practice both the quick-stick and faking moves with or without the ball.

- Practice on receiving a pass and incorporating a quick-stick move or fake move.

- When practicing on his own, a player should simulate game conditions and get a buddy to pass—taking passes on the run, pretending to ward off or beat a defender, and faking and quick-sticking to all parts of the net.

**Types of Close-In Shots:**
- Straight shot for near or far corner
- Fake short-side, shoot far-side top corner (best close-in shot move)
- Fake far-side, shoot near-side (second best close-in shot move)
- Fake short-side, shoot near-side (goalie doesn't move on first fake)
- Fake far-side, shoot far-side (goalie doesn't move on first fake)
- Fake high, shoot low
- Fake low, shoot high
- Hesitate by holding stick "still" like going to shoot far-side and look far, then shoot near-side all in one motion
- Hesitate or look near-side, shoot far-side
- Wave stick around all the way down floor (no fake)
- Two fakes—fake near-side, fake near-side again, then shoot far-side

- Two fakes—fake near-side, fake far-side, then shoot near-side
- Make three to four fakes, then shoot

**Close-In Shooting Drills (No Pass)**
Coach wants to find out who can score inside or close-in?

*1. One-on-Zero Single-Line Breakaway Drill (Close-In Shooting)*
a. Line of players taking "rapid fire" shots (no fake, no space)
b. Line of players "controlled" shots (pick and shoot or fake allowed, give space)

*2. Two-on-Zero Creaseman Shooting Drill (No Pass)* **(See Diagram #46)**
The coach puts the cone at the top of the crease and forms two lines in the corner areas. A left-handed shooter comes out of the corner position shooting past the cone and not before, then a right-handed shooter does the same thing. The lines can run continuously or alternate until the coach stops the drill or until one line scores so many goals. This is a reaction drill for the players and the goalie, therefore, players cannot fake, but just shoot. The left-handed players stay on the inside and the

**Diagram #46: Two-Line, No-Pass, Creaseman Shooting Drill**

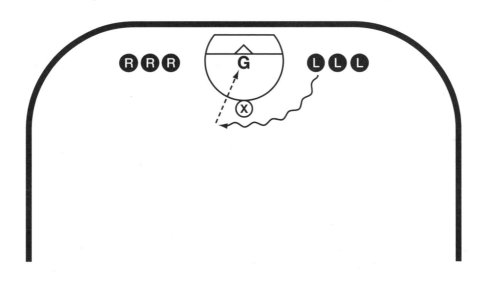

right-handed players stay on the outside, so the players don't run into each other. *(See Diagram #16)*

**Variation:** The drill is run in a more controlled manner with the players allowed to fake. Players still alternate, but they now shoot before the cone which makes it more difficult for the goalie since he has to move laterally quite a distance.

*3. Two-on-Zero Creaseman Step-Around Shooting Drill (No Pass)*
Two lines on each side of the net. Players start with a ball standing beside the net and just step around and shoot.

**Variation:** Players can step in front of net and make 3-4 fakes.

*4. One-on-Zero Two-Lines Shooting Off a Loose Ball Drill*
Players form two lines on each side of the floor. Coach places ball in middle of floor, rolls it into the corner, or rolls it off the boards. First player in one line retrieves the loose ball off the back board or in the corner, picks it up, and comes out looking to shoot a close-in shot then a player in the other line does the same thing.

**Close-In Shooting Drills (Off-A-Pass)**
*1. Two-on-Zero Creasemen Shooting Drill (Crease-to-Crease Pass)*
a.  25 pass across (no shot)
b.  25 pass across with quick-stick near-side corner
c.  25 pass across with step around to far-side corner
d.  10 pick and shoot (under glove hand, hip area, top corner, bottom corner)
e.  10 fake near-side, shoot far-top corner (No. 1 move, goalie commits)
f.  10 fake far-side, shoot near-side (No. 2 move, goalie commits)

g.  10 fake near-side, shoot near-side (goalie doesn't move on first fake)
h.  10 fake far-side, shoot far-side (goalie doesn't move on first fake)
i.  10 fake high, shoot low or fake high, fake high, shoot low
j.  10 fake low, shoot high
k.  10 hesitate far-side, shoot near-side (don't turn stick head, keep it still, can dip shoulder like going to shoot)
l.  10 hesitate near-side, shoot far-side
m.  10 fake near-side twice, shoot far-side
n.  10 fake near-side, fake far-side, shoot near-side
o.  10 make 3-4 fakes then shoot
p.  Two-on-zero cornerman on same side pass to creaseman—repeat
q.  Two-on-zero opposite cornerman pass to creaseman cutting—shoot far
r.  Two-on-zero opposite cornerman pass to creaseman cutting—shoot back to where you came from

*2. Two-on-Zero "Go" Shooting Drill (Crease-to-Crease Pass) (See Diagram #47)*
Form two lines beside the crease area. All the players have a ball except the first player in one of the lines. Coach places two cones about 10 feet apart in front of the net. The creaseman runs out of the corner area looking for a cross-floor pass from the other line. The goalie has to move back-and-forth in the crease to stop the shots. The shooter must shoot between the two cones in front of the crease. The players can alternate from side-to-side for the pass from the other crease or all lefts can continuously shoot while all the rights feed.

*3. Two-on-Zero Stationary Close-In Shooting Drill (Diagonal Pass) (See Diagram #48)*
One line of passers, in mid-side area, pass across to stationary player in the crease area

for a "quick-stick" shot. Stress passer looks at the net and be in a shooting position before making the diagonal pass for quick-stick shot. Alternate sides or run the "Merry-Go-Round" Drill. At first goalie doesn't move. He plays the ballcarrier to give confidence to the close-in shooter. Later he plays live.

**Variation:** Ballcarrier can shoot or make diagonal pass.

---

### Diagram #47: Two-Line, Pass, Creaseman Shooting Drill

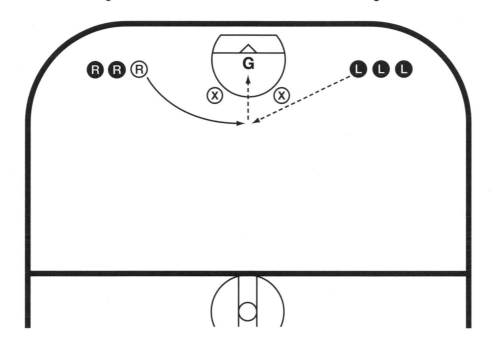

---

### Diagram #48: Creaseman Stationary Drill

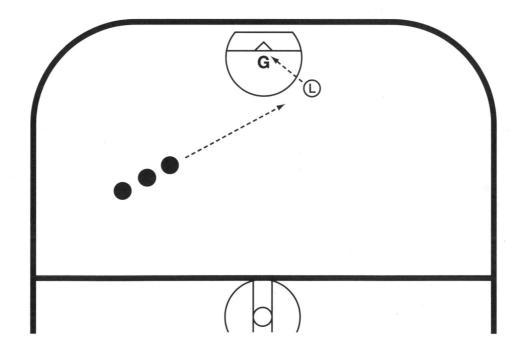

## IX. Shooter's Affirmations

- I am ready to shoot before I receive the ball.
- I catch and shoot from the same spot in my pocket!
- On the release of the ball from the pocket, I want the ball to run out smoothly in the pocket, but I like to feel the ball "tick" the top of the plastic to know it has gone.
- I know I can shoot faster than a goalie can move.
- I know what a great shot is! I know how to get the highest percentage shot.

### Shooting Rules

- I shoot from my proper side of the floor.
- When I shoot, I am at the proper angle and in the Prime Scoring Area.
- I shoot in my range. I shoot relaxed! (If I am not in my range, I know I will just "bomb" or force my shot.)
- Before I shoot, "My stick cannot be interfered with." (No stick or body in front of my shot.) I am one step ahead of my check ("wide open").
- My hardest shots are the ones I swing easy with. I do not try to swing or force the shot too hard.
- I can hit the open spot I am shooting at. I "pick" my shot in the Prime Scoring Area.
- I know accuracy is more important than hardness.
- I must have patience when shooting.
- I do not rush my shot, i.e., take "automatics." I take a split second to look for the open spot.
- I do not shoot around opponents—screen shots—unless they are playing off of me and cannot interfere with my stick.

- Seventy percent of all my shots bounce!
- I know the type of goalie I am shooting against (angle or reflex).
- I know in which hand the goalie holds his stick.
- I look at the whole net on my shot and pick the "open" spot.
- I do not look directly at the spot I am shooting at! (Some players look at one corner and shoot to other corner because they feel goalies watch their eyes.)
- I do not just shoot the ball straight and hard, I "think" my way around a goalie.
- I make it look like I am going to shoot to the far corner by holding my stick in a sidearm position, then I bring it over my shoulder in an overhand shot, shooting for near-side.
- If I am shooting straight on with the goalie, I step into the middle slightly to move the goalie sideways (away from near goal post)!
- Coming across the top, I look for far-top corner or mid-post, but if I can't see anything, I shoot a bounce shot inside the near corner.
- I must see an "opening" to shoot at before I shoot. (A lot of players end up just shooting at the goalie.) If I see no "openings" in top corners, I bounce! If I see no "openings" on far-side, I shoot near-side!
- I have "shooting discipline"—if I don't have a good shot, I don't shoot.
- I look to shoot all the time!
- If I wind up looking to shoot and the defender backs up, I keep shuffling in, faking my shot, then shoot.

# Chapter 9

# Face-Offs

I want to thank *NLL & CLA referee Bill Fox* on contributing to the face-off rules and interpretation.

## I. Face-Off Rules

### The Canadian Lacrosse Association Face-Off Rules

#### Start Face-Off at Center

All face-offs shall be conducted at the center Face-Off Circle to start the game, before each quarter/period, before an overtime quarter/period, and after every score. In today's game there is only one Face-Off Circle at center.

#### Referee Places the Ball on Dot

There is a 2" dot at center. To start the face-off the ball is placed on the dot. The referee shall place the ball on the floor between the two opposition players' sticks. Play shall start with a whistle. If a player or team delays the game prior to any face-off, possession of the ball goes to the non-offending team.

#### Positioning of Centerman Before the Draw

The "open face" of the centerman's stick must face his own goal. An easy way to remember the centerman's alignment is that his right shoulder is nearest his own goal whether he is a right-shot or a left-shot centerman.

#### Alignment of Stick

Players taking the face-off shall place the frames of their sticks flat along the playing surface at right angles to the length of the box. The open face of each player's stick shall face his own goal, and his feet shall not cross the Parallel Lines at the Face-Off Circle until the ball has left the two-foot-radius Face-Off Circle.

*Note: In Tyke and lower divisions, the persons taking the face-off are permitted to stand with their feet on (not over) the parallel lines.*

#### The Draw Motion

- The referee places the ball on the floor between the two players' sticks, who then contest for the ball. Play shall start with a whistle. The ball must come out of the circle.
- The two players are then permitted to gain possession of the ball by a straight draw backward.
- The first motion is continuous straight back draw until both sticks have cleared the face-off dot. Players are told to draw straight back and to keep their feet behind the parallel lines on either side of the Face-Off Circle.
- After a centerman draws his stick straight back, he then is allowed to trap the ball. The first motion must be a draw backward. Once that has taken place, a player can turn his stick over onto the ball to gain possession of

the ball, but the stick must continue past the face-off dot.

## Face-Off Violations

*"Dead Stick"*

Violation when centerman traps, clamps, or "dead sticks" which is clamping or trapping the ball and not moving his stick, with the intent to withhold play inside or outside of the circle. This is illegal and a technical penalty for illegal procedure shall be called. The ball shall be awarded to the non-offending team.

*Note: The referee, however, will allow some trapping if the centerman does it quickly with no delay.*

*Backward Motion*

Violation if a centerman does not comply to the first motion being backward, possession of the ball goes to the non-offending team.

*Movement of Centerman*

Violation, if a centerman "flinches," i.e., moves his stick or feet before the whistle, possession of the ball goes to the non-offending team.

*Ball Stuck in Stick*

Violation when the ball is stuck in the back of a player's stick upon facing off, possession of the ball goes to the non-offending team.

*Stepping on Opponent's Stick*

Violation for stepping on or kicking an opponent's stick, possession of the ball goes to the non-offending team.

*Cannot Touch Opponent's Stick with His Hand*

Violation if a centerman touches his opponent's stick with his hand or the netted portion of his own stick with his hand, possession of the ball goes to the non-offending team.

*Only Centermen Are Allowed in Center Zone*

When the ball is being faced-off, only the two centermen facing-off are allowed in the Center/

Neutral Zone. If another player enters the center zone before the ball leaves the two-foot-radius Face-Off Circle, possession of the ball goes to the non-offending team.

*Note: The ball must come out of the two-foot circle before non-face-off players are allowed to cross over the Restraining Lines.*

## The National Lacrosse League Face-Off Rules

- A new rule for the NLL is the sticks are now 8" apart rather than 2" apart for the beginning of the draw. Now players are going to have to experiment with the different face-off techniques to find which ones work the best.
- The rule used to be the walls of the stick must be approximately two inches apart so that when the ball is placed between them it can touch the floor. The sticks must not touch the ball.
- The big difference in the NLL from the CLA is that the centerman may trap or clamp first, then draw, but he must keep the stick in motion and not withhold the ball from play. Another difference in the NLL is that the face-off is a field-style face-off. Just get the ball out by pushing, pulling, pinching, and popping. A centerman does what he can to win the draw, but he has to make sure he keeps the ball moving and does not clamp too long or withhold the ball from play. In the CLA the first motion of the stick must be a straight drawback.
- Once the players have assumed their positions, the referee shall say, "set." Players taking the draw must remain motionless until the whistle is blown. Any movement after the "set" command shall cause possession of the ball to go to the non-offending team. In the CLA the referee does not call "set."
- The sticks must be placed so that they are parallel to the Center Line, and the players must keep their feet behind the Center Line.

In the CLA there is no Center Line on the floor diagram.

- In the CLA a centerman can take the face-off using the Side Stance or Straddle stance as long as his feet are behind the Parallel Line. In the NLL, a centerman can take the face-off using only the Side Stance as his feet must remain on his own side of the floor and not straddle the Center Line.
- Both hands must be on the handle of the stick and touching the floor. The feet may not touch the stick.
- Both hands and feet of each player must be to the left of the throat of the stick. Each must have both hands on the handle of the stick, not touching any strings and touching the floor. Their feet may not touch the stick. No portion of either stick may touch nor may either player be in contact with his opponent's body by encroaching in his opponent's territory.

**Other Major Differences in Rules Between CLA and NLL**

- In the NLL, the 10-second line is at center and once the team brings the ball over the 10-second it must keep it in the Offensive Zone for the remaining 30 seconds. If the ball goes over the Offensive Line, the offense loses possession of the ball. In the CLA the ball can go back over the center line without losing possession.
- The nets in NLL are 4' x 4'9". The nets in CLA are 4' x 4'6" or 4' x 4' (minor).
- Penalties: in the NLL, after the third man is penalized, it is a penalty shot. The NLL does not stack penalties. In CLA, teams can stack penalties, i.e., after two penalties the next penalties are delayed.
- In the NLL, the 30-second shot clock runs on all possessions. Now the Power Play team plays a one-man zone in the middle to back-up his teammates so that the Man Short cannot score as easily. The Power Play players know they will get the ball back in

30 seconds playing a conservative defense. In the CLA, the 30-second shot clock does not run if the team is short-handed. The man-short team can "rag" the ball for the full two-minute penalty. Now the power player players have to fight to get the ball back.

## II. Right-Handed Centerman Stance

### 1. The Side Stance for a Right-Handed Centerman

This is the most common stance and face-off method, called the "trap or clamp" method, used by centermen for taking the face-off.

**Body Position**

The main thing in taking the stance is to be balanced and feel comfortable. Take a semi-crouch or squat position with knees bent for a quick explosive move. Getting into this position gives one a low center of gravity which helps to maintain good balance, stability, and strength. So do not be flat-footed, but be on the balls of the feet, with knees bent, and be ready to attack any loose ball on the floor. The head should be tilted forward so a player can put his head on the opposition's front arm on the draw, now the body is lower than his opponent's. It is really important to stay low to the ground and be the last man to stand up. Usually the player to stand up last wins the draw.

**Photo 68:** The side stance for a right-handed centerman

### Placement of Feet

Get in a crouched position beside the stick with a wide-staggered stance. The front foot is parallel with the stick, while the back foot is turned sideways to give support and a solid brace to push from. A right-hand centerman stands on the same side of the stick as his own goal, i.e., on the outside of his stick. Some players like to kneel on one knee beside their stick, but this puts them at a disadvantage if they want to get up quickly.

### Grip of Stick

A player moves his top hand up to the throat of the stick while the bottom hand grabs the butt of the stick or moves it up the shaft, no farther than the mid-point. A strong centerman can place his hands close together, giving him a smaller radius to move his stick away or toward his body; while a weaker centerman should place his hands wider apart to make up for the strength factor. The knuckles of both the top hand and the bottom hand are flat to the floor. This position of the knuckles helps the centerman to draw and trap simultaneously. The power comes from both hands when rotating the stick inward to trap the ball, but the top hand is the key hand as most of the power comes from this hand, the right hand.

*Note: The old rules were such that the face-off was a straight trap as in the NLL. In this case, before the actual trap the wrist of the top hand would be rotated backward so that the back of the hand was underneath the stick and flat to the floor for more leverage. This position of the top-hand was important because more power could come from this hand as it now has farther to rotate forward. In this "power" grip position the opposition player would have had difficulty moving the head of the centerman's stick. This works on the same principle as turning a doorknob: the stronger somebody wants to turn a doorknob, the farther one rotates his wrist underneath before grabbing the doorknob, so that he will have more leverage to rotate his wrist.*

### Pressure on the Stick

A player can also put weighted pressure on the stick to help "muscle" the "back" of the pocket completely flush to the floor over the ball as he draws back. A player does this by staying low and exerting downward pressure with his body weight onto his front hand and front foot. The body's weight over the top hand helps to "muscle" the stick down on the trap. He can start the face-off with the body weight between the hands, but as a player begins his trap, the body rolls over the top hand and stays there. If a player can get away with it before the actual draw, he should lean the head of the stick slightly over the ball, rather than keeping it straight up and down, to give himself an advantage.

## 2. The Straddle Stance for a Right-Handed Centerman (CLA)

### Body Position

Take a squat position with knees bent and feet wide.

### Placement of Feet

In this position the centerman straddles the stick, i.e., the stick is between the legs, making sure the stance is wide and that he stays in this semi-crouched position. Not many players use this position of standing over the top of the stick, but those centermen who do, usually lefties, say they have more power and control.

**Photo 69:** The straddle stance for a right-handed centerman

The rules in the NLL do not permit a player to take this straddle position. A centerman has to stay on his own side of the Center Line.

### Grip of Stick

The top hand is placed at the throat of the stick while the bottom hand grabs the shaft halfway up.

### Pressure on the Stick

Similar to the Side Stance, the centerman leans forward over the stick almost looking straight down at the ball.

## III. Face-Off Techniques

There is really no wrong way when taking a stance to take the face-off. A centerman will take the stance that he feels comfortable and natural with. He will find the best and easiest technique to win the face-off, knowing he still might have to adjust this technique and have counters for certain opposition centermen. He has to be physically and mentally ready when taking the draw. The secret to becoming a good centerman is to learn from the experienced centermen he faces-off against.

*Note: Because of the new rule in the NLL that the sticks have to be 8" apart rather than 2" apart to start the face-off, centermen will have to experiment with these methods of taking the draw and find out which works for them best.*

### The "Trap" or Clamp Method

In this technique the centerman (black mesh in Photo 70) does a straight draw backward while simultaneously doing a quick forward rotation of the top-hand wrist, turning the "back" of the head of the stick over flat to the floor, thereby, trapping the ball under the mesh, while continuously drawing the ball backward in front of himself to scoop it up. The draw and trap is done in one continuous motion by

the top-hand wrist. Both the top hand and the bottom hand help to pull the stick back and both give power when turning the stick on the trap. Because the right-hander traps away from his body, he has a natural advantage of the body weight moving in the same direction as the wrist is turning. If the centerman gets his stick underneath his opponent's stick head first he will win the draw. This "Trap or Clamp" technique is not a finesse move, but mainly a power move. So players should just draw and trap in one continuous motion.

*Notes:*
– *Most of the face-off players in the NLL "trap" 95 percent of the time or at least partially trap the ball and adjust from there. The trap is the most effective way to get a win because it is the only way to really control where the ball goes. Using the other techniques is much more difficult to control where the ball goes.*
– *An NLL face-off player stated that the most effective way to get a win is to use the advantages that are listed here. He uses every one of the advantages. A face-off player needs to cheat in every little way he can. All of the little cheats add up to a one big win.*

**Photo 70:** The "Trap" or Clamp face-off method

### The Five Advantages:

To either gain a split-second or get more power, a centerman will try one or all of these methods to get an advantage. Remember to do these moves quickly so you don't get caught by the referee.

### Advantage No. 1—Lift the Handle

With the back hand lift the handle about two inches off the floor to help get more body weight into the trapping motion.

### Advantage No. 2—Lean Stick Slightly Over the Ball

By leaning his stick slightly over the top of the ball, the centerman can get underneath the

**Photo 71:** Advantage No. 1 for trap—with the back hand lift the handle about two inches off the floor

stick of the opposition centerman quicker and thereby trap first.

### Advantage No. 3—Push the Handle Out

Push the stick handle out to the left (toward opponent's net) and away from the body with the bottom hand (about a 20-degree angle to an opponent's stick). This movement is so that a player gets little resistance from his opponent's stick when he rotates his own stick downward. The thick end (the tip) of the head will now be in a position so that when he turns his stick to trap, the tip will go down without hitting his opponent's stick.

### Advantage No. 4—Move Stick Slightly Forward

The referee is supposed to place the ball in the middle of the pocket of both sticks. If a player can move his stick forward slightly, he will get an advantage as it is easier to clamp the ball as the pocket is narrower at the "throat" of the stick's head, making it quicker to go over the top of the ball. Besides all the power being at the throat, by moving the stick forward the centerman will have more netting to pull on.

If the centerman does the "Draw" method, and uses this advantage he will have a higher percentage of the ball popping out on his side of the circle.

**Photo 72:** Advantage No. 2 for trap—lean his stick slightly over the top of the ball

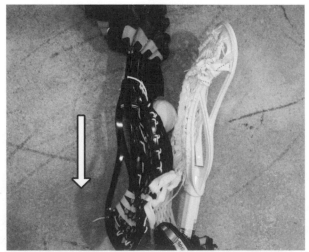

**Photo 73:** Advantage No. 4 for trap—move his stick forward slightly, pocket is narrower at the "throat" of the stick's head

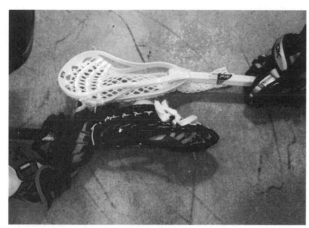

**Photo 74:** Advantage No. 5 for trap—Move the top hand closer to the throat of the stick, glove blocks opponent from trapping

### Advantage No. 5—Move Top Hand Closer to Throat

Move the top hand closer to the throat of the stick. This will give the centerman an edge by getting his glove involved in the trap, either to block his opponent's stick from turning or to use his glove as leverage to push his opponent's stick back.

*Steve Fannell, formerly of the Albany Attack of the NLL,* regarding the clamp: Steve draws a line across the middle of his stick's pocket frame, called the centerline, to help decide whether to clamp or create a stalemate.

"When I clamp against a player I can beat, I will clamp or trap the ball only if I can keep the ball above this centerline. I will clamp on the ball and either pull it back or rake it forward. If I clamp the ball and pull it back between my legs I will try to pick it up. After I trap, I try to block my opponent out by stepping or turning my body in front of him so he can't see the ball.

"If I am clamping to win I put more pressure on the head of my stick to get more strength into my trap. I do this by leaning more over my stick and putting my top-hand wrist bent with my palm flat on the floor so that when I turn up and over on the clamp I will have more strength. I also place my bottom-hand at the mid-point of the shaft for more power.

"If I want to clamp, not to win, but to 'hold' the ball, creating a stalemate I will keep the ball lower on the pocket to the throat of the stick, below the centerline."

### The "Draw" Method

- This is a quick move of pulling the stick back toward the body with both hands. With this drawing motion the ball is pulled by the netting in the same direction as the stick is pulled with the result of the ball coming out on the centerman's side of the circle.
- Remember, the referee tries to place the ball in the middle of the two sticks so neither player has an advantage. The trick is that the more netting a centerman can draw on, the better chance he has of winning the draw. So, just before the whistle, move the stick slightly forward to get the ball as close to the throat as possible. (Advantage No. 4) Do it quickly so you don't get caught. This maneuver will give the centerman more netting to draw on and thereby a higher percentage of the ball popping out on his side of the circle.
- Another trick is to lean the stick slightly over the top of the ball to get underneath the opponent's stick before the whistle to prevent the opponent from getting the advantage of putting his stick over the ball, "trapping," and getting underneath his stick

**Photo 75:** The "Draw" face-off method

first (Advantage No. 2). This move will put more pressure on the ball by the netting and the top edge of the tip of the stick as the centerman pulls the ball back. This "Draw" technique is a move of quickness versus the strength of the "Trap or Clamp."

*Notes:*
- *For this quick "Draw" method, players put pressure on the stick, but no weight on his hands as in the "Trap" method, and keeps his body weight on his feet, but no body weight on his front foot as in the "Trap" method, keeping his hands free and relaxed for fast stick action and to move quickly.*
- *If two centermen just draw straight back, the ball will stay in the middle of the small two-foot Face-Off Circle. A centerman must do different things to get an edge.*

***Steve Toll of the Rochester Knighthawks of the NLL,*** on the Draw method.
"All I do is just a quick clamp, pull the ball toward me, and scoop it up. I recommend staying low, keep your weight on your feet, and put a little pressure on the stick, but not on your gloves. I place my feet along the Center Line with all my weight on my front foot.

This keeps my hands free and relaxed so I can move quickly. I do not want to put pressure on my stick or on my hands, so I get this fast stick action. It is important to be physically and mentally ready on the draw."

## The "Double" Draw or the "Push-and-Pull" Method

The centerman puts his weight on his front hand near the throat of the head of the stick. He puts his other hand at the mid-point of the shaft rather than at the butt of the stick. This grip gives a centerman more flexibility and power on his draw. In the Push-and-Pull method, as the opponent draws, the centerman goes with him by moving his stick forward attempting to push the ball to the "throat" of his stick (Advantage No. 4). With the ball at or near the "throat," the centerman stops his forward draw and now starts to draw back because he now has more "netting" to draw on. Thus, the ball pops out on his side of the Face-Off Circle. Also, as he moves his stick forward, he is turning it inward (Advantage No. 2) to help put more force on the ball by the netting to stop it from being pulled by the opposition's netting. This maneuver works against a centerman who also likes to "Draw."

**Photo 76:** The "Double" draw or the "push-and-pull" face-off method—the push

**Photo 77:** The "Double" draw or the "push-and-pull" face-off method—the pull

*Brad McArthur, formerly of the Toronto Rock of the NLL,* talks about the Push-and-Pull method.

"I push forward with my top hand on the front of my stick and at the same time tilt my stick at about 45 degrees to stop my opponent from trapping the ball under his stick. I then pull the ball straight back down the center of the floor to a teammate."

## The "Hesitation Draw" Method

### Stance

For best results with this technique, the right-handed centerman should take a kneeling stance and align his left knee with the face-off dot or with the tip of his opposition's stick. He does this to get a subtle advantage because now he has to place his stick on the outside of his left knee with the result of the stick being slanted at an angle to his opponent's stick which should be straight (Advantage No. 3) Being down on one knee may give a player less mobility, but this stance helps in setting up the "Hesitation" draw because the stick is at an angle—plus leaning the stick against his left leg gives his stick stability. A player may be slower to get up with one knee on the floor, but if he gains possession of the ball, he does not have to worry about getting up quickly.

### Grip

The top hand is placed at the throat of the stick with all his body weight on it and his bottom hand grips the stick about two-thirds of the way down the shaft for more strength. The bottom hand and stick rests against his left knee for more stability and strength.

### Setting Up the Hesitation Draw

Start the face-off with the stick straight up and down, but as the referee moves away turn the stick inward a quarter turn to lean the stick slightly over the top of the ball to get an advantage (Advantage No. 2). Rotating the stick a quarter turn helps to put more physical pressure on the ball by the netting portion of the stick. As the opposition centerman draws back, the ball will be restrained by the netting, the shooting strings, and the tip of the centerman's stick.

### The Hesitation Draw

Let the opposition centerman draw first, making sure the centerman's stick is kept still. He must be very quick and anticipate his opponent's move. As the opponent starts his draw, the centerman does not draw, but merely holds his stick, preventing the ball from being drawn back. This drawing action by the opposition centerman does not bring the ball out because the ball is being restrained by the netting, the shooting strings, and the tip of the centerman's stick. The ball now ends up at the opposition's tip, where he will lose strength. This is because the farther the ball gets away from the middle of the netting, the less power he will have; however the ball will still be in the middle of the centerman's netting for a powerful trap.

## The "Flip" Method

With this technique, as the centerman continuously draws, he traps, i.e., turns the back of his stick downward, then, continues the stick around, knocking or flipping the ball back to his goalie with the back of his stick. From the beginning of the move to the end, he turns his stick 180 degrees. The wrist rotates forward on the trap and continues rotating around so that the wrist actually pushes the stick backward. The "flip" move must be done quickly with no hesitation on the trap.

*Steve Fannell, formerly of the Albany Attack of the NLL:* When "clamping" against a player I can beat, another technique I use is I will trap the ball and spin or turn my stick back around [180 degrees] and knock the ball back to my teammates or goalie.

## The "Up-and-Over" Method

This technique is a move of split-second quickness and finesse, with the centerman going over the top of the ball with his "head," getting his stick between the opponent's stick and the ball, then knocking it back with the "face" of the pocket. He can either lift up the throat end of the stick to bring it over the ball while at the same time using the handle to block his opponent's stick from trapping or just lift the whole head of his stick over the ball. The centerman tries to use his shaft to block the opponent's stick, but in a game he usually uses his glove to interfere with his opponent's stick. To get an advantage, he can start the face-off holding the stick's head in the air rather than resting it on the floor. Some players even wear bigger gloves to help keep the stick off the floor.

**Variation:** This is the strength move of going "Up-and-Over." The centerman concentrates on his opponent's stick rather than the ball at the beginning of the move. He picks up his stick and uses his shaft to prevent his opponent's "head" from trapping down. By moving his top hand forward just before the draw he can use it also to help block his opponent's stick. Here he must use all his strength to get underneath the stick of the trapping opponent. The centerman must keep "digging" and be persistent so he eventually will get under his opponent's stick head and push it from the ball, letting the ball go under his own stick, then knocking the ball back to a teammate.

## The "Block" Method

This technique is a defensive maneuver to counter a centerman who wins by "trapping." In this situation, the plastic head will bend and flatten out quickly. With the "Block" technique, rather than the shaft being used to block the head of the stick, as in the "Up-and-Over" technique, the tip of the head is used to interfere with the opponent trapping down on the ball.

As the referee moves away from the face-off, the centerman pulls the butt-end of the handle toward his body, placing the head at roughly a 45-degree angle to the opponent's head, with the tip straight up and down, and pushes it in toward his opponent's stick. The stick is now in a good position to block the opponent's stick as he tries to turn his stick to trap the ball. The centerman then turns this into an offensive move by sweeping the ball out from underneath his opponent's stick.

**Photo 78:** The "Up-and-Over" face-off method—lift stick at throat and block opponent's stick from trapping then coming over top of ball front facing your goal

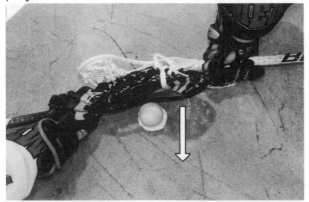

**Photo 79:** The "Up-and-Over" face-off method—knock ball back

**Photo 80:** The "Block" face-off method—pull stick toward body

## The "Sweep" Method

The "Sweep" technique occurs when the centerman pulls the end of the handle toward his body, but this time he turns the stick "face" down on the floor and goes underneath his opponent's stick, and sweeps the ball from underneath his opponent's stick with the frame of his stick. His opponent can only trap the ball into the back of his stick's pocket. This is strictly an offensive move.

*Steve Fannell, formerly of the Albany Attack of the NLL,* says, "When clamping against a player I can beat another technique I use is the "Sweep" method in which I will go under the opposition centerman's stick and sweep the ball back to a teammate or goalie."

# IV. Left-Handed Centerman Stance

*Notes:*
– *The disadvantage for most left-handed centermen is that they are natural right-handed people and the power hand is the left hand which is his weaker hand.*
– *Centermen in the NLL cannot take a left-handed stance as it is against the rules, because you cannot step over the Center Line. This left-handed stance is done about 20 percent of the time in the CLA.*

## 1. The Side Stance

### Body Stance

Same body position as a right-handed centerman.

### Placement of Feet

A left-handed centerman has the same stance as a right-handed centerman, except he stands on the same side of the stick as the opposition's net, i.e., he stands on the inside of his stick.

## Grip of Stick for Various Techniques
*Reverse Grip*

For all these techniques, the left-hand centerman can also take a reverse grip with the left hand, similar to a hockey centerman on a backhand face-off. This grip allows more leverage and power as a player can grip the stick on the outside of the shaft with the wrist at a 45-degree angle to the floor. On the rotation a player can then use not only his wrist and forearm, but also his upper back for more strength. Again, the difference with this left-handed reverse grip is that the trap comes only toward the body where he can scoop it up rather than away from the body or toward him for a scoop up like the right-handers do.

a. **The Trap**

For the "Trap" technique, he can take a normal grip with his left hand at the throat and rotate his wrist backward, turning his stick toward his body to trap. Again, he is at a disadvantage because this is his weaker hand and the rotation backward is not a natural one.

b. **The Draw**

For the "Draw" technique, he has the same advantage as a right-handed centerman.

c. **The Flip**

For the "Flip" technique, he can turn his stick toward his body by rotating his top-hand wrist backward to get the head flat to the floor, and then he continues rotating his wrist to end up with the back of the wrist under the stick and pushing the stick backward with his palm. This is a difficult and tough move to execute.

d. **"Up-and-Over"**

For the "Up-and-Over" technique, he picks up his stick's shaft to prevent his opponent's head from trapping down while at the same time pushing his opponent's stick head away from the ball and then knocking the ball to a teammate with the shaft or head. This is a more natural move than trying to trap the ball, and is a good move against a hard trap.

## 2. Straddle Stance

This stance is more commonly used by the left-handers. Use the same stance as a right-hander except that the top hand is the left hand. The objective is to counter the power of the right-hander by using quickness and being in a better position to react to a loose ball.

## V. Qualities for a Centerman on the Face-Off

The essential priorities of a centerman taking a face-off are:

### Concentration

Shut everything out and focus on the ball, the referee's whistle, your technique and what the opposition centerman is going to try to do.

### Stance

A player should be comfortable and balanced so he can concentrate on his drawing technique—weight on the front hand and front foot if he is going to "Clamp."

### Grip

The top hand for a right-hander is the most important because this is where most of the power comes from.

### Alignment of Stick

Try to get an edge by tilting the stick inward over the ball and slant the shaft at an angle pushing it outward from the body.

### Anticipation

Anticipate, or "cheat" by making your move just slightly before the referee's whistle and your opponent's action. This is important for a player who relies on the "Draw" technique

### Combination of Strength, Quickness, and Technique

A centerman must learn to use his asset, whether it is strength or quickness, to complement his technique.

*Note: An NLL face-off player: "I think face-offs are mostly technique, but obviously the faster and stronger a centerman is the better chance he has of winning the draw. I have never been the fastest or strongest, but I feel I can consistently beat most of the guys in the NLL league."*

### Intelligence

Be smart enough to analyze the opposition centerman and figure out why he is winning or losing.

### Competitiveness and Determination

Fight for and pursue all loose balls.

## VI. Face-Off Tips and Strategies for Centermen

### Facing-Off is All About Getting an Advantage

The basic philosophy for a centerman is to do whatever he can do to offset the advantage of the opposition and/or to do whatever he can do to get the advantage. Most times whoever gets the best advantage before the actual face-off wins. Things such as tilting the stick inward slightly over the ball, pushing the stick out slightly at an angle when trapping, putting the feet over the Restraining Line, and moving the stick's head forward slightly to get more netting to draw on the ball, all lead to advantages. He should try to do what he is most comfortable with and make his opponent beat him. But do not become predictable.

Any advantage or "cheating," such as trapping early before the whistle, should take place after the referee places the ball between the sticks and starts to move out of the circle. If you can control the ball, that is, win the face-off, you must know where you want the ball to go. General rule for face-offs is "cheat until you are caught."

## Some Face-Off Players Have a Strictly Face-Off Stick

Face-off players have pinched their stick to use strictly for taking face-offs, especially if they rely mainly on the trap. Some centermen use a face-off stick for face-offs and have another stick for the rest of the game. Face-offs destroy the stick and NLL face-off men go through three to four face-off sticks per season and one stick for the rest of the season.

## Get Possession Over Creating a Loose Ball

Possession is the most important thing. If the centerman can win 60 percent of his face-offs, he is doing an excellent job. He obtains this high percentage by picking up the ball, directing the ball to a teammate, or just plain old fighting and winning loose balls. If a centerman can pick up the ball from the face-off, then "pick it up" rather than knocking it to a teammate or back to his goalie.

*Note: A NLL centerman thinks everyone would like to pick up the ball, but only a few great face-off men can do it on a consistent basis. Certainly picking the ball up yourself is the best option if you can do it.*

## On Winning the Face-Off, the Centerman's Options Are:

All the players on the team should know where the ball is going, so the good centermen should have a signal or a set play so their teammates can anticipate and react to the loose ball. Also before the draw look at your players to see who are the fresher players. Read their energy level and draw the ball to the side you feel your players are fresher.

### 1. Pick the Ball Up

The best thing to do is win the draw and scoop up the ball facing it. In a regular game, 60 percent of the time the centerman, if the centerman controls the draw, is trying to knock the ball to a teammate, knock it back to his goalie or pick it up, but it may still just go loose. The other 40 percent of the time the centerman is trying to get the ball free from his opponent's control.

In today's game the art of actually winning the face-off, with the result of the centerman picking it up, has disappeared. Most centermen just knock the ball loose or draw it to a teammate, because the opposing players are too close, and too quick getting in on the Face-Off Circle and hitting the centerman.

If a centerman wins the draw, he tries to knock the ball to a teammate about 80 percent of the time and pick it up 20 percent. As a centerman, try to pick up the ball off a face-off, this happens about 20 percent of the time, as the rules permit protection for the centerman in the face-off area as he cannot be checked by the other players. The only thing the other players can do is reach in the center circle with their sticks for a loose ball.

### 2. Hit the Loose Ball to Goalie

The centerman, after winning the draw, hits the ball directly back to the goalie.

### 3. Knock Ball to Teammate

The centerman, after winning the draw, knocks the ball directly to a teammate. When drawing directly back to a teammate, make sure the ball goes to the side of the teammate who hopefully has sealed or boxed out his opponent.

Draw, trap, and knock the ball to a teammate, who is usually coming in behind him. He can knock it back like a sweeping motion with the back of his pocket, or he can knock it back with the tip of his stick. He can also knock the ball forward to a creaseman in the Offensive Zone, or he can knock it backward to his goalie in the Defensive Zone.

Most times a centerman wants to pick up the ball off a face-off, but knocking it to a teammate might be just as advantageous, depending on who is on the Restraining Line, a good loose-ball man, and how the opposition has lined up.

*Note: When executing the "Trap" in the Straddle position, the centerman draws, traps, and knocks the ball between his legs. He does this so his teammates, not he, can pick it up, although he can pursue it as a loose ball.*

### 4. Draw Ball Out Behind Himself

The centerman, after winning the draw, draws the ball directly out behind himself for either his creaseman (forward) or cornerman (defenseman).

### 5. Push the Ball Behind Opposition Centerman

The centerman, after winning the draw, pushes the ball behind the opposition centerman so a teammate can pick up the loose ball.

### 6. Force the Draw into a Loose Ball

Centerman draws and traps with the idea of letting the ball go loose, then pursuing it as a loose ball. Just as a good centerman does not use the same technique every time, he does not hit the ball to the same spot every time; sometimes it is easier to go forward, sometimes is easier to go backward, or to a certain player. Everybody pursues all loose balls, the closest player and centerman.

### 7. Pick Ball Up and Look for Breaking Offensive Player

The centerman draws and traps and then picks up the ball looking for the creaseman breaking toward the net. The creaseman can just break and beat his defender on sheer speed or the other creaseman can set a pick on the breaking creaseman's defender. On this pass from the draw, the centerman stays down on the draw, and even on the pick-up, the pass is gone before he stands up.

## Strategies to Counter Opposition Centerman From Winning the Draw

- Before getting into his stance, a centerman should get a mental picture of what his opponent did on the last face-off.
- If a centerman is getting beaten and knows what technique his opponent is going to use, he should use this same technique as an edge. He just copies what the opposition centerman does. If he cannot beat him, he copies him.
- Centerman must be ready to get a split-second jump on his opponent by executing his technique before the whistle is blown by the referee.
- Centerman might have to change his style against a good opposition centerman and take a little more of a defensive approach.
- Centerman must take an "advantage" position with his stick. (See section on Advantages)
- Centerman must have a countermove.
- Centerman can try a "Draw" or "Rake" technique to get the ball out quickly to prevent his opponent from trapping.
- Centerman can try mixing up his techniques against his opponent and try getting him rattled a little bit.
- Centerman can try to outguess his opponent.
- Centerman grabs his opponent's webbing with his top-hand fingers underneath his stick.
- Centerman can think of staying on the defensive side of the floor and go to where his opponent likes to pop the ball, where he can have a better chance of preventing him from picking up the ball.
- Centerman can try to keep the ball loose by leaning all his weight on the top hand and "raking" the ball straight back with all his strength.
- Once his opponent traps, the centerman traps over top of his opponent's stick and

the ball. The ball will either pop out or both players will be called for a stalemate and will be kicked out of that particular face-off.

- The "Sweep" and the "Up-and-Over" moves are used to counter the trapper.

*Steve Fannell, formerly of the Albany Attack of the NLL,* recommends to "stay with your two best face-off moves and keep one in 'the closet.'

"When playing against someone who is better than you, just let them win and pursue the loose ball. Clamp down to start, but when you are ready to pursue release the clamping pressure. As your opponent goes down to clamp over the ball, you are on your way up in pursuit of the hopefully loose ball."

## Rightie Versus Leftie

Some centermen feel a right-hander has a natural advantage over a left-hander because his top hand and his body weight is moving in a natural forward motion, but there are many left-handers who have great technique and are tough to beat. Lefties are only in the CLA.

## Analyze His Opponent

Centerman should look to see if his opponent is a clamper or is a quick-draw man. Some feel a "trapper" will always beat a straight "draw" man, but it still boils down to strength, quickness, and technique. A combination of good technique, quickness, and strength will win most of the time no matter what type of technique a player uses. So unless a centerman has all these qualities, he needs to figure out how to beat his opponent. A player must analyze his strengths and how to use them, and analyze his opponent's strength and how to adjust or counter.

*Note: A centerman gets better by analyzing and copying opposition centermen.*

## Reading and Working the Referee

- Get to know the tendencies of the referees. Referees will for the most part have the same time factor for each face-off—ball down, centermen in, ready, three-steps back, and blows his whistle. Good face-off specialists get to know referee's routines. Count from the time the referee leaves the Face-Off Circle until he blows his whistle; a face-off guy might pick up on a pattern he has, depending on where he backs out. Some face-off guys may even watch the referee's mouth as they might be able to tell when he is going to blow his whistle to start the play.
- If a centerman can get away with some things, he should keep doing them. Watch as the referee backs away, a face-off man can sometimes start to roll his stick over if the ref is not looking or get away with something else. Most referees are looking for a safe way out and not at the stick. Referees let players do what they want as long as they do it quickly, especially in tight games. If players delay the trap, they will be called for "withholding the ball from play."
- On some nights a referee will let things go and on other nights another referee will call a game tightly, so a centerman has to be smart enough to know what he can get away with, with certain referees.
- The draw man will always work his opponent trying to beat him and work the referee a little, hoping to place attention on his opponent's illegal moves and off him.
- If the opposition centerman is very good at cheating by anticipating the whistle and going early. A centerman has to get on the ref about this right away.
- If the opposition centerman keeps winning by taking an unfair advantage, complain to the referee. Especially for a very important face-off tell the referee, so the opposition can hear, that for example, "his foot is over the Parallel Line." This could get the

opposition slightly distracted because now he is concentrating on not putting his foot on the line rather than the face-off. Also, the referee might get distracted about what the centerman is doing by watching that the opponent does not step on the line.

- If the centerman has lost a draw for a violation, ask the referee what you did wrong at the next face-off. Learn from your mistakes and what they are calling that night.

    *Brad McArthur, formerly of the Toronto Rock of the NLL,* on face-offs. "Five keys for becoming a good face-off man: 1) You need strength and conditioning. 2) You need to set up your opponent properly. 3) You need quick reaction on the draw. 4) You need a good, low, solid stance. 5) You need good weight distribution."

## VII. Face-Off Alignment

### Players' Stance on the Restraining Line

- Be physically ready, i.e., be low and crouched with stick in ready position to scoop the ball up. If a player is standing up straight he is definitely not ready to go after a loose ball.
- Be mentally ready and alert to attack the ball immediately. The attitude is, "that's my ball." It is man-against-man, so make sure your check does not get the ball.
- Try to anticipate where the ball is coming out from the draw.
- All five players should talk beforehand and have a signal or set play where the ball is trying to be placed.
- Stress aligning-up on opponent's stick side to interfere with his stick or to align on the outside, to the sideboards, of an opponent depending on the situation.
- Do not try to pick up the ball with just the stick exposed, use the body to protect the ball, and use two hands on the scoop.

*Note: The ball must come out of the two-foot-radius Face-Off Circle first before the non-face-off players can break over the Restraining Line to go after the loose ball.*

### Positioning on the Restraining Line

**1. Centerman's Responsibility on Loose Balls**
The centerman pursues the ball wherever it goes, unless he picks it up or wins it or knocks it completely back to the goalie. He must stay low to keep a low center of gravity for better balance. In pursuit of the ball be relentless, aggressive and persistent. Scoop the loose ball up with two hands on the stick and then protect it with the body. Stress keeping the butt of the handle low to the ground for an easier scoop pick-up.

**2. The Defensive Players on the Restraining Line (Cornermen and Pointman)**

- Defensive Players General Rule is, "If your man goes, you go. If your man doesn't go, you don't go." If a defensive player questions whether he can get a loose ball he stays back. He plays cautious defensively as he always errs on the side of defense.
- The back two defenders do not go after loose balls unless they know absolutely they can get it.
- The defensive players must never back off on the face-off, especially if their team has a chance of obtaining the loose ball. The defender, on the side of the ball where it comes out, cheats in for the loose ball, while the other defender balances the floor.
- "The opponent beside you does not get the ball." The defender must interfere with him and cannot let him pick it up. On all face-offs, the ball could come out loose every time and a team could lose every battle. Keep these attitudes: "Your man does not get the ball!" "It's our ball." "We must dominate the face-offs."
- The defensive players try to get on the outside, sideboards side, or stick side of

their opponent. They interfere with their opponent's stick by putting their own stick over the opposition's stick, or interfere with the opposition's fast-break from the face-off by putting their leg behind the opposition's leg.

- If the opposition tries to shoot in to check the centerman or go after a loose ball, the defensive player will again interfere with him by putting his stick in front of his body or step in front of his opponent's body to hold him or at least slow him down. Be careful not to make it so obvious when using the stick that the defensive player is called for "holding" by the referee.
- Against a great loose-ball player a defensive player can face-guard him and cross-check him to stop or deny him from getting the ball. If nobody interferes with a great loose-ball player he will beat a defender to the ball all night. So face-guard him and deny him a straight line to the loose ball.
- If the centerman knows he is going to win the face-off, he places the two defensive players on the inside of their checks to form a "cup" where he can place the ball between them down the middle of the floor.
- If the centerman knows the opposition centerman is going to win the draw and try to knock it back to his goalie, he places one defensive teammate behind the opposition centerman, on the outside of his check, and the other defensive player in the middle of the floor to counter his teammate.
- After picking up the ball, tuck it in or throw it back to the goalie.

## 3. The Offensive Players on the Restraining Line (Two Creaseman)

- If the ball is loose from the draw, they pursue the ball on their side of the floor every time.
- A team needs tough players on the face-off unit who are quick, big, not afraid to get hit, and good at getting loose balls.

- On the face-off, it is a "one-on-one" battle, in other words, "the man beside you does not get the ball." Everybody plays every loose ball like they "want it." The offensive player must clamp down on the man's stick beside him and does not let him pick up the ball. Does a player play on his opponent's stick side or on the outside? It depends on who the centerman is and who is beside the offensive player.
- An offensive player has to be in first for any loose ball. The toughest thing in this game is to pick up a loose ball knowing one is going to get hit. So attack all loose balls with total abandonment.
- An offensive player must attack the loose ball rather than running in the opposite direction down the floor for a fast-break. Getting possession of the ball is number one priority.
- Offensive forwards have to fire in and "cheat" off the line for any loose ball. Referees seem to miss a lot of plays with players cheating or moving in early.
- Offensive forwards can "cheat" more on the line going after a loose ball because they don't have to worry about being scored upon.
- If the opposition is in first for a loose ball, an offensive player never backs off and just lets him pick it up. He must play his stick to stop him from picking it up or bang him into the boards. The good loose ball teams send two players after every loose ball.
- Most centermen pull the ball out behind them most times. So the forward or creaseman playing on that side plays on the outside of his opponent on the Restraining Line to go after the loose ball.
- If opposition centerman knocks the ball back to his goalie, put an offensive player halfway back between the opposition's goalie and Face-Off Circle.
- If the centerman knows he can win the draw, he sends the offensive players on a

break from the face-off to get a goal rather than getting a loose ball.

- In the NLL, players can move along the line before the ball is drawn to get a jump or cheat to go after a loose ball. *Jim Veltman, formerly of the Toronto Rock of the NLL,* likes to stand behind his opponent and run around him anticipating the loose ball coming out.

## VIII. Face-Off Game Adjustments

Coach has to be prepared to make adjustments or do something to the opposition to take away their advantage, such as change the centerman, change from two players back to three back on defense, change the alignment, or change the face-off group to a different group of players.

### No. 1 Rule: No Goals Off the Face-Off!

Follow this rule even to the point where the coach will put three players back in the defensive end. He would rather neutralize the other team, meaning give them possession rather than give up a goal. It is much better to play five-on-five lacrosse rather than give up a goal from the face-off. Coach does not worry about wins and losses on the face-off, he worries about getting scored upon. He still wants aggressive pursuit of the ball, but not to the point where his team gives up an odd-man situation.

### Put Three Men Back on Defense

If the opposition fast-breaks from the face-off, coach should put a third defender back. By putting three players back the coach protects himself from a fast-break. He has the option of being aggressive by "firing" one of the offensive players from the Defensive Line to go after any loose ball, or he can become totally defensive by putting the third defender halfway back to the net in the defensive zone.

### Change Players

- If the centerman is losing, the coach has to put in a new centerman.
- Coach can send into the game two centermen. The first centerman can cause a stalemate by trapping the ball along with the opposition centerman, then both of these centermen will be thrown out of the face-off. Then, the second centerman comes in to take the draw.
- If a centerman cannot beat a certain type of opponent, let another teammate centerman take the face-off. It seems that certain centermen have more success against certain opposition centermen. So a player should not be so stubborn to prevent another teammate from taking the face-off. Some nights a centerman feels he can beat anybody, then there are other nights when he just can't beat anybody. Those are the nights he should let a teammate take the face-offs.

### Loose Balls Off Face-Off

Some teams plan on creating loose balls from the face-off rather than picking them up because their centerman is weak. If the ball goes in the Defensive Zone from the face-off, some teams send only one defender after the loose ball, while the other defender protects the net. The centerman follows all loose balls along with the offensive forward on that side.

### Going Against a Strong Face-Off Centerman

- Coach goes with a big centerman against a big opposition centerman for the strength factor on the draw. If that doesn't work, then go for quickness. Coach must make adjustments against a big strong face-off player.
- If the big face-off centerman can put the ball wherever he wants to, such as knocking the ball back to his goalie, coach must put a player halfway back between the Face-Off Circle and the opposition net.

## Aligning Teammates on a Draw the Centerman is Going to Lose

- The centerman makes sure one of his teammates lines up behind the opposition centerman and fires in to check him.
- If the opposition centerman keeps knocking the ball back to his goalie, put a player halfway back between the center Face-Off Circle and the opposition goalie's crease.
- If all else fails, put three players back on defense to relinquish possession of the ball and to protect the goal if the opposition gets possession.

## IX. Face-Off Drills

The best way to get better as a centerman is to just take a lot of face-offs. A coach doesn't want to have four or five guys taking face-offs, especially in the NLL. He should take his two best guys and let them take them all. A centerman can't get better only taking four or five draws in a game. Repetition is the key. The more draws a centerman takes the better he gets. There are some centermen who have a variety of drills that they use to practice their face-offs. Then there are other centermen who have never practiced taking face-offs or done any drills. For them it's been on-the-job training. Some centermen have been taking face-offs since they were tyke (four years old) and have developed their skills on the job by taking thousands of face-offs. In the NLL a centerman averages around 25 draws a game.

## 1. One-on-One Centermen Face-Off Drill

a. One centerman gives token resistance.
b. One player traps the ball while the partner does a countermove.
c. One player draws the ball while the partner does a countermove.
d. Do a "live" face-off.

## 2. One-on-One Loose Ball on the Restraining Line Face-Off Drill

Coach rolls a ball from the Face-Off Circle while both players are on the Restraining Line ready to go after the loose ball.

## 3. One-on-One Loose Ball on the Restraining Line Face-Off Drill (Eight Pairs)

Coach rolls ball from Face-Off Circle and a designated pair fight for possession, one player opposite the other on the Restraining Lines.

## 4. Two-on-Two Loose Ball on the Restraining Line Face-Off Drill

Coach squats in the center Face-Off Circle with a bucket of balls. Offensive and defensive players are on both sides of the Restraining Lines. Coach throws ball toward the sideboards on their side and both sets of players go for the loose ball. The pair that gets possession of the ball gets a point. Play to five. Losers run.

**Variation:** Players after possession go for goal at both ends. Work both sides of the Face-Off Circle.

## 5. Four-on-Four Loose Ball on the Restraining Line Face-Off Drill

Coach in Face-Off Circle rolls ball in various directions. All eight players fight for it: four defensive players and four offensive players standing on their respective Restraining Line. Although all four players on the same team are fighting for possession, they have to "read" the play as they may have to back-up their teammates who are in the midst of a loose-ball situation. On possession, the offensive team goes to score.

## 6. Two-on-Two Face-Off Drill

Two centermen and two sets of partners on the Restraining Line behind each centerman. If ball comes out one side, one set of players go after the loose ball; if ball goes other side, the other pair go after the loose ball. Centermen does not pursue.

**Variation:** Centermen and one set of players go after ball. I. On possession, the drill is over. II. On possession, the possession team tries to score.

### 7. Three-on-Two Fast-Break From Face-Off

Both centermen fight for possession from face-off. Nobody touches the ball except the centermen. The centerman who gets possession runs a three-on-two with his offensive players on the Offensive Line. There are four defensive players and four offensive players standing on their respective Restraining Line.

### 8. Three-on-Three Face-Off Drill

Centerman takes draw and all three sets of players play the ball live. There are two defensive players and two offensive players standing on their respective Restraining Line. I. On possession, the drill is over. II. On possession, the possession team tries to score.

### 9. Four-on-Four Face-Off Drill

Centermen are involved with loose ball. There are three defensive players and three offensive players standing on their respective Restraining Line. I. On possession, drill is over. II. On possession, the possession team tries to score.

### 10. Five-on-Five "Battle" Drill

Teams fight for loose ball from face-off. I. On possession, drill is over. II. On possession, the possession team tries to score.

# Chapter 10

# **Goaltending**

*Note: Goalie rules and information on goalie equipment is from* **Bill Fox, a referee in the OLA and NLL.**

The position most coaches either ignore or just don't know about is the goaltending position. How many times has a goalie been left alone in practice to work on his game by himself? "Go keep yourself busy until the shooting drills" is said a lot of times by coaches. So what do you do as a goalie when left all alone? Well, if this does happen to a goalie, here are some drills that he can do so that being on his own is not a waste of time. This section talks about goal positioning and the importance of it, the types of saves a goalie make, how to put on the goalie's equipment, goaltending drills, and the importance of communicating—always communicating—on the floor with your teammates.

Goaltenders do make a difference. They can make a bad team into a good team and a good team into a championship team. Goaltenders are the backbone of the team as they can make up for a poor-effort on defense and help to generate an offense by their quick initiation of the fast-break. Yet goaltenders are often neglected in practice, sometimes used as targets in practice by their teammates, and are usually told by their coaches to figure out the skills of their position. A common saying by most coaches is "I don't like to work with

goaltenders because I don't know much about the position. So I let them develop on their own." The answer to this saying is to bring in an experienced goalie coach who is still playing or who has retired from playing and wants to stay involved in the game, or read this section about goaltending.

## I. Terminology for Goaltenders

### **Floor Terminology**—*(See Diagram #1)*

**Short Side**—the goalie's "short side" or the shooter's "near side" is the side of the net closest to the shooter. This is the smallest part of the netting a shooter can see.

**Long Side**—the goalie's "long side" or the shooter's "far side" is the side of the net farthest from the shooter. This is the largest part of the netting a shooter can see.

**Net or Goal**—in Minor, the size is still 4' x 4', the size in Major and Junior is now 4'6" x 4', and in the NLL the size is 4'9" x 4'.

**Goal Line**—a line from goal posts. If the ball goes past this line it is a goal.

**Crease**—a 9' radius from the center of the goal line in a semi-circle pattern. Offensive players cannot step on this line or the goal will be disallowed or the offending team will lose possession of the ball. *Note: Size of crease in the NLL is 9'3".*

**Diagram #49: Playing the Angles**

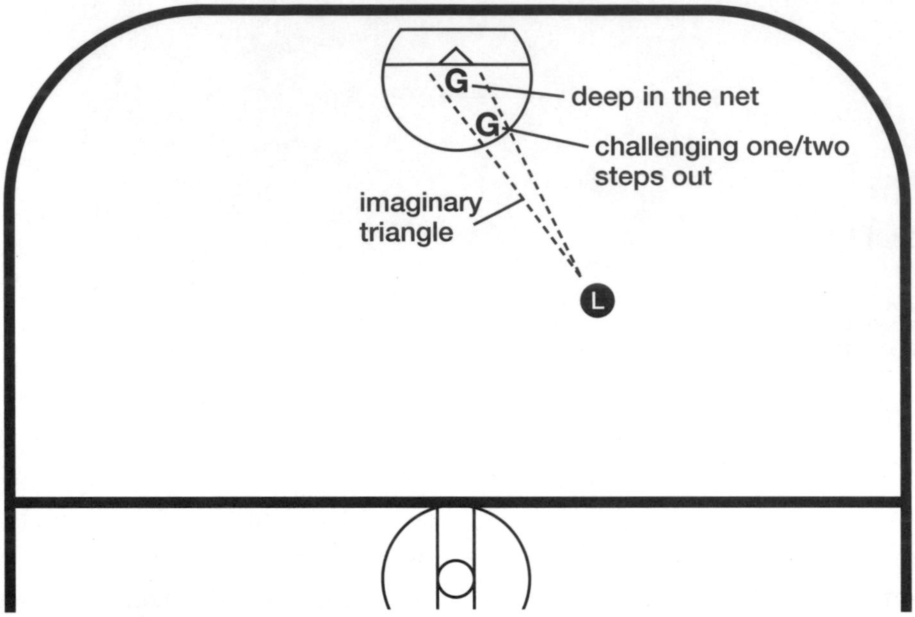

**Defensive and Offensive Zone Lines**—lines across the width of the arena from sideboard to sideboard to distinguish the Defensive and Offensive Area.

**Imaginary Center Line**—this is an imaginary line down the middle of the floor, parallel to the sideboards that break the offensive area into ball side and off-ball side.

**Imaginary Semi-Circle Line**—This is an imaginary line that the goalie should be aware of, because from 15' to within this line from the crease the ballcarrier is a threat to score.

## II. Equipment of a Goaltender

This is what Mark Brown, the owner of Blades in Whitby, Ontario (who has been in the hockey and lacrosse business for 30 years), and Andrew Faric of Lax Shack in Pickering, Ontario, have to say about buying lacrosse goalie equipment.

*Notes:*
– *Today there are only two goalie manufacturers STX or NAMI, and Boddam.*
– *The rule of thumb on equipment and protection is if a goalie gets hurt in certain areas, fix it so that*

*he will not get hurt there again. But it is more important to protect all areas of the body before he gets hurt. As the saying goes, "better to be safe than sorry." Goalies can get welts and bruises on the arms, legs, shoulders, toes, and thumbs, so be certain these areas are well protected. Goalies are always adding foam inside pads, gloves, and shin guards.*

– *Mark says make sure the equipment fits comfortably and is both protective and flexible. This is tough to do sometimes because parents tend to overprotect and make their young goalies so protected they can't move.*

**CLA Rules Regarding Goalie's Equipment**

• Goaltenders shall be allowed to wear only one chest protector and one set of arm pads.

• The chest protector and arm pads may not be altered in any way from the manufactured form.

• No additional padding of any sort may be sewn, taped, glued, or added to the chest protector and arm pads in any location.

• The goalkeeper shall not be allowed the use of abdominal aprons or a sweater extending down the front of the thighs on the outside of the pants, below the crotch area. This prohibits the use of any type of material added to the team sweater.

The goalkeeper shall be allowed the use of approved chest, shoulder, and arm pads, as well as leg guards and pants. All this equipment must conform to the shape of the body and must not include anything that would give the goalkeeper undue assistance in keeping goal.

- Goalies cannot use any add extra padding anywhere—not on the inside of their hockey pants; no "wings" on the side of their pants; not on their shoulder pads, usually football pads; not on the side of their chest protectors.

*Note: The lacrosse rule says that the goalie pads have to form to their body, but they really do not conform. The main theme for goalies today are big, bulky, and the bigger the better*

## I. Plastic Goalie Stick

### I. Depth of Pocket

Usually the depth of the pocket of the plastic goalie stick is about a ball depth below the frame.

The trade-off with the shallower pocket is that there is less winding up to throw with the result of an easier and quicker pass, but more chance of rebounds because of less cushioning effect of the shot with this type of depth.

The trade-off with a two-ball depth pocket, which is deeper than normal, is that it will help absorb shots, i.e., keep the ball in the netting and thereby prevent a rebound. However, this deep pocket will present a problem in throwing, since a goalie must take a bigger windup, i.e., drop the stick farther back behind his back, to throw the ball resulting in a slower release, a more arching pass, and possibly less accuracy. So the trade-off with a shallow pocket is it could give more rebounds, but gives a goalie a quicker release for his team to run; the trade-off with a deeper pocket is less rebounds but a slower release on the break out.

**Photo 81:** Equipment on a goaltender (front view)

**Photo 82:** Equipment on a goaltender (back view)

*Gee Nash, formerly of the Colorado Mammoth of the NLL,* says, "Try and make the pocket deep enough so the ball does not bounce out easily on a shot allowing for an unnecessary rebound, but that it is not deep enough that the ball may hook upon release of the ball."

*Bob Watson of the Toronto Rock* says his pocket is one to two balls in depth.

*Gee Nash, formerly of the Colorado Mammoth of the NLL,* advises having the pocket in the upper-middle part of the stick as it allows for a quicker ball release, which is very important when starting the fast-break.

> *Note: Andrew Faric recommends these goalie sticks: the Gait Quad, the Warrior Wall, and the Gait Web.*

## II. Number of Shooting Strings

Approximately two to four shooting strings seem to be the normal criteria for goaltenders to help get the proper arc on a pass. Each player will have to experiment to find what is most comfortable for himself. Goalies have found that with the smaller plastic stick they can get away with making a deeper pocket than the old wooden-stick pocket without much hindrance in their ballhandling.

*Gee Nash, formerly of the Colorado Mammoth of the NLL,* says, "shooting strings depend on the goalie's tendencies. If they are like a lot of shooters, then they should put in as many shooting strings as they need."

*Bob Watson of the Toronto Rock* uses three to four shooting strings. Bob likes to put in a string shaped in a V-formation in front and back of the pocket for consistent ball exit.

## III. Width of the Head of a Plastic Goalie Stick
*CLA Goaltender's Stick Rule*
The goalkeeper's stick may be of any desired length, but shall not be more than 15" in width and less than 12" in width measured from the inside of the plastic frame. Nothing may be added to or attached to the outside of the stick.

*The Width of the Head of a Plastic Goalie Stick*
The standard plastic goalie stick is approximately 13–14 inches wide (normal width) and, because it is lighter and smaller, both adults and young goalies use it to improve their passing.

For the true Fast-Break goalie, however, a 13-inch-inside width is the best width, because he is interested as much in starting the fast-break as he is in stopping shots, and a smaller and lighter plastic head gives the goalie more speed, quickness, and accuracy in his passes.

Mark Brown feels goalies have a problem passing or catching now because they are so bulked up. Some goalies now put football pads over top of their regular goalie equipment and then they can't lift their arms. They try to pass the ball and their arms are at their hip area when passing and that doesn't work. They have to bring their arms up above their shoulders to pass properly.

*Gee Nash, formerly of the Colorado Mammoth,* says, "I would recommend the STX Eclipse plastic stick for young goalies because of its durability, light weight, and its arc structure, allowing a goalie to feel the ball more. The stick is used for stopping shots as well as passing."

*Notes:*
– *The Warrior goalie stick—the "Wall Stick"—is becoming very common because it is square on the bottom and therefore lies flat on the bottom of the floor. Parents like this stick because it takes up a lot of the net (15" width from the inside) and*

*therefore will help their son become a better goalie. But because of the size they are going to have problems throwing the ball.*

— *The better goalies in the NLL, such as Bob Watson of the Toronto Rock; Dallas Eliuk, formerly of the Philadelphia Wings; and Gee Nash, formerly of the Colorado Mammoth, were not only great stoppers, but great passers because they used a smaller stick.*

*The Width of the Head of a Wooden Goalie Stick*
The wooden goalie stick is still used in some leagues, but it seems to be disappearing. The saying "the wider the stick, the better" is not always true. The trade-off for a wide wooden stick, 15" inside width, is that it will cover more of the net and thereby help in stopping shots, but it will definitely be a hindrance in passing as it is a bit heavy and cumbersome to get it up and pass quickly. It seems the 13–14-inch-width goalie stick has become the most common stick on the market. The width of the biggest wooden stick is 15" and the width of the smallest wooden stick is about 12". The youth's wooden goalie stick is a standard 13" inside width.

*Notes:*

— *So the trade-off with a 13"-width stick is it covers less netting, but gives a goalie a quicker release for his team to run; the trade-off with a 15"-width stick is it covers more of the net, but because of its bulky size it is harder to get the stick up and therefore gives a slower release on the break out. The question is, "Does the coach wants his team to run a fast-break or break out slowly?"*

— *In minor/youth leagues about 5 to 10 percent of goalies use wooden goalie sticks, but in Junior and above it is 20 percent wooden and 80 percent plastic. The wooden goalie stick is made by Mohawk International Sticks. Warrior and STX make the best plastic goalie sticks.*

## IV. Length of Stick

A long handle is better for lever action on the pass, but a goalie does not want it too long because the stick then gets caught in the netting of the goal. A goalie has to find the point on the shaft where the stick is balanced. This will help give the goalie an area to grab when passing. If the goalie finds the stick "head" heavy, the stick is too short. With the plastic stick, the goalie must adjust his release because it has a tendency to produce a higher arc when throwing. Recall the CLA rule of the goalkeeper's stick: it may be of any desired length.

*Gee Nash, formerly of the Colorado Mammoth of the NLL,* says, "A goalie may choose to leave the shaft long enough so that when he is in his stance the shaft ends up over his shoulder approximately six to eight inches."

*Bob Watson of the Toronto Rock of the NLL* believes the length of the stick is a personal preference, just remember not to make it so long it gets caught in netting of net.

*Gee Nash, formerly of the Colorado Mammoth of the NLL,* says, "I use an STX Eclipse goalie head with a Throttle shaft. It is a thick composite handle that allows the goalkeeper to hold onto the shaft easier which helps to prevent the shaft from spinning in your hand as much when a shot hits the stick sidewall."

## V. Taping the Shaft

Tape the aluminum shaft of the stick from the throat to 6" up the shaft, where the stick is gripped with the stick hand when stopping shots. Some goalies tape the shaft of the stick from the butt or end of the stick to about 6" down, where the stick is held with the bottom hand when throwing outlet passes. Again some goalies prefer to leave the bottom area untaped.

Some goalies even tape the middle of the shaft where they would hold the stick with the top hand for passing.

During the course of the game, the shaft becomes slippery from the goalie's sweat, resulting in the stick's twisting easily in the hand when passing or stopping shots. The tape helps the goalie grip the shaft better and prevents this spinning motion. It is a good idea to change the tape often during the season.

## 2. Goalie Jock

Goalie should put padding behind the cup with a sponge or towel for extra protection. Mark Brown recommends that some goalies wear a regular jock under a hockey-goal jock for extra protection, including the lower tummy area. Andrew likes Boddam, STX, or any other goalie hockey jock.

## 3. Goalie Pants

Goalie pants protect the thigh and waist area. Most goalies wear hockey pants unless they get a good lacrosse pant, such as STX, who have cut out the back of the pant in a horseshoe shape so the goalie can run better without the back of the straight hockey pant restricting them.

To customize the goalie pant and protect the thighs, put compressed foam behind the thigh fibers in the pants to absorb the impact of the shots.

*Notes:*

– *Goalies were at one time allowed to alter their pants. In the inner thigh and crotch area of the pants, they would sew in pockets on the inside of the pants from top to bottom and stuff these pockets with compressed foam for added personal protection. If cost permitted, an alternate choice for the lacrosse goalie was to buy hockey goalie pants and do some alterations on them, such as padding on the inside of the top of the legs. Most hockey pants do not have this padding and it's important to have for box lacrosse as this is a "hot spot" for shots. So when the goalie's legs are together, with these pockets, there is less space for the ball to go through.*

– *But the new CLA lacrosse rule is goalies can't alter equipment. The manufacturers are now starting to put wings on the side of their pants and padding on the inside of their legs. Now if the manufacturer makes the pants that way, goalies can wear them as long as they meet the CLA specifications on size allowed for each age group.*

## 4. Goalie Shin Guards

Goalie shin guards are hard plastic and protect the thighs, legs, ankles, and the top of the feet. Most shin guards come with a flap protection for toes, toenails are always getting hit so make sure toenails are clipped, and there are hard-toed running shoes for added protection. Foam should be added around the arch of the foot area, tucked in the shin guard, like a tongue on a skate, for additional protection. To help absorb the impact of the ball on the leg, tuck some foam inside the shin guard between the plastic and the cloth. All manufacturers make good shin guards. Mark Brown and Andrew both recommend STX (NAMI) Gladiator series and Boddam for goalie leg guards.

## 5. Hockey Knee Pads

Sometimes it is necessary to go down for shots, depending on a goalie's styles, so hockey knee pads for quad and knee protection should be worn at all times.

## 6. Chest Protector and Shoulder Pads

### Shoulder Pads

Shoulder pads protect the arm, bicep, and shoulder areas. Goalies use ordinary lacrosse players' shoulder pads and attach the large kidney pad fibers, from the ordinary lacrosse player's kidney pads, upside down to the shoulder and bicep area for protection over the padding. Be sure to strap or tape the fiber to the whole arm to ensure that the equipment will stay in place.

It is especially important for younger players to wear this extra fiber protection because a younger goalie will become frightened of the ball if he gets hurt too often. Some goalies like to tie the shoulder pads to the pants to help keep the pants up and the chest protector intact if braces are not desired.

### Chest Protector

Chest protector protects the chest area. Most of the goalie chest protectors and arm guards now come in a one-piece combination, such as STX Gladiator Series and Boddam Extreme Flex.

Some goalies attach the plastic strip from the ordinary lacrosse player's kidney pads, on the shoulder part of the chest protector to help absorb shots. A flap of compressed foam could be sewn on the side of the chest protector to protect the kidney area.

When getting dressed, some goalies like to tuck the chest protector inside the pants to get rid of the bulkiness, while others like to wear the chest protector outside the pants.

Some goalies like to tie the braces for the pants together to stop them from sliding down over their shoulders and to help keep their chest protector flat. Most goalies now use a belt-like system to keep their pants up and to keep their chest protector flat to see the ball better in the feet area.

> *Dallas Eliuk, formerly of the Philadelphia Wings of the NLL,* says, "I don't use bulky padding for stopping shots, as I feel it will hinder a goaltender's movement and thus hinder in developing his goaltending skills. Most goaltenders bulk up on padding and rely on this bulk to stop shots rather than on their goaltending ability in stopping the ball."

### 7. Elbow Pads

Elbow pads should be worn to protect the elbows in case of falling.

> *Gee Nash, formerly of the Colorado Mammoth of the NLL,* says, "I wear players' elbow pads and/or slash-guards under my arm pads for added protection."

> *Bob Watson of the Toronto Rock* wears elbow pads when he plays in the NLL to prevent turf burn.

### 8. Helmets/Throat Guards

At the minor or younger levels, goalie helmets must be approved by the CSA (Canadian Standards Association) or NOCSAE (National Organizing Committee for Safety in Athletic Equipment), since it is now legal to wear field lacrosse helmets in box lacrosse. Some goalies use field lacrosse helmets at the minor level. Mark feels the field helmet is a better mask because it is heavier and has a stronger structure. Make sure the helmet fits snugly and is comfortable so it doesn't move around and interfere with the sight of the ball.

Field lacrosse helmets seem to be the choice of older goalies. The Cascade helmet is a good field lacrosse helmet that goalies use in box lacrosse. Hockey style facemasks are being used more and more.

*Note: Andrew likes the Cascade CPX, Cascade CPV, Cascade Pro 7, Warrior Fatboy, and Olli Goalie Helmet.*

Make sure a throat guard or protector is worn and securely attached to the facemask, which is a flat fiberglass hanging down from the helmet so the ball doesn't come up under the mask and hit the goalie in the throat or neck. Andrew likes Cascade throat guards.

> *Gee Nash, formerly of the Colorado Mammoth of the NLL,* feels ice hockey goalie masks are ideal because they are shaped to deflect the impact to either side of the face whereas field helmets usually take the impact directly on the face.

### 9. Mouthguard

It is recommended that an internal mouthguard be worn. This is essential for the protection of the teeth and concussions.

### 10. Goalie Gloves

Use good-quality lacrosse gloves for the best protection. For the free hand, because the goalie should use the back part of the hand as a blocker, put some fiber or hard cover and compressed foam on the inside of the glove to absorb the impact from the ball. For the stick-hand, put some fiber or foam around the thumb and wrist area.

Mark thinks the best protection still comes from an upper-end hockey glove. Lacrosse manufacturers make goalie gloves, which are basically a lacrosse glove with padding on the back.

*Notes:*
- *Do not cut the palms out of the goalie gloves for extra grip on your shaft. This will result in a game misconduct for altering your equipment.*
- *It is important for a goalie to keep up his equipment maintenance, such as tightening screws, and replacing straps. After every game and practice make sure the goalie equipment is "aired out" so it is completely dry and not wet when he plays the next game and it doesn't mildew and rot from too much moisture.*
- *Andrew Faric of Lax Shack recommends Warrior Fatboy Goalie Glove (12", 13", and 14")*

## III. "Ready Stance" for a Goaltender

This Ready Stance is called a position of "readiness," because the goalie is balanced and relaxed, yet ready to react quickly. He is in the best stance to move forward, backward, and laterally (side-to-side) in relation to the ball. Since this stance covers as much of the net as possible, it is important that the goalie stays in this Ready Stance at all times when the ball is in the Defensive Zone.

### 1. Stance

The goalie takes a crouching position with knees slightly flexed, back straight, shoulders and chest square to the ball, feet shoulder-width apart, keeping the body's weight on the balls of the feet and holding the stick between and in front of the legs, and resting his stick hand on his thigh.

### 2. Position of Glove Hand

There are three styles of holding the glove hand:
- The goalie can hold the glove hand to the side of the body, ready to move, and turned, with the back of the hand facing outward to block any shots while keeping the arm flexed with the elbow out to the side to cover more of the net.
- The goalie can rest the glove hand on the hip area in a position ready to react.
- The goalie can drop the glove hand down and let it hang near the thigh in a natural position.

**Photo 83:** Front view of "ready stance" for a goaltender— stance, position of glove hand, grip of stick

All positions of the glove hand depend on the goalie's style and what feels comfortable to him.

## 3. Grip of Stick

### Types of Grip

- A goalie can grab the plastic stick with the fingers and thumb naturally wrapped around the shaft in a firm grip. The thumb is along the side of the shaft.
- He can wrap his fingers around the stick with the thumb on top of and along the shaft.
- With a wooden stick the goalie grabs the stick at the throat, i.e., the place where the "head" meets the handle, making sure the grip is firm. Some goalies grab the stick with the thumb in the throat, but with this grip there is always a chance of getting the thumb jammed by a shot against the head of the stick. As well with this grip, a goalie has a tendency to drop the stick shoulder, depending on his size. It is very important to have both shoulders square to the ballcarrier's stick.

### Placement of the Stick Hand

#### a. Plastic Goalie Stick

The plastic stick's throat is much lower than the wooden stick. The plastic goalie stick netting is approximately 18" from tip to throat of the "head." If a goalie grabs the plastic stick at the throat and still keeps the stick on the floor, he will be off-balance by bending at the waist and leaning too far forward with his shoulders or dropping his stick shoulder lower.

To prevent this, goalies put taped knobs around the shaft of the stick, about 7–8" up on the handle from the throat, as a reference point to grab behind or above, some goalies actually grab the knob, to help them keep the stick on the floor and still maintain a good stance with the shoulders square to the shooter. The goalie puts the knob at the best spot where he can maintain a comfortable and balanced position, i.e., in a crouched position that does not require bending over at the waist and dropping the shoulders forward, so that the shoulders are square to the ball and the stick is still on the floor.

#### b. Wooden Goalie Stick

The adult wooden stick netting is approximately 24–25" from tip to throat. Most goalies can grab the shaft at the throat and have the stick touching the playing surface while maintaining the goalie's stance: knees bent, legs shoulder-width apart, shoulders square over his feet, and stick arm straight or slightly bent.

The goalie may have to adapt the placement of his grip to keep his stick on the floor by moving his hand up the shaft slightly, but he may lose some control over his stick with this hand placement position.

Some goalies even move the hand up and down the shaft to maintain the stick on the floor permanently. The stick does not have to remain on the floor all the time, as a goalie will be stiff and rigid, but the stick should be kept on the floor until the shooter takes his shot; then the goalie moves his stick accordingly to where the shot is going. (See section on Using the Stick for Stopping Shots)

# IV. Styles of Goaltending

A goalie has to learn the basic mechanics of goaltending before he can develop his own style. Most goalies learn about goaltending from watching older goaltenders that they try to imitate, or through trial and error, teaching themselves rather than learning directly from a coach, unless the coach is a former goalie.

Basically, there are two parts to goaltending: the reflexive part and the angular part.

## 1. The First Style is the Reflex Goaltender

The reflexive part of goaltending relies heavily on the goalie's lateral reactions to get his body, his leg, his arm, or his stick in front of shots. It also relies on anticipating the shot from years of experience and from knowing the shooter or situation (See section on Qualities of a Goaltender)

The pure "reflex" goaltender thinks he can react more quickly than the ball. His basic principle is to set the shooter up by "giving and taking away" shots. He does this by luring the shooter to aim where he wants him to shoot by giving him a tempting target, i.e., an open area of the net, which is usually the short side of the net, then he takes it away by stepping in front of his shot.

*Bob Watson of the Toronto Rock and Dallas Eliuk, formerly of the Philadelphia Wings both of the NLL,* are both more of a reflex-style goalie than an angle-style goalie. They still move out to cut down the angle, but because of their quickness and size, both are smaller than a lot of NLL goalies, they have to rely on their reflexes to make saves. (See section on Reflex Goaltending)

*Bob Watson of the Toronto Rock of the NLL,* on goaltending: I feel a smaller or more athletic type of goalie is more suited for [the] reflex-style of goaltending. With larger nets, especially in the NLL, unless the team defense is very strong, one has to display a stronger ability in stopping balls. I think playing for a weaker defensive team in the early years of developmental years is an asset. It makes a young goalie stronger mentally and prepares him physically for the future.

## 2. The Second Style is the Angle Goaltender

The angling part of goaltending relies on good body positioning in the crease by stepping out and cutting down most of the net area, leaving the shooter little or nothing to shoot at.

The pure "angle" goaltender does not cheat or guess on shots, but plays the shooter's stick straight on. His positioning is such that the space between the net and both sides of his body is the same. He is so sure of having good position that he rarely moves on a fake, because he believes a shooter has to make a great shot to score. (See section on Angle Goaltending)

## 3. The Third Style is the Standard Goaltender—A Combination of Reflex and Angle Goaltending

The "standard" goaltender who combines both the "reflexive" and the "angular" techniques has to rely on both stepping out, getting good positioning, and stopping shots with the body or the stick by moving laterally or stepping sideways. Some goalies may be stronger at playing the reflexive game because of their quick reaction, and some may be stronger at playing the angle game because of their big size and the ability to take a good position before a shot. But no matter what style a goalie plays, to be good he must be strong in both styles to stop shots. As he becomes more experienced, each goalie will develop his own style.

## V. The Reflexive Part of Goaltending for Stopping Shots

### 1. Being Out and in a "Ready Stance" for Stopping Shots

Goalies try to stop every shot from their ready stance, but they still need the reflexive part of goaltending in stopping shots. From the ready stance, a goalie has to react laterally to get something in front of the ball whether it's his body, his stick, his arm, or his leg. If they start to drop or flop it is because they are out of position, or have made a mistake and have to recover with a "spectacular save," or they are just tired.

By "being out and set" (stopped) in a ready stance before the shot occurs, a goalie is ready to move laterally, either way—near-side or far-side. He must always remember that he cannot rely strictly on angles to stop the ball; no matter how well he plays the angle, there are still many openings. Good players will not aim at the goalie, but for these openings, so the goalie still has to rely on his reflexes to stop shots. A major problem for goaltenders is getting caught in transition, i.e., still moving out when the shot is taken, and being unable to move laterally when moving forward.

*Note: There are some goalies who play the Butterfly position, down on both knees with legs flared out to the side, for stopping shots.*

## 2. Using the Stick for Stopping Shots

The stick is the main weapon used to stop long, low shots. Always keep the stick between the legs, in front of the feet, and on the floor, because it spreads out the legs farther, thereby covering more of the net. All shots below the waist on both stick and glove side should be played mainly with the stick. To cut down on rebounds, the goalie "cushions" the ball by

**Photo 84:** Reflexive part of goaltending—being out and in a "ready stance"—using the stick for stopping shots backed up by leg

moving his stick backward as the ball makes contact with the netting. The goalie is surer of catching the ball with the stick than deflecting it with his glove hand or shin guard.

Usually, low shots on the stick side are played with the stick backed up by that leg by stepping sideways and low shots on the off-stick side are played by moving the stick to that side backed up also by that leg moving sideways. It is important to step sideways as the goalie brings the stick over to block the shot so the leg acts as a brace for the stick and stops it from twisting on the shot. A goalie must maintain a firm grip, to have control over his stick or else the hard shots can turn the stick in his hand and the ball could end up in the net. When the goalie has to make a stick save from a hard low shot without the leg for a backup, he must turn the stick into the direction from which the shot came.

*Notes:*
- *In some cases, the head of the stick has to be used to cover the top-corner shots when the arm/shoulder cannot get there fast enough.*
- *When using the stick to stop the ball, think of "catching" the ball, to start the fast-break, rather than just stopping the ball.*

## 3. Using the Upper Body for Stopping Shots

In stopping high corner shots most saves are made with the upper body. There are three methods used:

**Use Middle of Chest to Stop Shots**
In the first method for stopping high corner shots, the goalie tries to stop all high shots in the center of the chest, following the principle of keeping as much of the body as possible in front of the ball. However, it is only possible to move the chest one foot in either direction, so shoulders and elbows are backups to take away top corner shots until the chest can get over to cover this area. With these high shots

**Photo 85:** Reflexive part of goaltending—being out and in a "ready stance"—using middle chest for stopping shots

## Use Shoulders to Stop Shots

For the second method for stopping high corner shots the goalie starts with his shoulder first, then his body. He gets in front of the shot with his shoulder and chest by stepping over laterally. He keeps his feet on the ground, to push off with the stationary foot while stepping sideways with the other foot in the direction he wants to go. On the step his leg's shin guard will face the boards. When moving laterally, he stays on his feet.

## Use Elbows to Stop Shots

With the third method for stopping high corner shots the goalie takes a stance like a scarecrow with both elbows out and bent at 90 degrees. He steps sideways in the direction of the shot, but this time he merely stops the shot with the protruding elbow or flicks the arm out straight to block the corner area of the net.

*Note: Beginning goaltenders have a tendency to turn their body on shots with the ball hitting their side or their back. Coaches must give them confidence that they can't get hurt through drills and by making sure they are well protected.*

on either side of the body the goalie steps out slightly and hops sideways to get the chest in front of the shot. On the hop, his feet will leave the floor with both shin guards facing the shooter.

For example, if a left-shot shooter moves in tight around the crease, he will generally move in the direction of his stick side. The goalie will maintain his position between the ball and the net. If the goalie ends up moving right over close (tight) to the far goal post, he has to be conscious of the left-shot shooter shooting back for the near top corner. In this case the goalie has to move quickly laterally to that particular (near) side to take away the top corner with his upper chest.

High shots that are in the middle of the net are easy to stop with the chest, but be aware of "cushioning" the ball by "giving" or moving back with the chest to cut down on any rebounds.

**Photo 86:** Reflexive part of goaltending—being out and in a "ready stance"—use elbows to stop shots for far-corner shot

*Gee Nash, formerly of the Colorado Mammoth of the NLL,* says, "I practiced five times a week with my team and would work with my stick every day after a scheduled practice. For top-corner shots I would take round after round of shots to the corners and practiced my lateral movement from side to side. And on the low shots I took round after round and would try to catch the lower shots in my stick. And I always practiced passing to players on the run."

## 4. Using the Upper Body Against a Stick-Fake for Stopping Shots

When a goalie faces a stick-fake by a shooter he must stay square to the shooter's stick, relying on his angles and positioning. The key is to have patience and not overcommit. Always let the shooter make the first move, in other words, wait out the fake. Many shooters who use fakes will state that when a goalie does not commit, but stays square, they will often second-guess themselves and end up either shooting at the goalie or missing the net.

### Far-Corner Fake

On a fake shot to the far-side, where a goalie will get the majority of his shots because it is supposed to be his weakest side, a goalie should not bring his stick up to block the shot or react with his upper far-side shoulder. The shot may be a fake, leaving the shooter with the open near-side of the net. Instead, he should be shuffling in small side steps staying even or in front of the shooter's stick, if it is a fake to the far-side he does not move, now he is in a position to take a side step sideways to the near-corner using his upper body and glove-hand shoulder, ready to block the near-corner shot while keeping his stick between his legs in the ready stance. Even if the near-side shot is a fake (second fake), he still has his body and the shoulder on the stick side to come back and make the stop with one step sideways.

**Photo 87:** Reflexive part of goaltending—being out and in a "ready stance"—using upper body against a stick-fake for stopping shots, fake at stick side or long-side, wait out fake (do not bring stick up on that side on fake)

**Photo 88:** Reflexive part of goaltending—being out and in a "ready stance"—then step sideways to near-side corner to stop shot using his upper body and glove-hand shoulder

### Near-Corner Fake

On a fake shot to the near-side, where a goalie could also get a majority of his shots because it is supposed to be his weakest side, especially if it is his glove side, a goalie should not swing his stick up or react with his upper near-side shoulder to block this near-corner shot. The shot may be a fake, leaving the shooter with the open far-side of the net on the stick side. Instead, he should be shuffling in small side steps staying even or in front of the shooter's stick. Now he is ready to step sideways in either direction—step with his body and near-side shoulder to the near-side or step sideways with his body and far-side shoulder to the far-corner ready to block the shot.

The goalie should know the types of shooters he is going against so he can anticipate what they like to do and possibly out-think them. A goalie should be ready for "automatic" moves by the shooter, i.e., if the shooter fakes the goalie up, the goalie should know he is coming down for a low shot.

*Note: Beginning goalies will react to fakes, but good body position will compensate for this overcommitment. Beginners have to fight the tendency to tighten up, or blink on a fake. Just stay relaxed and wait it out.*

*Bob Watson of the Toronto Rock of the NLL,* says, "By knowing the type of shooters I am playing against will help me anticipate their moves. On a stick-fake I must have patience and not overreact to the first fake, I just wait-out the shooter and let him make the first move. The problem for shooters is when I don't do what they think I am going to do, that is, react to the fake.

*Gee Nash, formerly of the Colorado Mammoth of the NLL,* says, "On a fake shot I try and wait the shooter out and try to dictate to the shooter where to shoot by leaving an open spot in the net

so I know where he is likely going to shoot. Do not 'jump' on every fake and always stay on the balls of your feet so you can be properly ready to move from side to side."

## 5. Using the Legs for Stopping Shots

Most often the goalie has his stick between his legs and makes the stick-save on low shots. The legs are basically to back-up the stick saves, but occasionally he will use a leg as a reflex move to kick a shot away from the net. The one exception occurs when a shot is taken from the side of the net a goalie can keep one leg tight against the post with the other leg close beside it and the stick at his side.

## 6. Using the Glove Hand for Stopping Shots

Recall that low shots on the glove side should be played with the stick. It is easier to catch the ball with the stick than to deflect it with the

**Photo 89:** Reflexive part of goaltending—being out and in a "ready stance"—using the glove hand for stopping shots

back of the glove. But occasionally the goalie may have to use the glove hand as a blocker for stopping waist-high shots on the glove-hand side of the net.

**Remember:** The glove-hand arm should be held to the side of the body around the hip area, flexed, relaxed, and ready to move with the back of the hand facing outward.

## VI. The Angular Part of Goaltending for Stopping Shots

### Definition of "Playing Angles"

"Playing angles" is when the goalie moves out from the net toward the ball to take a position in the crease area for the purpose of cutting down on the shooting area of the net, i.e., the shooter has nothing or very little of the net to shoot at, with the result that the ball hits the goalie or forces the shooter to shoot wide. All goalies should remember that forcing a shooter to shoot wide, or hit the post, is part of a successful job and is as good as a save.

To explain "playing angles," think of a triangle formed by two imaginary lines from the ball to each goal post. If a goalie plays deep

in his net, he will give the shooter more net to shoot at. If the goalie moves out to "challenge the shooter" he will cut down on the amount of net to shoot at. The problem is how to move out (See section on "Ready Stance" for a Goaltender), when to move out (See this section, Rule No. 4), and how far to move out. (See this Section, Rule No. 6) *(See Diagram #49 pg. 180)*

The ideal position occurs when the ball hits the goalie rather than the goalie having to move to get in front of the shot. So, playing angles is a very important skill in helping to stop the ball. By playing the angles correctly a goalie can save himself a lot of unnecessary work, but a goalie never takes away everything so he must be ready to react and move laterally to protect the rest of the net. (See section above on Reflex Goalie)

It seems that the most natural shot for shooters is to shoot to their far-side of the net or the goalie's long-side. It does not matter if it's the goalie's stick side or the glove side. If a goalie understands this, in getting his positioning, besides following the principles of "playing angles," he can anticipate this shot more than those aimed for the short-side. *(See Diagram #50)*

## Diagram #50: Goalie's Long Side and Short Side

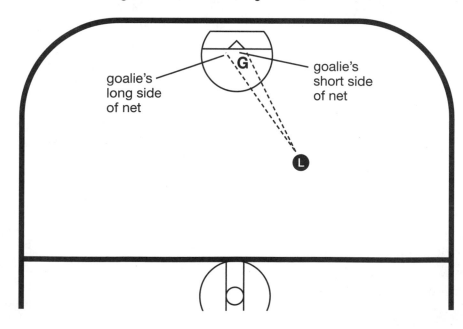

goalie's long side of net

goalie's short side of net

**Remember:** *Goaltending is playing angles.* Here are some rules for playing angles:

### Rule No. 1 for Playing Angles: Keep Eyes Centered on the Top-Hand Area

When the ball is being passed around on the offense, the goalie should keep his eyes on the ball all the time. When the long-ball shooter is winding up he should be focusing on the top-hand wrist, the ball, and the stick, but not on the shooter's body.

Since some shooters, especially close-in, can get the stick going one way and the ball the other, by using their wrists, some goalies feel it is too difficult to watch just the ball with all this faking, so they watch the top-hand wrist area, and peripherally the ball, and the stick's head, to get the overall picture of what the shooter is trying to do.

Some goalies get into a bad habit of watching just the shooter's eyes to see if he telegraphs his shot, but good players, knowing this, look one way and shoot the other.

### Rule No. 2 for Playing Angles: Follow the Ball with the Body

The goalie should not only be following the ball as it moves around with his eyes, but with his body as well, keeping it square to the shooter's stick. So to keep the proper position, the goalie concentrates on the shooter's stick rather than his body.

### Rule No. 3 for Playing Angles: Start All Movement From the Center of the Net

The goalie should start all movement from a centering position. He does this by standing on the goal line and grabbing both posts with his hands to know where he is and to get his body centered in the net. Some goalies like to grab one post with the free-hand and hit the other post with the stick. The idea is that if a goalie knows where he is—centered-set position— before he moves out then he will take a better angle to cut down on the shot.

**Photo 90:** Rule No. 3 for playing angles: start all movement from the center of the net, turn the body on the goal line square to the stick

### Rule No. 4 for Playing Angles: Turn the Body on the Goal Line Square to the Stick

From the "center-set position" on the goal line, the goalie turns to face the direction the shooter is coming from. This is called "squaring to the stick." As the shooter crosses the Defensive Zone Line, the goalie turns his body while on the goal line, facing the shooter's stick; he then steps out to get the best angle. This procedure keeps the goalie centered in reference to the net as he moves out in the direction of the shooter's stick.

### Rule No. 5 for Playing Angles: Move Out on the Imaginary Shooting Line

The goalie moves out on an Imaginary Shooting Line formed with his body, the ball, and the center of the net. By straddling this shooting line he knows there is even space between the net and both sides of his body. He now only has to move one foot either way on a shot. If he moves out off-centered, he will give the shooter too much of the net to shoot at on one

## Diagram #51: The Imaginary Shooting Line

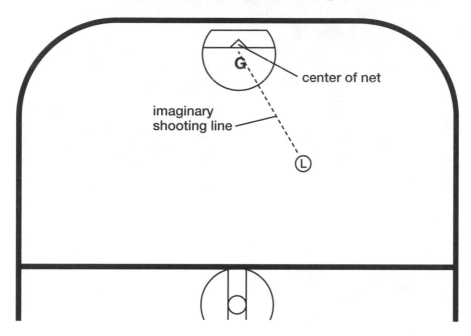

center of net

imaginary
shooting line

particular side, although some reflex goalies do leave one side open to entice the shooter to shoot at this opening, then, by anticipating the shot, takes it away. *(See Diagram #51)*

### Rule No. 6 for Playing Angles: Move Out One Step, Two Steps, Three Steps

*One Step Out*

The goalie centers himself on the goal line, turns his body on the goal line, square to the stick, and starts to move out on the Imaginary Shooting Line. Now, the important question is, "How far should he move out?" A goalie usually takes one step out from the goal line, i.e., "challenging the shooter," to cut down on the amount of the net to shoot at, but the distance of stepping out depends on the size of the goalie (adult, one normal step; small adult, a large step; a young goalie, perhaps two steps) and the size of the net (minor/youth nets 4' x 4', Junior and Major nets 4'6" x 4', NLL nets 4'9" x 4'). Other factors that determine the distance of stepping out include where the shooter is standing, and who is shooting. The goalie takes

**Photo 91:** Rule No. 6 for playing angles: front view of moving out one step

**Photo 92:** Rule No. 6 for playing angles: side view of moving out one step

**Photo 93:** Rule No. 6 for playing angles: front view of moving out two steps

one step out or comes out as far as he can as long as he can touch one post with his glove hand extended, with the end of the shaft of his stick, or with his leg nearest the post extended. Thus, he now knows that he is in a good position; not too far out, not too deep in his net. All he has to do is take one step back and sideways to get to the far-goal post in the event of a diagonal-crease pass. (See section below on Types of Shots and Goalie's Expectations)

*Two Steps Out*
Some goalies move two steps out to get good positioning, but because of variation of the size of nets and size of goalies, goalies will have to do some experimenting to find out the perfect spot that reduces the shooting area the most. By moving out two steps, a goalie must be aware of recovery back to the far post on any cross-floor or diagonal pass.

**Photo 94:** Rule No. 6 for playing angles: side view of moving out two steps

*Gee Nash, formerly of the Colorado Mammoth of the NLL,* says, "On long shots I try and step out about two feet from the goal line so I cut down the shooters' angle as well as protect against a quick pass to the crease or a quick fake, because at two feet out I can still recover in time if the diagonal pass is made or the shot is faked."

*Dallas Eliuk, formerly of the Philadelphia Wings of the NLL,* says, "On a good defensive team a goalie can take an extra half to full step out, i.e., two steps out, because of the bigger nets, to cut down on the amount of net to shoot at. But on a weaker defensive team it's best for the goalie to stay close to his goal line (one step out) so he doesn't have to scramble to follow a cross-floor pass or a quick pass to the crease for a quick-stick shot. Also, by staying on or close to his goal line, it gives the goalie a longer look at the ball from a long shot and more time to move/react."

### Recovery

Coming out is important but recovery is just as important. For this recovery the maximum is two steps. If a goalie takes three steps out, or moves almost to the edge of the crease, the shooter can shoot over a goaltender's shoulder as the shooter's stick is higher than the goalie, or the shooter can cut across in front of the net, and shoot around the goalie into the open net. So be careful not to move too far out.

### Three Steps Out to Edge of Crease

Depending on the situation, such as it is only the goalie and the shooter alone and the goalie reads the shooter's body language that he is going to plant and shoot long, moving out to the edge of the crease might be a good option as he doesn't have to worry about fake shots and diagonal passes.

**Photo 95:** Rule No. 6 for playing angles: front view of moving out three steps or top of crease

**Photo 96:** Rule No. 6 for playing angles: side view of moving out three steps or top of crease

Another angling method some goalies use is to move out early, three steps from the goal line to about the top or front of the crease as the shooter comes over the Defensive Zone Line. If the shooter shoots from the scoring area, the goalie is far enough out to cut down the angle and still have time to move on the shot on goal. If the shooter does not shoot and still advances toward the net, the goalie gradually moves backward one to two steps. If the shooter ends up on the crease, the goalie will have moved back and be stationed about one step out from the goal line and centered in respect to the shooter's stick. The problem with this "coming out and retreating back" method is that the goalie could lose his relationship to the net.

*Note: The general rule is the farther the shooter is away from the net, the more the goalie can move out, such as to the top of the crease, to reduce the amount of netting to shoot at.*

### Experiment for Best Position

This one-step rule is a general rule and there are always goalies that make an exception to it because of their style and preference. Some goalies play right on the goal line for long shots and others come right out to the top of the crease to play long shots. So a goalie has to experiment to find out what position is best suited for his style.

*Gee Nash, formerly of the Colorado Mammoth of the NLL,* says that standing on the goal line for long shots gives

the goaltender more time to see a shot coming in and therefore, more time to react to it. This idea is something to think about and experiment with.

### Rule No. 7 for Playing Angles: Trace Out a Half-Moon Pattern When Moving Across the Net

The movement pattern for a goalie in the crease is usually the shape of a half moon from post to post. Following this imaginary half-moon pattern gives a goalie a basic position to follow as the ball moves around on the offense. As the ball moves from one side of the floor to the other, the goalie shuffles with small side steps staying in the ready stance—with both shin guards facing outward, keeping his stick between his legs and on the floor, keeping his body facing and square to the ball in this half-moon pattern. He takes one step off the goal post, one step to the middle of the net, and one step back to the other goal post.

A young goalie will take two steps forward off the post, two side steps across the top of the half moon, and two steps back to the other post. *(See Diagram #52)*

**Diagram #52: Imaginary Half-Moon Pattern**

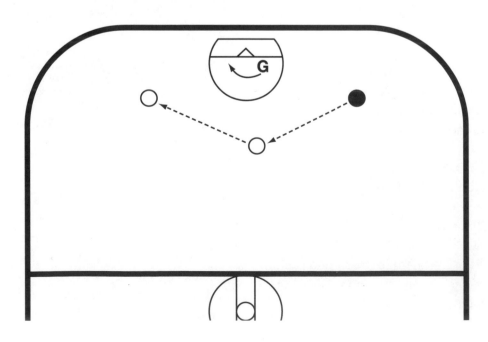

## Rule No. 8 for Playing Angles: Use Floor Markings as Reference Points to Find the Ideal Position

If a goalie does not know where he is in relationship to his net once he moves out, he is at a disadvantage. A goalie needs reference points in regards to the net, the crease, the posts, floor marking, and arena markings to tell himself if he is in the best spot to cut down the angle and still recover quickly backward to the net. One of his best friends is his goal posts, which can tell him where he is in certain situations. But a goalie has to know his ideal position, i.e., where he is in relationship to the net, especially when out from the goal line and in front of the net near the crease where he cannot touch the goal posts and he does not have time to turn around. He then can use marking on the arena floor and the arena itself as reference points by aligning his body with them, such as:

- Using the center Face-Off Circle as a reference point
- Using markings on the sideboards as a reference point
- Using other markings in the arena as reference points

It is not a good idea to use the crease as a reference point in getting the proper angle since most times he will be focusing out in front of his net with little time to look down.

## Rule No. 9 for Playing Angles: Position of Angle Goaltender to Specific Positions of the Ball

For a goalie, most of the game is spent moving forward, backward, and sideways in this half-moon pattern following the ball. Every time the ball moves, the goalie must move to be in the best spot when the ball is shot. It is important for the goalie as he moves to always stay in his ready stance with his stick on the floor.

### I. Goalie's Angle Position When the Ball is in the Corner Area of the Floor

The goalie places his outside foot against the nearest goal post with his body and leg hugging tightly to it. His outside arm or stick are on the outside of the post. His inside leg is slightly forward, off the goal line. He stays in the net with his body facing outward. He should be turning his head back and forth while watching the ball in the corner and checking in front of the net area to see where the opposing players are and what is going on, anticipating what is going to happen such as a quick pass out and shot.

**Photo 97:** Goalie's angle position when the ball is in the corner area of the floor

## II. Goalie's Angle Position When the Long-Ball Shooter is in the Cornerman's Area (Mid-Side Area or Wing Area) of the Floor

The goalie steps away from the post at an angle to play the ball honestly, i.e., the body square to the stick and ball. He first step out is with his inside foot to line up this foot with the stick and ball, then shuffles his outside foot to square up to the shooter. If he can touch the post with the shaft of his stick, with his glove hand, or with his outside leg, the leg nearest the post, this will tell him where he is and that he is in a good position when the ball is in the mid-side area of the floor.

## III. Goalie's Angle Position When the Long-Ball Shooter is in Front of the Net

The goalie is standing one to two steps out from the goal line either by stepping straight out from the Center Set Position or taking one side step from the position when facing the mid-side area of the floor. He may not have time to center set. This is a very difficult position to play because the goalie does not have the goal posts to use as reference points. He can pick other reference points, such as markings on the floor or on the boards, to maintain his floor awareness. He should always know how many steps are needed to get back

into his net or to get to the post. If he knows a shooter is winding up for a long shot, he can take another step (third step) out to the top of the crease to challenge the shooter and cut off more of the net to shoot at. This move comes from reading the shooter's body language and from experience on knowing what certain shooters like to do.

## IV. Goalie's Angle Recovery Move When the Ball is Passed Across the Floor *(See Diagram #53)*

Following Rule No. 2 for playing angles (as the ball moves the body moves) the goalie, after taking one or two steps out from the post, gets in a ready stance to play the shooter. On a quick cross-floor pass or a diagonal pass to the opposite crease, he steps back to the far post as a recovery move in case of a quick-stick shot rather than the normal move of stepping sideways around the imaginary half-moon. If there is no quick shot, he steps out again (third step) to play the ball square.

*Bob Watson of the Toronto Rock of the NLL:* "I step out to stay square to the stick and just follow him across in front of the net with small side steps in my

**Photo 98:** Goalie's angle position when the long-ball shooter is in the cornerman's area (mid-side area or wing area) of the floor

**Photo 99:** Goalie's angle recovery move when the ball is passed across the floor—playing shooter

**Diagram #53: Recovery Move for a Goalie**

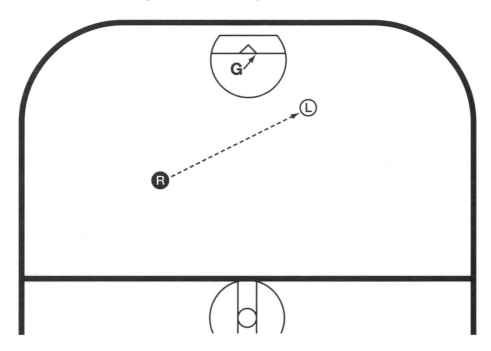

ready stance. My concern on stepping out is my recovery in case the shooter tries to get in closer to the net."

## V. Goalie's Angle Position for Playing the Long-Ball Shooter Cutting Across in Front of Net

Goalies should come one to two steps out from the goal line and stay square to the long-ball shooter and then, following him across in front of the net by doing small side steps. Keep the feet shoulder-width apart with the stick between the legs to be in a position to go back the way he came from by pushing off with the opposite foot. A goalie has to be aware of how many steps he has to take to get back to the post.

## VI. Goalie's Angle Position for Playing the Close-In Shooter

*A. When the Shooter is Coming Across in Front of the Net for a Close-In Shot*
The goalie starts on the post and as the shooter comes out from the side of the crease, he follows him across the net. The position

**Photo 100:** Goalie's angle recovery move when the ball is passed across the floor—recovery move across

is about a half-to-one step out from the goal line. If the goalie gets out too far, the shooter can put the ball over his shoulder. He should stay a little closer to the net playing the close-in shooter than when playing the long-ball shooter. Most shooters either like to reach around the goalie and shoot at the goalie's long-side, or fake his shot to the long-side and put the ball back to where they came from, the goalie's short-side. Because the goalie should be shuffling in small side steps staying even with the shooter's stick, if the shot is a fake to the long-side he does not move, now he is in a position to either take a side step sideways to the short-corner using his upper body and glove-hand shoulder ready to block the short-corner shot; or if the shot is an actual shot to the long-side the goalie is in position ready to step sideways with his upper body and stick-side shoulder to block the long-corner shot. A goalie must anticipate these moves. The good angle goalie plays the shooter's stick square and is in his ready stance poised to react accordingly.

*Bob Watson of the Toronto Rock of the NLL,* says, "When playing a close-in shot I like to stay a little deeper in the net and play the shooter's stick square."

*B. When the Shooter is Coming Down the Side of the Floor for a Close-In Shot*
The goalie still follows the principles of coming out, being set, and being ready to move laterally, but as the shooter comes closer to the net, down the side of the floor, the goalie must shuffle backward to maintain his proper positioning. If the shooter carries the ball down the side toward the goal line extended, or if the shooter cuts in toward the net from the side, the goalie might have to attack the shooter by stepping into the shot. The key is to step out, not when the shooter is drawing his stick back to shoot, but just as he begins bringing his stick forward to shoot.

**VII. Goalie's Angle Position for Playing the Long Bounce Shots**
The key in playing the long bounce shot is to attack the ball by stepping forward, and making sure to get out in front of the bounce. First, he must try to catch the ball with the stick before it bounces or ricochets off the floor. If he misses the ball, at the spot it hits the floor or just after it bounces, he must try to put his body in front of the ball to stop it with either his shin guards or his chest protector. He should not just stab at the ball with the stick, but have a backup: either the body or the legs together. Goalies must be aware that when shooters bounce the ball they look to bounce the ball on the outside of the goalie's legs so that it ricochets up into the mid-side area or top corner.

**Photo 101:** Goalie's angle position for playing close-in shooter cutting across in front of net—on step out from crease, stay square to stick before shooter

**Photo 102:** Goalie's angle position for playing close-in shooter cutting across in front of net—shot is an actual shot to the long-side the goalie is in position ready to step sideways with his upper body and use shoulder to block the long-corner shot

## VIII. Goalie's Angle Position for Playing the Breakaway Shooter

The goalie starts from his "center-set position" on the goal line. He waits until the shooter comes into the Defensive Zone, then he turns or keeps his body on the goal line, square to the ball, and moves out his one normal step along the Imaginary Shooting Line. The goalie works on the principle of playing the shot as it comes. He should be a comfortable distance to play a long shot or to retreat quickly to play a close-in shot. By moving out to eliminate the long shot option, he has forced the close-in shot. When moving backward as the shooter approaches the net for the close-in shot, it is important to maintain a distance between the goalie and the shooter where the shooter still does not have a good long shot.

The goalie is now in his ready stance, waiting: (A) for a close-in straight shot or fake shot. The goalie should anticipate that as the shooter gets closer to the net, the scoring area is reduced so he might rely more on his fake-shot or his straight close-in shot. Most often the shooter wants to fake first so the goalie should just hold his ground and let him make the first move. (B) Be ready to move backward or sideways for a cut across in front of the crease shot. If the shooter's stick passes the mid-point of the goalie's body, be ready to step sideways to the far post or be aware of the shooter shooting back to the near side in which case he has to move laterally to that side with his upper chest to take away the shot. (C) For the shooter who likes to run straight down the side, past the goalie, and try to put the ball in behind him, the goalie just steps back sideways to the near goal post and anticipates a shot to the far-corner.

*Note: The goalie can try to fake out the shooter by "giving him something and taking it away." (See section above on Reflex Goalie)*

**Gee Nash, formerly of the Colorado Mammoth of the NLL,** says, "On a breakaway I usually step back to the goal line and get set up in my net. From there I take about a step out, no more than one step, because any more than one step a shooter can put the ball over the goalie. I try not to stay flat-footed and I am on the balls of my feet so I can react to a fake and make a save."

**Bob Watson of the Toronto Rock of the NLL,** says, "I start at the goal line and center set. I take one step out to challenge the shooter. As the shooter attacks, I move backward. I know patience is the key, so I let him make the first move, but I hold my ground. I feel the toughest save to make, especially on a breakaway, is the Over-the-Shoulder shot.

## IX. Goalie's Position When Playing the Ball Behind the Net

The goalie can play this position of the ball behind the net in one of two ways:

a. **Facing the Play**

He faces the players out in front and watches for the pass coming out front, periodically turning his head side-to-side to look over his shoulder for the ballcarrier. He keeps his back tight against the crossbar so the ballcarrier cannot bang the ball off his back into the net. He is not concerned with intercepting or deflecting any passes, but watching the play developing out in front or the ballcarrier coming out from behind the net. Playing the ball behind the net this way, his body is always facing the play, and he is in a position ready to make a save.

b. **Facing the Ballcarrier**

In the other position, the goalie faces the ballcarrier and hugs the crossbar with his chest, holding his stick up to prevent the ballcarrier from completing the pass out in front of the net. Goalies who play this way feel more comfortable watching the passer. There is no right or wrong way to play the ball when it is behind the net, just do what is comfortable.

*Gee Nash, formerly of the Colorado Mammoth of the NLL*: In the NLL where players can now dive from behind the net and "dunk" the ball in ("Air Gait"). The goaltender needs to be aware of where the shooter is at all times by facing the shooter as the dive can come in from over the top or from the side of the net. It is important in today's NLL that a goalie communicates with his defenseman and each person will choose a post to "hug" so that a player has a small chance of finding a good place to dive too.

### X. Goalie's Position in Regards to Crease for Receiving a Pass

CLA Passing Rule to the goalie in the crease: a player cannot pass the ball into the crease. A goalie must have both his feet outside the crease to receive a pass. He cannot touch any part of the crease including the line. The crease line is used just like the 10-second line, if you touch it you're in it. So, even one foot on the line and a goalie is still in the crease.

So a player cannot pass the ball into his own crease. That is why the goalie must stand outside the crease in certain situations, such as in case a teammate gets into trouble and wants to knock or pass the ball back to the goaltender. He can hold the stick's head in an "up" position as in catching a ball, make sure he stands to the side of the net, or he can hold the stick's head in a "down" position as in scooping up a loose ball.

Another CLA rule regarding the crease a goalie should be aware of is that if he leaves his crease for a loose ball he cannot go back into his crease with the ball.

*Note: In the pro (NLL) league a player also cannot pass the ball into the crease to the goalie or a teammate. Also, an out-player in the crease may be stick-checked, but a goalie may not be stick-check in the crease.*

## Position of Reflex Goaltender to Specific Positions of the Ball

The reflex goalie relies heavily on his quickness and reflexes in stopping shots. This goalie's style is a little different from the standard goalie's angling, so he is discussed here separately.

### I. The Reflex Goalie's Principle of "Give-and-Take-Away"

The reflex goalie likes to set the shooter up by luring him into shooting at a tempting target, i.e., an open area of the net, then, anticipating that the shooter will aim at the given target, moves laterally to block the open area and hopefully the shot. He thinks he can react more quickly than the ball, so he relies heavily on his reflexes to get in front of shots. Because he relies on his quick reactions and anticipation of shots, he does a lot of moving, swinging of arms and stick, flopping, and diving.

### II. Reflex Goalie's Position When the Long-Ball Shooter is in the Cornerman's Area of the Floor

His positioning with regard to the long-ball shooter is different from the angle goalie. When the ball is in the cornerman's spot (the mid-side area or wing area), the reflex goalie to play the angle steps away from the post straight out with his outside foot first, then shuffles his inside foot out. This move does not leave him square to the shooter. (See section on Angle Positioning Rule)

He steps out this way to cut off the long-side of the net, thereby leaving a little bit more on the short-side of the net to shoot at—the principle of "giving the short-side to shoot at, then taking it away." By stepping straight out rather than coming out at an angle, besides taking away the natural shot for a shooter, i.e., the larger opening to the far-side of the net, he is also in a better position to take away the quick cross-floor pass and shot or the ever-dangerous diagonal-floor pass to the crease.

### III. Reflex Goalie's Position When the Long-Ball Shooter is in Front of the Net

His positioning with regard to the long-ball shooter in front of the net is different from the angle goalie. When the ball is in front of the net, the reflex goalie overplays the shooter's stick by half a step to take away the shooter's far-side shot and "give" the long-ball shooter the short-side of the net. The reflex goalie wants to take away the difficult save to the long-side and make the easy save coming back to the short-side.

### IV. Reflex Goalie's Position When the Close-In Shooter is Coming Across in Front of the Net for a Shot

A reflex goalie's position with regards to the close-in shooter coming across in front of the net is also different from that of the angle goalie. When playing close-in shots where the shooter is coming across in front of the crease, the reflex goalie wants to take away the shot around him to the long-side, by staying about a half a step in front of the shooter's stick so the shooter has to come back to the short-side, on which the goalie should now anticipate this shot. Basically, the reflex goalie is telling him to shoot at the short-side by taking away the long-side.

### V. Reflex Goalie's Position for Playing the Breakaway Shooter

The reflex goalie's position with regards to the breakaway shooter is also different from that of the angle goalie. When playing the close-in fake shot or playing the breakaway, as already stated, reflex goalies like to "toy" or "play mind games" with the shooters by always keeping them guessing what they are going to do. The shooter questions whether the opening is there because the goalie is making it inviting for him to shoot at, or because the goalie does not know he's left an opening. This gives the reflex goalie an advantage, because each time he can play the situation differently: one time he can play the player straight up as an angle goalie; next

time he can play the shooter on the principle of giving him something to shoot at, then taking it away.

## VII. Types of Shots and Goalie's Expectations

### Playing the Overhand Shot

The overhand shot can be one of the most deceptive shots because the shooter has more options: he can shoot straight down at the goalie around the hip area by releasing the ball later beside his head, he can shoot for the top corners by releasing the ball early behind his head, he can shoot for the low corners or a bounce shot by again releasing the ball late, or he can fake the shot. (See Chapter 8, Fake Shooting) Most of the time with the overhand shot, the goalie should expect the ball coming high. This overhand shot, along with a combination of a sidearm-overhand shot, called the three-quarter shot, has become a more common shot in lacrosse. In the sidearm-overhand shot the stick is held vertically about a 45-degree angle to the floor and is released from the side of the body.

### Playing the Sidearm Shot

With the sidearm shot, the goalie should expect the ball to come around him on his long-side, as it is difficult for the shooter to pull his shot to the short-side of the net. The sidearm shot is usually about waist high on the goalie or to top-corner high.

### Playing the Underhand Shot

With the underhand shot, the goalie should expect a ball low and parallel to the floor with it periodically rising. This shot, because of the windup, is a very hard and heavy shot. Again, he plays the low shot with his stick backed up by the leg on the side of the shot or he can go down into a butterfly position like a hockey goalie.

## Playing the Over-the-Shoulder Shot

The goalie should expect the over-the-shoulder shot to occur when he has taken away the long-side of the net leaving only the short-side. This shot occurs when the shooter has passed the halfway mark going across in front of the net. Because the shooter now has nothing to shoot at on the long-side his only option is going back to the short-side which has now opened up bigger. Only a few players can execute this shot accurately so a goalie should know who they are.

## Playing the Screen Shot

*Dallas Eliuk, formerly of the Philadelphia Wings of the NLL,* says, "Today there are more screen shots than ever before. In fact, a lot of the outside shots are scored these days from screen shots where a defender gives the shooter a large gap and the shooter ends up shooting around him. So, a goaltender must stay alert and be ready for any type of shot. Shooters are shooting around and over players more and catching and shooting with a quick release where there is no wind-up."

## Playing the Toughest Shot

*Gee Nash, formerly of the Colorado Mammoth of the NLL,* says, "The toughest save to make in the NLL is probably when the opposing team is on the Power Play and the Pointman on the top of the Power Play or the Shooter on the side of the Power Play looks as though he is going to shoot, but ends up making a diagonal-pass across to the opposite creaseman. This play is tough to defend because I am already committed to his long shot and I have to react fast to the opposite side of the net knowing there is at least one less person on defense to knock it down due to the penalty. But it feels great when I am able to make this type of save."

# VIII. Passing to Start the Offense

A goalie has to learn to pass the same way as a player does (See Chapter 4, Passing). In minor/youth lacrosse, there are goalies who are gifted in passing up the floor accurately and quickly and there are others who are slow and inaccurate. If a goalie is weak in passing, then the coach has to practice over and over again with the goalie to work on his speed and accuracy.

A Fast-Break goalie is like a catcher in baseball: defensively he catches the ball from the pitcher and offensively he must be able to throw the ball quickly and accurately to second base. When a Fast-Break goalie stops the ball with his stick, he thinks of "catching the ball" rather than just using the stick to stop it. Once he has caught the ball, he is already starting the up-motion of the stick to pass. This helps to increase the quick outlet pass, which is so important on starting the fast-break.

The grip for a goalie for passing is similar to a forward: grabbing the stick at mid-shaft with one hand and at the butt end with the other hand. So, once a Fast-Break goalie makes a save, he should control the rebound and know exactly what he has to do with the ball. He should look to pass long first, which happens only a few times in a game, and pass short second, usually to the off-bench side of the floor to a player moving up the floor which happens most of the time. The ball-control goalie who has a hard time passing just looks to dump the ball into a player's stick in the crease.

*Note: The CLA and NLL rule is a goalie has only five seconds in the crease with the ball before he has to get rid of it.*

A Fast-Break goalie will be pressured, delayed, or looking to intercept the pass by an opponent waving his stick in front of him while trying to make the breakout pass. To counter this delay tactic the goalie flicks the bottom-hand wrist and flaps the front elbow as if he is going to pass, thus faking the pass. This will "freeze" the opponent as he will now look to intercept the so-called pass. This will allow the goalie time and space to move sideways and pass, or make a pass unmolested by passing around his stick or bouncing a pass to his teammate.

*Note: It is a good idea for a young goalie to step to the side of the net when throwing a pass. Since he might accidentally drop the ball or it might roll out the back of the pocket when he stands in front of the net.*

*Gee Nash, formerly of the Colorado Mammoth of the NLL,* says, "My strength as a goaltender would be my ability to get the fast-break started with a quick release from my goal crease to a player up the floor in order to get into the offensive end."

*Dallas Eliuk, formerly of the Philadelphia Wings of the NLL,* says, "The ability to pass accurately and quickly in the NLL is important for a goaltender. But don't sacrifice ball possession with an ill-advised breakaway pass, i.e., turning the ball over, with a low-percentage pass. Too often goaltenders try to throw the 'Hail Mary' pass or 'Hope' pass, more often than not where the breaking player is covered. If the pass is missed, the opposition has another 30 seconds of possession."

*Gee Nash, formerly of the Colorado Mammoth of the NLL,* says, "A minor goalie can improve his ball-handling ability very easily. 'How?' By having a ball in his stick at all times during practice when there are no shots being taken at him. He can aim for spots on the net or on the boards when the drills or plays are in the other end in practice. Another way to improve his ballhandling is when the goalies are doing passing drills in practice, always have the players running at game speed so there is no adjusting period for the goalie once the game begins. All in all: Practice! Practice! Practice!"

## IX. Loose Balls

When retrieving a loose ball, trap it first, then scoop it up, and pass to a teammate. If a goalie has good ball-handling skills, speed, and confidence leaving his crease to obtain a loose ball, it gives his team a great advantage.

## X. Qualities of a Goaltender

### 1. Physical Qualities of a Goaltender

*Bob Watson of the Toronto Rock of the NLL reviews the basics of goaltending:*

- Be in a ready stance—knees flexed, body crouched, shoulders and chest square to the ball and over the knees, stick between the legs and on the floor.
- Keep your eyes on the ball.
- Move the body when the ball moves and keep the body square to the ball.
- Start all movement from the center of the net on the goal line.
- Turn your body on the goal line square to the shooter's stick.
- Come out at least one step to "challenge the shooter."
- Move out on the Imaginary Shooting Line.
- Be stopped and in your ready stance for the shot.
- Trace out a half-moon pattern when moving across the net.
- Keep your stick on the floor even when moving.
- Get in front of the ball with your body, stick, arm, or leg.
- On close-in shots and breakaway shots, "wait out" any fake.
- Be ready to step back or sideways if necessary.
- Playing long low shots by catching them with the stick backed up by a leg.
- Playing long high shots, try to get in front of them with the center of the chest backed-up by shoulders and elbows.

*Bob Watson of the Toronto Rock of the NLL,* says, "To improve my ball handling when I was younger I spent a lot of time with my stick, passing with my friends or finding a wall and passing against it. To improve my stopping ability I would get my dad or somebody to take a video of my performance and then I would diagnose my stance and angles. And finally, I watched a lot of different style goalies and learned from them."

*Gee Nash, formerly of the Colorado Mammoth of the NLL,* says, "A minor goalie can improve his stopping ability by always practicing the basics. If they have trouble in a certain spot on the net, then take a round of shots to that area until it becomes an easy save. Go back to the basics, use tennis balls if a goalie is "scared" of the ball at the beginning. Also make sure the goalie is well padded to prevent injury, which will enhance his stopping ability and his confidence of not getting hurt. Coaches should always take time in practice to work with their goaltenders."

### Be Athletic, a Good Passer, and Verbal

The main physical quality for a goaltender is the ability to stop the ball. He should be a good athlete with quick reflexes and good eye-hand coordination. A goaltender cannot be afraid of the ball. This is especially true for beginners.

It is essential for a goaltender to have the skill of passing the ball up the floor accurately and quickly. He should be aggressive when going after loose balls around the crease area, when controlling rebounds off his body, when throwing the ball up the floor, and when even running the ball up the floor to initiate the fast-break.

The goaltender has to be verbal by giving instructions to his teammates on where they should play on defense and on where the ball is on the floor. It is important that he keeps this communication on the floor between himself and his teammates to get rid of any indecision. He sometimes yells at teammates for lack of

effort or cheers them on for their great effort. With all this communication he becomes the leader on the team, plus all this talking keeps him mentally in the game.

## 2. Mental Qualities of a Goaltender

### Anticipation—Being Mentally Ready

A goalie has to anticipate what is going to happen before it happens by "reading and reacting" to the situation rather than just reacting or guessing. In other words, he has to anticipate what is going to happen before it happens. He has to be continually "reading the play" (Is it a pass across the floor or a shot?) and "reading the shooter" (Is it a fake or a shot? Is he going to cut across or come down the side of the floor? Is he going to shoot at the far-side or near-side of the net?) Quickness of mind and alertness are extremely important assets for a goalie.

He must understand the whole concept of the game of lacrosse, usually through experience—as good judgment comes from experience—to help him anticipate what could happen. For instance, he must realize that most goals are scored from offensive plays initiated out in front of the net rather than being initiated from behind or from the corners. He must realize that there are hardly any deflections or screen shots with an opponent standing in front of the net. But in today's game, there are more long-ball screen shots where the shooter shoots around his defender using him as a screen.

In helping him to anticipate, a goalie must know the opposition shooter beforehand so he knows what to expect. He must know what type of ballcarrier he is: a playmaker, a close-in shooter, or a long-ball shooter, in order to anticipate what to expect from him.

He must be able to read "visual cues" from the opponents' actions and body language to help him anticipate. He can watch the ballcarrier's eyes to get an idea if he is going to shoot or pass. If there is eye contact between the ballcarrier and another teammate, the goalie can anticipate a pass-and-cut play. Similarly, by watching the overall picture of the shooter, i.e., the top-hand area, the ball and the stick's head, the goalie can anticipate better what is coming: a shot, a fake, or a pass. He must remember that "shooters are habitual liars they never do what you think they are going to do."

**Concentration During the Game**

In a game a goalie must focus on one thing (the ball), and yet be aware of everything going on around him and in front of him. He has to stay mentally alert every second of the game. He has to block out all distractions from his mind except what he has to do—stop the ball.

He has to stay in the "present moment" and not worry about the past, the last goal scored against him, nor worry about the future: "How am I going to play?" or "We have to win this game." A goalie should focus on his performance rather than the score. When a goalie is "on his game" or "in the zone" his thoughts and his actions are one, everything seems to "be in slow motion" where he knows what is going to happen before it happens rather than everything "speeding up" where he reacts or guesses what he thinks he should do and ends up "fighting the ball."

One of the problems of goaltending is that goalies will periodically have mental lapses or let their mind wander and occasionally allow in soft goals. Here are some tips on how a goalie can concentrate better and stay mentally in the game:

- His challenge is to concentrate 100 percent for the whole game and not to relax for a moment or have no momentary lapses.
- He can do a play-by-play to himself to help himself stay focused.
- He can talk to himself or give himself a pep talk. "I will watch the ball," "I will watch the top-hand area," "I will not emotionally overreact to a bad goal or a bad call by a referee," "I will challenge all shooters," "I

love playing against great shooters," "I will stay mentally alert," "I love pressure and tight situations."

- He can give verbal instructions to his teammates to stay mentally in the game: "Pressure your check," "Watch the man in front," "Watch the cutter," and "Loose ball."
- He can break the game into five-minute segments of total concentration, then take a break.
- He can follow the principle that when the ball is in the Offensive Zone, i.e., when he will have no shots, this is "his time." He does things that help him keep loose, such as just relaxing from concentrating, taking a break, walking around in his crease, adjusting his equipment, cheering on his teammates, or coming out of his net in case any loose balls come back down the floor.
- If he finds his mind wandering, he can drop down on his knees or side step around the crease like he is stopping a shot or just do something physical. Some goalies' rule is that they only stand straight up when they want to rest.

*Dallas Eliuk formerly of the Philadelphia Wings of the NLL:* To stop a shooter you have to focus on the ball and only the ball.

*Bob Watson of the Toronto Rock of the NLL* believes a major quality of a goaltender is staying focused in a game. "Our mind has a tendency to wander and it is a job in itself to keep yourself mentally in the game at all times. Whether it is using five-minute segments to focus on or to talk to yourself to stay focused, you must find your own way to stay focused in the game."

### Attitude

A goalie has to have a positive attitude because he knows that the way he thinks is the way he plays. He knows that goals will be scored, mistakes will be made, bad calls will be made by the referee, and games will be lost, but as long as he does his best nobody can blame him. He must maintain a smile and a sense of humor throughout all these adversities.

He must maintain an attitude of great confidence, bordering on cockiness, in his ability to stop the ball, and especially in his ability to make the "big save" at crucial times in the game. Making the "big save," besides giving his team a lift, maintains his leadership role. The bottom line is a goaltender must be a competitor who loves the pressure of being the last line of defense. Here are some sayings to help a goalie keep everything in the proper perspective:

"I will do my best and let the chips fall where they may."

"I want the challenge of stopping the best."

"I do not have to stop the shooter as much as the shooter has to score on me."

"I have an attitude of just doing my best and not worrying about anything else."

"I have confidence from all of my hard work in practice and the knowledge I have of playing this position."

"I am going to clench my teeth and defy anyone to score on me."

"I will never let in two bad goals in a row."

### The Emotional Part of the Game—How Does a Goalie React to Mistakes?

**a.  Being Scored On**

How he reacts when being scored upon will determine his success or failure. A goalie must realize that he is going to be scored upon and not let it throw him off his game or discourage him. He cannot show any negative emotions because this will be taken as a sign of weakness and lack of confidence. He cannot get emotionally upset, show negative emotion, or get rattled by banging his stick on the floor, displaying a posture of defeat, i.e., hanging his head and dropping his shoulders. He must keep his cool when the opposition scores on him, whether it was his mistake or not. A lacrosse goalie must understand that he can have 15 goals scored upon him, yet his team can still win the game. Not getting upset helps the goaltender stay mentally in the game ready for anything and helps him remain confident for the remainder of the game.

There are goalies who get upset and end up "throwing their game off," especially when the opposition talks to them. If a goalie has this type of reputation the opposition players will get on him all the time trying to upset him. Here he must learn not to get upset when bad goals are scored on him or when the opposition is constantly talking to him. Besides if he is really focusing on the game he shouldn't hear anybody talking to him.

**b.  A Bad Goal**

So when a team does score a bad goal on him, he must analyze it—by realizing what he did wrong, learn from it, forget about it, and then do something to get his mind off what had just happened to get back into the "present moment," such as walking away from his crease, never looking at the ball in the net or the opposition, and starting to focus on the next face-off.

*Bob Watson of the Toronto Rock of the NLL* believes a key quality for a goaltender is to remain confident because in lacrosse there are no shut-outs. "You will be scored upon, so don't get too high and don't get too low. When scored upon, analyze how they scored, learn from it so you won't do it again, and then forget it."

**c.  How to Relax**

Here are some techniques to help a goalie lower his tension level, to stay relaxed, to keep his cool, and to remain confident throughout the game: taking deep breathes; giving himself positive self-talk; having a refocusing plan to replace negative thoughts with positive thoughts, such as saying "Relax," "Smile," or "Be cool"; and keeping a sense of humor. A goalie must understand that goals will be scored, mistakes will be made, and games will be lost, but it is the ability to bounce back after mistakes that is the criterion of being a great goalie.

## XI. Major Problems in Goaltending

- The goalie lets his mind wander and loses his concentration of where the ball is and what is happening on the floor.
- The goalie is not mentally and physically ready to move laterally to get in front of shots.
- The goalie starts to play cautious or passive by retreating back into the net too quickly, thereby leaving too much of the net open.
- The goalie plays too far out from the net when the shooter is cutting across and he either shoots around him or shoots over his shoulders.
- The goalie loses his floor awareness or ideal position in regards to the net with the result of leaving too much of one side of the net open.

## XII. Preparing for a Game

For a goalie to play well he has to have certain good feelings, such as being physically relaxed, yet energized; being mentally calm, yet alert; being confident and optimistic. To get these feelings a goalie must have a physical and psychological pregame plan. Here are some techniques a goalie can use in his pregame routine.

**Visualization for a Pregame Routine**
Goalie can isolate himself, close his eyes, and picture himself stopping the ball and making great saves. He should visualize his best games to create a proper frame of mind.

Visualization is like going to the movies and seeing yourself doing everything perfectly, making save after save in the upcoming game.

*Dallas Eliuk, formerly of the Philadelphia Wings of the NLL,* says, "I visualize before each game, whether it be the night before or on the way to the arena. I pre-play the game and visualize each player approaching the net shooting from the outside and doing what he does best. I in turn see myself making those saves, controlling rebounds, and jump-starting the fast-break. So when the whistle is blown and the ball is dropped in the real game, I've already faced this team and beaten them. I find this technique helps build my confidence and concentration."

*Bob Watson, of the Toronto Rock of the NLL,* says, "After the last warm-up I take several deep breaths to relax myself. When totally relaxed I visualize myself making saves, controlling rebounds, and making good passes. It is important that I keep all my thoughts positive, which is sometimes easier said than done."

**Self-Talk or Self-Affirmations for a Pregame Routine**
A goalie gets confidence by talking to himself with positive thoughts. He repeats to himself strong, powerful, positive words that stress how he wants to play and what he wants to do. "I love playing goal," "I have fun playing goal," "I love the challenge," "I am the best," "I am ready and prepared to play," "I am going to play relaxed, daring, and aggressively," "I love pressure situations," "I am going to stay focused," "I am going to stay up and stay out," "I am going to control all rebounds," "I am going to talk to help my teammates," "I am going to play relaxed, yet intense, alert, and daring," "When I get excited, I am going to take deep breaths," "I am going to take great positioning in the crease," "I am going

to challenge all shooters," "I love pressure situations," "I am going to keep my composure after bad goals or bad calls by the referee," "I love playing against great shooters."

These types of sayings will make him feel relaxed, confident, energized, focused, and prepared to play.

### Relax by Taking Deep Breathes for a Pregame Routine

- **Muscle Relaxation Exercises for a Pregame Routine**
  Goalie tightens up his hands and then shakes them out loosening the muscles.

- **Pregame Routine**
  Coach should insist all players be in the dressing room one hour before game time, although most players are on the floor working on their shot two hours before game time. Some goalies like to be busy up to game time to avoid thinking too much and worrying about the game. Some like to walk, stretch, or listen to music; some find a teammate to shoot tennis balls at him in the adjoining hallway. Others like to isolate themselves in order to visualize their best performance or to look over a prepared list of opposing players so they can anticipate the upcoming moves and shots of the shooters. The important thing for a goalie is to find the routine that works best for him. Using the right pregame routine will get the goalie in the right frame of mind: relaxed, confident, and with positive feelings.

  **Bob Watson, of the Toronto Rock of the NLL,** follows the same routine before every game, "I take five minutes throwing the ball around to warm up and get used to my stick. When I am half-dressed I go for a jog and then stretch for 20 minutes with the team. The next 20 minutes I take shots in the official warm-up. Then, lastly in the dressing room just before I go out on the floor, I relax and focus on the game and my job."

- **Pregame Routine of Getting Dressed**
  *Gee Nash, formerly of the Colorado Mammoth of the NLL,* says, "When getting dressed before a game I usually follow the same routine. I make sure my under clothing is comfortable and dry before I put it on. To prevent rashes from leg equipment I usually wear cut off long-john underwear just cut around the knee area and longer socks to protect the back of my legs. On top I wear a long sleeve, either tight fitting or loose fitting 'Under Armour' sweat-absorption shirt. This shirt is excellent for moisture management. From there I put all my bottom equipment on, such as my running shoes, my athletic support and cup, then my leg pads, and my goalie pants, followed by my upper equipment, such as the upper-body chest protector and shoulder pads and apply electrical tape where needed."

## XIII. Goaltender Drills

(See also Chapter 8: Shooting, for more drills)

The coach should keep the goalie busy and active during the entire practice, but there are two major times in practice that are strictly for him: stopping shots and passing.

In the shooting drills for goaltenders, the goalie can work on his angles, on his reflexes, on stopping long shots, on stopping close-in shots, and on his weaknesses.

*Note: A coach can make up random shooting drills using tennis balls for younger goalies who sometimes duck and shrink on shots because they are afraid of the ball. A tennis ball can't hurt them and builds up their confidence. Do not forget to warm up the goalie.*

### I. Progression Drills for Goalie While Receiving Shots

- Goalie sits back in net on crease (doesn't move) for shooters to work on their accuracy.

- Goalie sits back in net on crease and works on his reaction and stopping ability.
- Goalie takes one step out (doesn't move) for shooters to work on their accuracy.
- Goalie takes one step out and works on his reaction and stopping ability.
- Goalie drops into butterfly position, if he uses this style (doesn't move), for shooters to work on their accuracy.
- Goalie drops into butterfly position and works on his reaction and stopping ability.
- Players shoot long shots only at the far top-corner for the goalie to work on his stopping ability for this type of shot. Players can take all types of shots (bounce, close-in, etc.) to work on the weak area the goalie wants to improve on.
- Goalie plays every shot "live."

## 2. Stretching Exercises

Goalies can get stretching exercises out of books written on stretching exercises. A goalie should make sure he stretches his groin, his hamstring muscle (back of upper leg), the quadriceps muscle (front of upper leg), and the shoulder muscles.

## 3. Agility Drills

Agility is the physical ability to move backward, forward, and laterally quickly. Again these drills can be found in most exercise books. Here are some suggestions:

- Any type of skipping, hopping, or jumping can really help to develop agility.
- The Wave Drill: the goalie moves in the direction the coach points—forward, backward, side-to-side, and down-and-up, while staying in his ready stance. Remember no more than two to three steps in any direction.
- The Mirror Drill: the goalies are in pairs with one goalie imitating the movements of the other goalie.

## 4. Structured Warm-Up Drills for Practices and Games

Warm-up shooting is strictly for the goaltender, not for the shooters, to build up his confidence, get him use to being hit, and to work on his angling and reflexes. For all these shooting drills look at Chapter 8 on Shooting.

- Work on progression of the distance—team starts far out from goalie for shots and work their way in.
- Work on progression of hardness of shots— players don't wind-up and shoot hard, but place their shots.
- Players shoot at different corners working on their accuracy rather than their scoring ability.

## 5. Reaction Drills

- Line up all the players in a straight line with a tennis ball and shoot long-shots one after another about 15' out from the goal line to work on the goalie's reflexes.
- Then have two players each shoot a tennis ball at the same time to help him improve his quickness and reaction time.
- Players turn the net around facing the end-board about 3' away. The goalie also faces the end-board standing exactly in front of the net. His three teammates, one standing beside each post and the other behind the net, each with a tennis ball, bounce a ball off the end-board with the goalie reacting to the balls ricocheting off the boards trying to stop them from going into the net.

## 6. Drills to Teach Angling

### I. Using Two Ropes to Teach Angling

The coach ties a rope to both goal posts and at the point where the ball would be in the shooter's stick. The two ropes and the goal line form a triangle. To help goalies understand the importance of angling, one goalie stands on the goal line while the other goalie stands where the shooter's stick would be to show him how much a shooter can see to shoot at, the shooting view. The goalie on the goal line then moves out showing the other goaltender how much of the net he can cut down on to shoot at. As he moves out, he practices staying even between the two sides of the rope, i.e., the Imaginary Shooting Line. *(See Diagram #54)*

The goalie can also show the different positions taken when he centers on the ball versus centering on the shooter's body.

*Note: Remind the goalie not to move out too far—one, two, or three steps depending on the size of the goalie and where the shot is coming from—as a shot could go over his shoulders easily.*

## II. Using a String for the Imaginary Shooting Line

The coach can also tape a string in the middle of the net at the goal line and stretch it out to the position of the ball. The string represents the Imaginary Shooting Line. The goalie stands on the goal line centered, then moves out on the string staying squared to the ball. The coach gives him feedback as he moves out.

## III. Finding the Ideal Position

Things a goalie has to do to find the ideal location in the crease for stopping shots in reference to the ball. Goalie has to:

- Center himself on the goal line
- Turn his body on the goal line square to the ball
- Move out one to two steps on the Imaginary Shooting Line
- Where he stops is the ideal spot for stopping shots
- Now he is ready to uses his reflexes to take away the open spots

In this drill, players shoot from different spots on the floor and the goalie stands in his crease in what he believes is his ideal spot and does not move while a player shoots at him. He gets a sense of his position by the results of the shots, if they go off him or if they go into the net.

## Diagram #54: Finding the Ideal Spot

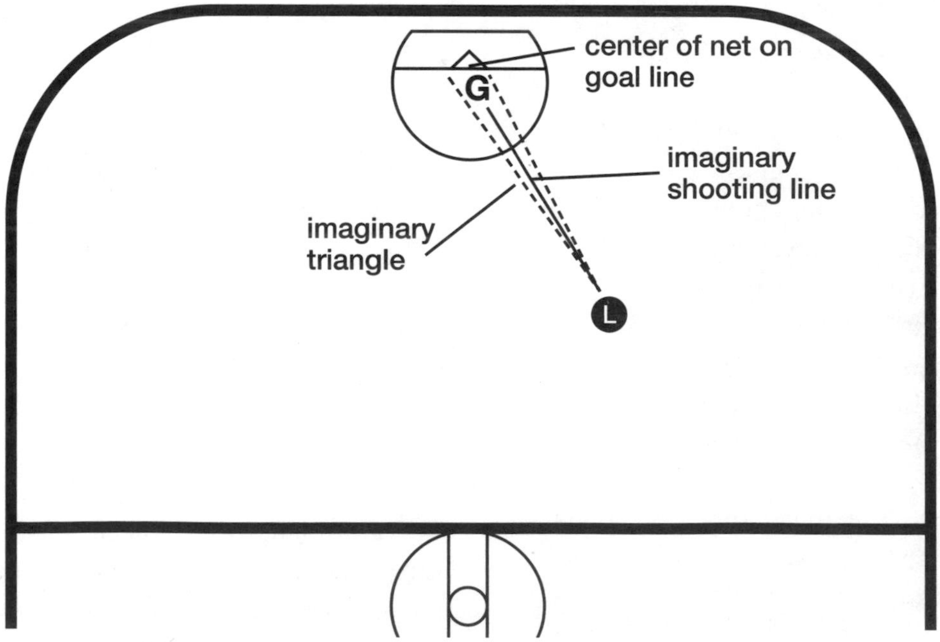

## IV. Five Players Shooting to Work on Goalie's Angling

To help teach angling five players in different positions on the floor and each with a ball will shoot at the goalie, one at a time. The coach stands behind each shooter to check the goalie's angle. This is a controlled drill.

## V. Teaching Angling in the Half-Moon Line

To teach a goalie to move around on the imaginary half-moon line, align five players around the net in good scoring positions. These offensive players pass the ball around slowly as if they are running their offense and the goalie moves around on his imaginary half-moon line accordingly. The coach can check his position and give him feedback.

In the next progression, the players pass the ball around and shoot. The goalie, through this experience, will get to know his relation to the ball and the net, and his floor awareness in the crease.

## 7. Drills for Stopping Long-Ball Shots

All these shooting drills for goalies are the same as the "Shooting Drills" in Chapter 8: Shooting, except the purpose is different—they are strictly for the goalie. In all these drills the coach will tell the players to take certain types of shots, usually shots that will improve the goalie's weaknesses, or help improve his stance.

Coach can tell players to take certain types of shots:
    a. Players shoot long, top-corner shots (near or far)
    b. Players shoot long, bottom-corner shots (near or far)
    c. Players shoot long mid-area shots (stick side or glove side)
    d. Players shoot long bounce shots for top corner
    e. Players shoot long bounce shots for mid-waist area (stick side or glove side)

- Work on angle or reflex: Goalie can sit back in his net for reflexes or he can take a step out and play normal angling.
- Speed of drills: These drills can be run in either a controlled manner where the shooters are spaced out to give the goalie time to get set between shots so he can work on his technique, or at high speed, where the shooters shoot in rapid-fire continuously one after another so the goalie does not have time to get set and thereby works on his quickness and reflexes.

## I. Individual Shooting Drill

Goalie works on stopping shots from different areas of the floor. After receiving a pass an individual shooter shoots from the crease area, the corner area, or from the middle of the floor. He shoots repeatedly at a specific spot that the coach tells him. The passer has a bucket of balls from which he just feeds the shooter.

## II. Breakaway Long Shot Drill

A group of players with balls line up at center floor and run in on the goalie. The players can be spaced out to shoot or shoot one-after-another. The goalie can make the drill more difficult on himself by not using his stick.

## III. Single-Line Drill

Players with balls in a single file cut down the side and shoot or cut across the top and shoot. The goaltender works on his angling and positioning.

## IV. Semi-Circle Long-Shot Drill

Each player with a ball will line up around an imaginary semi-circle line about 15' out from the crease. A goalie can work on his angling by staying on his imaginary half-moon by having players shoot slowly and continuously around the semi-circle; or the goalie can work on his reflexes and lateral motion by having the players shoot rapidly and continuously around the semi-circle, or by alternating from side to side of the semi-circle. Goalie can play with his stick or without his stick. Coach can vary the drill by having the players shoot only long bounce shots, shoot for far top corner, etc. And have them shoot at a certain speed—50 percent speed, work up to 75 percent speed, and then 100 percent.

## V. Semi-Circle Shooting Screen Shot Drill (No Pass)

Players with a ball form three semi-circular groups about 15 feet from the crease behind each other. Players in the second semi-circle line shoot around the first line of semi-circle players continuously in succession around the horn starting at one of the ends. Then, after the players shoot, the players in the second line move up to screen for the third semi-circle line of players. The first group of players goes to the back of the line. Coach can vary the tempo of all these drills for the goaltender so that the players can shoot in "rapid fire" for reflex action or in a controlled manner for angling.

## VI. Two-Line Cornerman Shooting Drill (No Pass)

Players form two lines in the wing areas and alternate sides by shooting around a pylon placed in the middle of the floor. The goalie works on his reflexes. Or the coach can have all the players from one side cut across the top and shoot around the pylon so the goalie can work on his angling. Then the other line shoots.

Coach can run the same drill, but stress everybody shoots a certain type of shot: long, low bounce shots (goalie works on moving the stick to the ball with the body backing-up the stick), shoot only mid-area or hip shots, etc. Goalie can use only his stick to stop shots.

## VII. "Merry-Go-Round" Shooting Drill (Opposite Sides—Pass)

This is a two-line passing drill from the mid-side areas, the left-shots shoot continuously with the right-shots just feeding the cutters. Then, the players reverse roles. The cutters learn to move without the ball, cut quickly and hard, and cut with their sticks ready to catch and shoot. Again, the goalie learns to play the passer, then steps over to play the shooter who is cutting through the middle. A goalie can work on his reflexes by having the players running the drill quickly, or he can work on his angling by having the players running the drill slowly.

## VIII. Pass From Crease to Shooter in Middle of Floor

Players with balls play on both sides of the net in the crease area. The shooter is in the middle of the floor for a pass out from one side and shot. Then alternate to the other side of the net for a pass out and shot. Goalie works on stepping out from the side of the net and stopping a shot in front of the net. Option: can also put the passers in the wing area and have them pass to the middle of the floor for a shot.

## IX. Give-and-Go Shooting from Mid-Side Area of Floor (Opposite Sides—Pass)

Players work on their Give-and-Go technique while the goalie works on his movement and angling on cutting players. The coach puts two cones in the Prime Scoring Area of the floor. Players form two lines on opposite sides of the floor in the mid-side areas with a ball except for one player at the front of one of the lines. The first player in one line throws a cross-floor pass to the first player in the other line who has put his ball down beside himself. The passer then puts an offensive move on the cone and cuts to the ball for a return pass and shot. Then the former passer picks up his ball and passes to the next player in the line opposite him so he can work on his Give-and-Go move.

### X. "Go" Shooting Drill from Mid-Side Area of Floor (Opposite Sides—Pass)

In this drill, the players work on their cut or "Go" move. Again, form two lines on opposite sides of the floor from the mid-side area. Everybody has a ball except for one player at the front of one of the lines. Players alternate sides on their cut. They just cut and shoot. Goalie learns to play the passer and move across and out for the shot by the cutter.

## 8. Drills for Stopping Close-In Shots

- Coach can tell players to take certain types of shots:
  - Players shoot close-in shots with no fake (far or near side)
  - Players shoot close-in shots with one strong fake (far or near side)
- Goalie can work on angle or reflex for close-in shots: goalie can sit back in his net for reflexes or he can take a step out and play normal angling.
- Speed of drills for close-in shots: these drills can be run in either a controlled manner where the shooters are spaced out to give the goalie time to get set between shots so he can work on his technique, or at high speed where the shooters shoot in rapid-fire continuously one after another so the goalie does not have time to get set and thereby works on his quickness and reflexes.

### I. Breakaway Close-In Shot Drill (See Chapter 8, Shooting)

### II. Two-Line Creaseman Shooting Drill (No Pass)

One pylon is placed in front of the net and on the top of the crease. Players' options are shooting before the pylon or shooting after the pylon. Coach can alternate from left-side to right-side, or run all the right-shots continuously, then all the left-shots.

### III. Diagonal Shooting Drill

The goaltender works on stepping out for a good position on the shooter in the cornerman's area, then stepping back to the far post (recovery move) on a diagonal pass from the shooter to the opposite crease to stop a shot.

### IV. Two Lines Shooting Drill (Diagonal Pass)

Two lines—passers, in mid-side area, pass across to stationary player in the crease area for a "quick-stick" shot. Stress passer looks at the net and is in a shooting position before making the diagonal-pass for the quick-stick shot. Goalie plays the shooter, but on the pass to the crease he must recover over to the far post to stop the close-in shot. Work both sides of the floor.

**Variation:** Ballcarrier has option of shooting or making a diagonal pass.

## 9. Goalie Passes to Two Stationary Outlet Players

This drill is the beginning of the process of becoming a passing goalie. A shooter in the middle of the floor shoots at the goalie, and two receivers, each near the sideboards for breakout, receive a pass alternately from the goalie. The goalie learns to stop the ball and get his stick up quickly and make an accurate pass.

## 10. Starting the Fast-Break

Players are in two lines near the end-boards on their proper side of the floor. A player from one line rolls the ball to the goalie, who practices picking it up and throwing it to the same player who is breaking up his side of the floor.

## XIV. Goaltender's Affirmations

### Attitude Affirmations

- My challenge is to concentrate 100 percent for the whole game, no momentary lapses.
- I know that my opponent is really myself.
- The opposition is going to score only if I make a mistake, so I must stay alert.
- I have an attitude of just doing my best and not worrying about anything else.
- I am confident, aggressive, and daring. I do not play cautious or passive. I do not sit back in the crease.
- I am like a cat—physically quick, aggressive, a fighter, and mentally alert.
- I get my confidence from working hard in practice and knowing my position.
- I do not have to stop the shooter as much as the shooter has to score on me.
- I clench my teeth and defy anyone to score on me.
- I want the challenge of stopping the best.
- I love playing against great shooters.
- I know shooters are habitual liars; they never do what you think.
- I do not play two bad games in a row.
- I have a refocusing plan to replace negative thoughts and events, such as when scored upon. I say "relax," "smile," and "be cool."
- I do not overreact to bad goals or bad calls by the referee.
- If the opposition scores a bad goal, I learn from it, I analyze it, then I store it.
- I am the happy warrior: "I'll do my best and let the chips fall where they may."
- Goals will be scored, mistakes will be made, and games will be lost. But I know the ability to bounce back after a mistake is the criterion of a great goalie.
- I will stay focused.
- I will play relaxed, yet intense, alert, and daring.
- I love pressure situations.

### Technical Affirmations

- Stay up and stay out.
- I will not give any rebounds.
- I talk to help my teammates.
- When I get excited, I will breathe deeply.
- I take great positioning in the crease.
- I challenge all shooters.
- I am toughest in the third period.
- I start strong and I finish strong.
- I stay very active and move around to stay mentally in the game.

# Acknowledgments

When I was first writing this book I approached some of the best lacrosse players in Canada and the US to get their feedback on the skills of the game of lacrosse. With their input they added those extra special ingredients that will help make players, coaches, and parents understand the execution of these skills.

The old ideas from some of the now hall-of-fame players are still used in the modern game and will always be useful for the modern player. I have now added some new ideas from 15 great players from the National Lacrosse League.

I would like to acknowledge the following people for their time, energy, and contribution to this book.

## Photographer
John Smith of Creative-visions, Oshawa, Ontario, www.creative-visions.ca

## Pictures
John Chesebrough of Brooklin Redmen; Derek Suddons of the Edmonton Rush; James Hinkson of Scared Heart University (Fairfield) 2006; Nick Cotter of the Boston Blazers; Derek Hopcroft, formerly of the Calgary Roughnecks; Matt Holman, formerly of Portland Lumberjax

## Stick and Equipment
Gavin Prout of the Edmonton Rush of the NLL; Colin Doyle of the Toronto Rock of the NLL; Mark Brown of Blades Sporting Goods, Whitby, Ontario; Andrew Faric of the Lax Shack, Pickering, Ontario

## Passing and Catching
Terry Lloyd, Jim Wasson, Gaylord Powless, Ed Derks, Ron McNeil

## Long-Ball Shooting
Josh Sanderson of the Boston Bolts of the NLL, John Fusco, Larry Lloyd, Jim Meridith, Derek Keenan (Coach of Edmonton Rush), Kevin Alexander

## Close-In Shooting
Terry Lloyd, Peter Parke, Ed Derks

## Individual Offense
Josh Sanderson of the Boston Bolts of the NLL; Nick Trudeau, formerly of the Alabany Attack of the NLL; Terry Lloyd; Jim Wasson; Ed Derks; John Fusco; Gaylord Powless,

## Individual Defense
Brodie Merrill of the Edmonton Rush of the NLL

**Loose Balls**
Jim Veltman, formerly of the Toronto Rock of the NLL

**Face-Offs**
Steve Fannell, formerly of the Albany Attack of the NLL; Steve Toll of the Rochester Knighthawks; Bread McArthur, formerly of the Albany Attack of the NLL; Jim Wasson; Gaylord Powless; Elmer Tran; Derek Keenan; Kevin Alexander; John Fusco

**Goaltending**
Gee Nash, formerly of the Colorado Mammoth; Bob Watson of the Toronto Rock; Dallas Eliuk, formerly of the Philadelphia Wings; Shawn Quinlan; Merv Marshall; Ken Passfield; Ted Sawicki; Doug Favell; Bucky Crouch; Barry Maruk; Wayne Colley

In addition, the contributions of the following individuals were essential: Mike Keenan, former NHL coach, for his introduction, and Chief Irving Powless, for the history of the game.